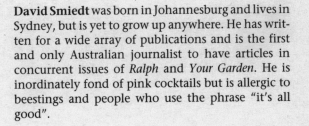

David Smiedt was born in Johannesburg and lives in Sydney, but is yet to grow up anywhere. He has written for a wide array of publications and is the first and only Australian journalist to have articles in concurrent issues of *Ralph* and *Your Garden*. He is inordinately fond of pink cocktails but is allergic to beestings and people who use the phrase "it's all good".

DAVID SMIEDT

Are We There Yet?

Chasing a
childhood through
South Africa

EBURY
PRESS

1 3 5 7 9 10 8 6 4 2

First published in Great Britain by Ebury Press in 2006

First published in South Africa by University of Queensland Press in 2004

Ebury Press, an imprint of Ebury Publishing.
Random House, 20 Vauxhall Bridge Road, London SW1V 2SA

Random House Australia (Pty) Limited
20 Alfred Street, Milsons Point, Sydney, New South Wales 2061, Australia

Random House New Zealand Limited
18 Poland Road, Glenfield, Auckland 10, New Zealand

Random House (Pty) Limited
Isle of Houghton, Corner of Boundary Road & Carse O'Gowrie,
Houghton 2198, South Africa

The Random House Group Limited Reg. No. 954009

www.randomhouse.co.uk

A CIP catalogue record for this book is available from the British Library.

Cover design by Two Associates

ISBN 9780091910747 (from Jan 2007)
ISBN 0091910749

Papers used by Ebury Press are natural, recyclable products
made from wood grown in sustainable forests.

Printed and bound in Great Britain by Bookmarque Ltd, Croydon, Surrey

Copies are available at special rates for bulk orders.
Contact the sales development team on 020 7840 8487
or visit www.booksforpromotions.co.uk for more information.

For Des Miller and Laurence Niselow – African gentlemen

No one is born hating another person because of the colour of his skin, or his background, or his religion. People must learn to hate, and if they can learn to hate, they can be taught to love, for love comes more naturally to the human heart than its opposite.

Nelson Mandela

Outside of a dog, a book is the best friend a man can have. Inside of a dog, it's too dark to read.

Groucho Marx

Acknowledgments

This book would not have been possible without the contribution – witting or otherwise – of a number of people on both sides of the Indian Ocean.

In South Africa, the Smiedts of Johannesburg and Kroonstad, the Dibowitzes of Cape Town and the Goodmans of Durban. I am also especially indebted to my sister Lynn and her late husband Laurence whose home I occupied, whose fridge I raided with impunity and whose patience I surely tested. Along the way, I was privileged to meet a number of South Africans willing to share insights to which I would have otherwise remained blind. So, thank you Oupa, Dolly, Maria, Foy, Fifi, Mona, Dave, Zinzi, Sipho and Ezekiel.

On the home front, I will always owe Phil Abraham big time for getting me started in the writing caper – ditto Maggie Alderson and Lisa Wilkinson. Any number of free drinks are also on offer to the following: Madonna Duffy for remembering a drunken conversation; Mark Abernethy and Todd Cole for whipping me into shape; Adam Hills for the example; John Birmingham and Mark Dapin for setting a standard; Nick Earls for blending humour with heart; Julia Stiles for masterful editing skills; John Burfitt, Lynne

Testoni, Tracey Platt, Jo Bates and Kerrie Alcorn for laughing harder than they had to; Marina Go and Lisa Green for allowing me to trail along; Fiona Inglis for her faith; and finally Paula Joye, Michelle Dunne and all the staff at *Cleo* magazine in Sydney for treating me like one of the girls. The unwavering support of my mum Renecia Miller, whose eager anticipation of each chapter rekindled my enthusiasm when it waned, is greatly appreciated. As are my brother Richard and his wife Stephanie. My last vote of thanks goes to Bryan and Mary Butler, without whom I wouldn't have had anyone to propose to on Table Mountain. Their daughter Jennie is everything I dared dream of. Her encouragement made this book a reality, while her tactful insights have made me both a better writer and human being.

Contents

CONTENTS

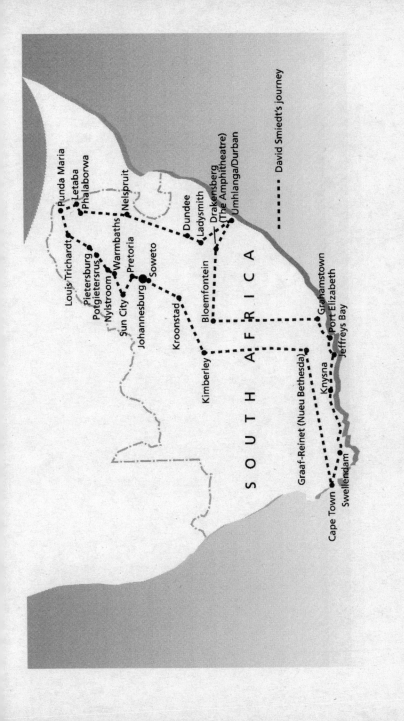

David Smiedt's journey

Punda Maria
Letaba
Phalaborwa
Nelspruit
Dundee
Ladysmith
Drakensberg (The Amphitheatre)
Umhlanga/Durban

Louis Trichardt
Pietersburg
Potgietersrus
Nylstroom
Warmbaths
Pretoria
Soweto
Sun City
Johannesburg
Kroonstad
Bloemfontein
Grahamstown
Port Elizabeth
Jeffreys Bay

Kimberley

SOUTH AFRICA

Graaf-Reinet (Nueu Bethesda)
Knysna
Swellendam
Cape Town

Chapter 1

Any African in You?

A Texan, a South African and a Sydneysider were standing on the deck of a cruise ship chatting under a blazing sun. During a lull in conversation the American produced a Cuban cigar as thick as his thumb, bit the end off, lit up, took two deep puffs then tossed it overboard. "What did you do that for?" asked the confused South African. "I only felt like a taste," came the drawled reply. "And besides, I've got a million of these at home."

Moments later the sweltering South African removed one of the sweat-soaked gold chains around his neck and cavalierly dispatched it brinewards. Faced with the incredulous expressions of his fellow travellers, he said, "It's really no big deal. I've got a million of these at home."

They passed the next few minutes in silence but the Australian felt the burden of expectation sitting on his shoulders like an overweight child. Unable to take it any longer, he grabbed the South African by the collar and tossed him overboard.

This joke was told to me by a colleague at the department store where I found my first job out of school, shortly after arriving as a new immigrant in Sydney. It was a test to see whether I had the wherewithal to take part in Australia's national sport: piss-taking. Having proved that I was as comfortable with urine extraction as the next bloke and that I could give as good as I got, a process of rapid integration began.

When I came to live in Australia, I was eighteen and had never made my own bed. Nor had I seen a photograph of Nelson Mandela or heard "Nkosi Sikele Africa", the hymn that would become South Africa's national anthem. Both were still banned when my family took our first trip Down Under, an exercise which was known at the time as an LSD trip: Look, Schlep, Deposit.

By the time I had completed my first year of a communications degree, the transformation was complete. I didn't merely support but "barracked for" the Wallabies (loudest when they were beating the Springboks), had swapped my "cor" for a "cah" and had developed the inability to use moderate quantities of hair gel.

Then it was time for cancer. A smudge on my father's lung, which had been dismissed during the physical examinations required by Australian authorities before they would grant permanent residency, metastasised and his health deteriorated.

Shortly after our worst fears were confirmed, Ronnie Smiedt left his adopted city, never to return. I helped load his bags into the car; we hugged in the garage and the last words he said to me before leaving to "sort out his affairs" were: "I feel like I've failed you as a father".

The next time I saw my father he was in a hospital bed in Johannesburg. His mouth was covered by an oxygen mask that fogged with each breath, and his sweat-saturated

pyjamas filled the room with the odour of a poorly venti-
lated gymnasium.

His crow's-feet danced a jig when he saw me. My mother,
sister, brother and I spent the next few days by his bedside,
refusing to acknowledge the inevitable. At around 4 pm on
Saturday 11 March 1989, with the hour beginning to dilute
the bright African sunlight piercing the windowpane, he
drifted to sleep. And by that I mean sleep, so try not to skip
ahead.

Mistaking his light doze for deep slumber, I reached for a
Mars bar on a nearby table and tore off the wrapper. The
noise roused him and he straightened his head on the damp
pillow. One of the traits I had inherited from him was a love
of all things sweet. When I was a child he would have me
shaking with laughter and glycaemic anticipation when he
slipped chocolate bars down his trouser legs and sleeves
before opening the front door and announcing, "The Chocolate Machine is here!" After which he would tremble and
flay until these treats magically shot from his extremities.

Now connected to an ECG and two drips, he looked
towards me in that vague and ponderous manner that comes
with being heavily medicated, then broke into a smile that
peeked around the corners of his respiration mask. It was his
last and I'm glad I prompted it. Two hours later he folded his
fists across his chest and collapsed into my arms as a cataclys-
mic coronary stilled his heart and stole the life from his eyes.

In accordance with Jewish tradition he was buried shortly
afterwards. My memories of the event are fragmented. I
don't recall a word of the rabbi's eulogy. However, the image
of the fifty black employees, who had been bussed in from
the distant family business warehouse, clustered around the
steps of the small hall at the entrance to the cemetery, each

wearing a borrowed yarmulke in a lurid shade of orange can be summoned as easily as an overly attentive waiter. The same applies to the moment when six of my friends acted as pallbearers – it is considered an honour to escort the coffin at a Jewish funeral and every few steps a new group is summoned. Encased in polished oak and resting on the shoulders of boys he drove to innumerable soccer practices and picked up at eleven-thirty ("a perfectly reasonable time") from so many parties, he was carried through a sea of granite headstones.

A part of me wishes I could remember more of the funeral – a part of me longs to recall less. Either way, returning to his grave has never been a particularly emotional experience for me. His spirit may well be in Africa but it's not hovering over a windblown Johannesburg cemetery that backs onto power-lines.

Life in 80s South African suburbia was pretty close to perfect. As long as you were the right colour and weren't burdened by a conscience. Our homes were expansive and opulent. A friend of my mother's even had an entire room given over to a multi-tiered rectangular conversation pit rendered in choc-olate plush pile.

The grounds surrounding our homes were lush, formal and tended by the "garden boys" who lived in cramped smoke-blackened rooms in the backyard. This term was applied as easily to teenagers as octogenarians and it prompted my first brush with white liberal guilt.

As we were between such employees at the time, my father had offered one of his long-time warehouse staff some extra cash for edging, weeding and watering. I had known Joseph – a soft-spoken man with downcast eyes and a toe that had been lost in a mowing accident – all my life. However, my eight-year-old brain was having trouble grasping the fact that he was now working in our garden instead of the family business. "Wow, Joseph," I said, genuinely impressed by his range of skills. "I didn't know that you were a garden boy."

He stopped where he stood, gently placed the rusting manual mower on the blade-flecked lawn and sat on his haunches so we were eye to eye. It was a tar-melting day and rivulets of perspiration were running down his cheeks. Without a trace of anger in his voice, he put a hand on my shoulder and said, "Dave ..." Joseph then paused, formulating a gentle way to express a rough truth. "I'm a man. I'm not a boy." I never used the term again.

These men, who by day chlorinated pools they would never swim in, were by night pressed and starched into liveried service for dinner parties. On these occasions they would be outfitted in a white suit of rough cotton, matching gloves and a red sash.

My grandmother employed one such manservant. He was called Willy – we never knew his last name, nor did we ask – and was required to don this uniform when we gathered around the dining room table on high holy days. One of my grandmother's favourite forms of amusement involved summoning him into the room by way of ringing a bell, then saying she had seen a mouse – a phobia that would send this portly giant of a man with kind eyes and a shaved head into a mild state of panic. Boy, did we laugh.

Willy toiled alongside an elderly maid named Josephine who had raised my father and uncle while my widowed-at-forty grandmother was transforming the small homewares import company her late husband had established into the largest such concern in South Africa. In this regard she was one of the few female CEOs in a country where men were men, women were housewives and blacks were "boys" and "girls".

It was much the same at our place. Every morning I was tenderly woken by our maid Martha who would present me with a warm mug of a chocolate drink called Bosco. She nursed me from infancy and by all accounts lavished me with loving attention as if I were her own. This was not an unusual phenomenon in South Africa, and while many white employers were undoubtedly callous, cruel and uncaring when it came to their domestic employees, this was certainly not always the case.

That was one of the most difficult things to explain to my new countrymen who would routinely ask me one of three questions: "Do you hate blacks?", "Did you have servants?" and "Is it true that they had to call your dad 'master'?".

No, yes and yes. It should, however, also be pointed out that in some cases the bond was characterised by genuine regard and affection on both sides.

For example, the family of my brother-in-law, Laurence, had a woman named Priscilla in their employ for thirty-four years. Reed-thin, quick-witted and possessing a rich knowledge of Jewish tradition, she mothered the five children in this clan, plus extended relatives such as myself, with love, compassion, lunches and laundry that knew no bounds. When she died recently, the family's grief was sustained and abiding.

In instances too numerous to be notable, white employers not only paid for the education of their domestic workers' children and grandchildren, but did so at the handful of exclusive private schools that opened their Latin-crested doors to all races of fee suppliers from the mid-80s.

By the same token – and I use the word advisedly – at the end of the Friday-night Sabbath dinners, my father would pour the dregs of the assorted Scotch, wine and beer glasses into a water pitcher to ensure the duo in our kitchen would not swig back an illicit shot or two as they washed the dishes.

Such trivialities were the extent of our concerns. Aside from our lavish domestic refinements, the greatest luxury that many white South Africans possessed was an unshakeable sense of security in our constitutionally enshrined position of racial privilege. Yes, it irritated us that we could not prove our sporting superiority against foes who objected to the way the country was run, but as long as they kept buying our gold, diamonds and platinum, we could live with the situation. While there was the odd white victim of a mugging or burglary, violent crime was a rarity and we felt safe in the knowledge that the vague threats posed by black masses in unseen townships could and would be dealt with by the police as they had been in the past.

By 1986, however, the writing was on the wall for South Africa and it read: "Get out now!" It was a message my father took seriously enough to book our look-see trip to Sydney, which in turn crystallised his decision to emigrate. The ramparts of apartheid were being eroded from within and without. Despite the assurances of Ronald Reagan that South Africa had "eliminated the segregation we [America] had in our own country" and Margaret Thatcher's attempts to prevent Britain and the Commonwealth countries from taking joint measures against apartheid, the international pressure being brought upon the apartheid regime was hitting where it hurt.

The American Congress passed the Comprehensive Anti-Apartheid Act (over Reagan's veto) which outlawed air links between the United States and South Africa, prohibited new investment and bank loans to the country, banned a range of South African imports and threatened to cut off military aid to allies suspected of breaching the international arms embargo against South Africa.

The South African government's attempts to placate the international community with a new constitution that introduced coloured (mixed race) and Indian voters into a three-house parliament divided on racial lines backfired. Black South Africans – the overwhelming majority of the population – saw it as a slap in the face and pointed out that an inherently discriminatory system can never be reformed. Only disbanded.

Petty regime window-dressing such as the repealing of bans on interracial sex and marriage, the reservation by law of particular jobs for whites and the permissibility of sporting contests between teams of mixed races only steeled the resolve of the protest movement.

While proudly proclaiming its reform program to the world, the apartheid government was taking a brutal approach to quelling the growing black resistance. On 12 June 1986 the government legalised despotism by declaring a state of emergency across the nation. During this time newspapers were published with inch after inch of copy blacked out as directed by government censors, and coverage of unrest was prohibited in the electronic media. As you do when you have titanic human rights violations to hide. Under the provisions of the state of emergency legislation, thousands were detained in solitary confinement without being brought to trial and without the knowledge of their family, friends or lawyers. During this period the police commissioner was empowered to ban any meeting he saw fit.

It was at one of these banned meetings that I first tasted tear gas. Equipped with a physique I describe as lanky but the rest of the universe insists on labelling skinny, I took to distance running with much enthusiasm and a slew of fifth places in the 800, 1500 and 10,000 metre events. When a Run For Peace around a nearby lake was announced, I believed the cause was so worthy and the event so benign that my parents didn't need to know that I planned on attending.

The starting gun at these events was usually fired at around 7 am so as to minimise traffic disruption and protect participants from unnecessary heat exposure. The liniment-scented crowd gathered in the usual way: lithe black distance specialists who loped along like gazelles and would account for the required kilometres before most of the field had hit the halfway mark loitered at the front of the pack. Behind them were the committed endorphin junkies who pounded pavements daily, followed by an assorted rabble of social joggers, teens and those who knew they would ache the next day but wanted to make a statement with their feet which was too dangerous to verbalise.

As tracksuits were shed and final stretches dispensed with, a convoy of fifteen yellow utes, each equipped with a cage welded to the flatbed, roared into a semicircular formation around thirty metres from the start line. Their doors sprung open and out poured police in riot gear. With rifle butts pressed into their shoulders, they dropped to one knee and trained barrels on the runners. From somewhere behind this line of sanctioned aggression came a slow voice on a bullhorn that screeched with feedback.

"Under the State of Emergency Act of 1985, I am bound to

inform you that this is an illegal gathering," drawled the commander.

Not quite able to reconcile what they were hearing with the reality of the situation, the confused runners turned towards one another with quizzical expressions. The crowd then scattered as three tear-gas canisters were shot towards us on trajectories so low that a freckled teenager four metres to my left brought one to a halt with his cheekbone. Those who saw the blood running down the side of his face assumed he'd been shot. It was only then that we noticed the metal canister spinning at his feet. Sputtering thick smoke with every rotation, the tear-gas enveloped us in a searing cloud. Because your pulse and therefore your breathing inevitably quickens during times of stress, yawning gulps of this vapour are inhaled within seconds.

One of the reasons tear gas is so effective is that it not only attacks the eyes but also the other mucous membranes. Clutching at faces and throats, many of the runners collided with one another at speed as they attempted to escape the smoke. After copping an unintentional elbow to the solar plexus, I staggered from the crowd winded and gasping. It felt like someone had strapped me down, opened my eyes with toothpicks and then rubbed freshly cut brown onions over my corneas. This was, of course, after they'd inserted a Tabasco drip into my arm and dusted my windpipe with chilli powder.

I thought my parents were going to scale new heights of apoplexy when I told them where I'd been, but in hindsight I think they were merely relieved that I hadn't been hurt or arrested, or arrested then hurt.

My father did, however, make me promise not to attend any more political rallies. My mother realised that the word "forbid" makes teenagers do crazy things and asked me simply to inform her if and when I was planning to take part in any more protests. That was the abysmally trivial sum of my experience with apartheid resistance.

Although the decision – as opposed to the discussion – to migrate was already in place, my potential political proclivities helped justify it. As did my looming conscription, the turbulent state of South African society and the fact that it was now easier than ever for a white boy with admirable intentions to find himself in the wrong place at the wrong time. But for Ronnie Smiedt to move forward, he had to look back one last loving time.

My father was born in a small town in the centre of South Africa called Kroonstad and died fifty-four years later in Johannesburg, the city where he had lived most of his life. He was a fierce patriot who would stand if the national anthem was played on TV, an old-school gentleman whose handshake was a contract, and a man who walked away from financial security, a lucrative family business and the only life he had ever known to start a new one in Sydney.

I don't think my father was particularly fond of Johannesburg, but he didn't despise it either. It was where he lived and was part of a community. So entrenched was the Jewish network that I never used the Yellow Pages before I came to live in Australia. A group of cousins, the Raisins – "The Current Specialists" – were our electricians. Our plumber was related to an aunt's side of the family by marriage (we stopped using him after the Affair) and when we went retail, it usually involved requesting the manager by name, who would in turn give us a discount.

Dozens of women sporting pioneering plastic surgery that

left them looking perpetually astounded would besiege my father's showroom on a Saturday morning in search of some cost-plus-ten Wedgwood. He never took umbrage at these discount divas. Somewhere along the line, they, their husbands or their children would eventually respond in kind.

My father never saw me negotiate, as I did, the modern Australian man's rites of passage – marriage, mortgage and divorce. His advice never came to mind when decisions had to be made, I never felt his spiritual presence the way my sister does and although I wear the gold-faced Omega watch he received for his twenty-first birthday, I struggle to recall the pitch of his voice.

What I do recall is that he used the words "of late" when everyone else said "lately" and that our annual holidays were sacrosanct. Aside from Jewish holy days, he spent six days a week, forty-eight weeks a year at the business he ran with his mother and brother. In early December, however, Louis Smiedt Wholesalers – importers and distributors of fine china, Parker pens and everything your servants in the kitchen might need – shut down for precisely four weeks.

Because my brother and sister are eight and nine years older than me respectively, they were holidaying with their friends by the time Dad decided that our traditional seaside sojourn year after year would simply not do. In hindsight, I believe that with migration on the horizon he yearned for some farewell road trips around South Africa. He was going to give his youngest child the opportunity to experience as much of his homeland as possible before it went to hell in a hand basket.

In the weeks leading up to these trips I would find small piles of maps and highlighters beside the toilet, where –

between exertions – he would pore over routes, attractions and detours.

Being a man who effortlessly bounded what for most people is a chasm between organised and obsessive-compulsive, he would have a test run at packing the boot with empty suitcases and polystyrene eskies. On the morning of the trip, however, his finely tuned calculations would be fatally compromised by the dreaded luggage bulge. With the boot refusing to close and him loath to force it into submission, every item was then removed and the logistical process began all over again.

Having been roused from bed when dawn was slicing a carpaccio-thin slice out of the indigo night, I would crawl onto the rear seat and slip easily back to sleep.

On the highway out of Johannesburg we would zip past slumbering apartment blocks where the only lights visible where those in the servants' quarters on the roof as the Doras and Dorothys rose to make somebody else's breakfast before having their own.

With the first museum or natural phenomenon of the road trip usually six hours away, boredom accompanied me in the back seat trip after stultifying trip. This was partly because I was alone and partly because there was nothing to look at but a wasteland of mine dumps which gave way to a landscape that resembled a beige billiard table.

My dad was a Mercedes man all his life. Not the flashy sports variety, but the sturdy workhorse model. This was a person who considered fuel injection an optional extra and regarded the idea of sheepskin covers on the back seat as ostentatious. The inside of these cars was cavernous and it felt like my parents were in first class while I was in third.

Second class was reserved for what was known as "the cool

bag", a mobile pantry of fare that matched the rest of the journey in its tedious predictability.

Surrounded by water-filled plastic blocks that had been frozen overnight were four smoked salmon and cream cheese bagels, dotted with capers, cut in half and wrapped in foil; a bottle of water; half-a-dozen cans of assorted soft drinks; and a handful of apples which would remain untouched.

Before he had pulled out of the driveway, my father knew exactly where we would be pausing to refuel. Aside from toilet breaks, this was the only valid reason to stop the odometer ticking over. Because from the moment he turned the key he was overtaken by a muted obsession with "making good time".

The only good thing about these journeys was the music. Ella Fitzgerald, Count Basie, Sarah Vaughan, Billie Holiday, Frank Sinatra and Dean Martin seeped from the speakers. I was also allowed to supply a tape of my choice, which was invariably *The Beatles' Greatest Hits*. Somewhere between "Hard Day's Night" and "Lucy in the Sky with Diamonds" my father would announce, "They were such a fantastic group until she came along."

Cue argument. "How can you say that Yoko Ono broke up the Beatles?" my mum would ask.

My parents always took great care never to argue in front of me and there were only two ways I could tell their respective hackles were rising. The first was the use of the phrase "with all due respect" at the beginning of my father's sentences. The second was a pet name before every full stop.

"It's obvious. She arrived and the group disintegrated, honey."

"I don't think this is your field of expertise, sweetheart."

"Hey, I know my pop, angel."

"Not as well as you think, darling."

For an hour the car would be filled with Lennon, McCartney and unresolved tension, until my father would reach across the automatic gear stick and hold my mother's hand for a few moments. I wanted to vomit. Not only then, but most of the time.

Motion sickness waited around every turn and in each dip. My parents attempted to regulate my outbursts with a drug called Dramamine. It did little to quell my nausea but induced a sleep marked by luridly trippy dreams. Goblins with the faces of chameleons would lead me through valleys of enormous poppyseed bagels with a cream cheese river and caper stepping stones.

I would emerge from the narcosis about five or six hours into every journey to see the signs begin to appear. Because most of the major global fast-food chains boycotted South Africa until the fall of apartheid, our highways weren't marked with the illuminated posters indicating how near you were to clogging your arteries at KFC or Burger King.

In the absence of such multinational grease peddlers, local one-off operations with names like Wendy Burgers and the Doll's House flourished in South Africa. What appealed to me most about these establishments was that they were not merely drive-through but drive-in. No sooner had you parked in a lot facing the restaurant than a smiling black waiter with a jaunty bow tie would appear to affix steel trays to the car doors.

I would only do the elongated pleeeeeeassssse once and the response was always the same: "It's not necessary. Have another bagel and there are still lots of apples." I learned early not to press the issue or Dad would threaten to bring out The Belt. Although the threats were sporadic, he made good on it just once. I don't recall what prompted the discipline, but I do remember giggling when he removed his belt. It was the last time I laughed at him and it was the only time he laid a hand on me in anger.

Because he had to leave school in year ten when his father died and another set of hands was needed in the family business, my father always viewed his education as being somewhat deficient. This manifested itself in a desire for knowledge that stayed with him all his life.

As we wandered around whatever museum, national park or monument was on the day's itinerary, something strange would happen to my dad. His face would crease into the gentlest of smiles as he peered into the dusty display case bearing the Bible and spectacles of Phineas Dystopia, whose inadvertent discovery of dioxy-methyl-who-gives-a-toss revolutionised the art of anodising. He pored over the plaques most others rushed by and would murmur some admiring superlative before summoning me over to share his peanut brittle and epiphany. It is only now when I find myself riveted to a Discovery Channel special on the mating rituals of the hummingbird or logging onto the *New Scientist* website when I should be working that I understand the pleasure that new information gave him. In an uncertain world, facts were steadfast and knowledge was power. And so it was that he sought destinations where extraordinary men did improbable feats, or where nature underlined man's impermanence.

In an era where dads weren't exactly comfortable with verbalising their feelings for their children, it was his actions that spoke volumes. Although he never got beyond an "ILY" at the end of his notes to us, there were no limits to the generosity he displayed with his time and energy. He was on the sidelines at every weekend soccer game from the time I was six until I was twenty. He taught me that being a gracious winner was as important as being a gracious loser. When he went to watch a provincial rugby match, there was never any doubt I would be taken along. His time was my time.

Now that I was on the verge of proposing to a girl he would never meet with plans to produce children he would never hold, I felt the need to connect with him in some way. In so doing perhaps I would discover why I couldn't make it to the end of *Field of Dreams* without choking on tears. Was it simply that I missed the old man or was it regret at thanks left forever unsaid and admiration never articulated?

It wasn't so much that I had to make peace with him being removed from life too soon, but rather that it was time to cast aside the foolish preconceptions I had about the manner in which he might make his enduring guardianship known.

For too long I had been vainly searching for some sign that he was watching over me. A decade and a half after his death, I realised that instead of seeking his presence, perhaps the time had come to start appreciating his presents. To see his attitudes, follies and foibles in my own. To value the principles, thirst for knowledge and appreciation of nature he gave me, instead of dwelling on what his absence had removed.

If there was one thing he'd taught me with all those trips it was that lessons were most effectively learned on the road. And where better than his homeland? Perhaps I might even catch up with the old man on some bushveld highway. Or at the very least do a practice run on packing the boot.

Curious to contrast the South Africa I grew up in with the postapartheid nation, and facing an imminent charge of grievous bodily harm against the builder who was carrying out my agonisingly slow and costly renovations, I journeyed to the Rainbow Nation with a wish list that grew daily.

I wanted to see elephants in the wild. I wanted to hear someone respond to "How are you?" with "Sharp!" I wanted to see sunsets saturated in the apricot shades that understandably aggrieved bridesmaids wear just once. I wanted to hear a Zulu spiritual on a Sunday morning and kwela jazz that night. But most of all I wanted to have a Castle Lager in the shadow of Table Mountain at a certain Camps Bay bar which is situated on a rocky outcrop surrounded by a tinfoil sea. Here, amid the gentle jibing of Springbok fans and the hushed urgency that comes with questions about property prices and wages in Sydney, I would tell a joke that goes like this:

A Texan, a South African and a Sydneysider were standing on the deck of a cruise ship chatting under a blazing sun ...

Chapter 2

The Walled-Off Astoria

The first notice you encounter when arriving at Jan Smuts Airport in Johannesburg is located above the wooden booths manned by customs officials. There's always plenty of time to take it in as the staff in question are usually embroiled in a heated competition to see who can make a line of jet-lagged visitors stand still longest. The board reads: "Should you have any complaints about the service offered by the Department of Immigration, please enquire about the register in which such complaints can be registered". Not a good sign, given that your grievances are already being anticipated this early in the visit.

There's a lot to bitch about in South Africa, and Johannesburg has it worse than most. It's a city where there are counsellors who specialise in carjack trauma, the police instruct you to proceed with caution through red lights if travelling alone at night, and for a fee you can equip your vehicle with an undercarriage flame-thrower that will render any would-be assailants medium rare at the touch of a button.

With that in mind, it was probably best that I got the robbery out of the way on day one. I had gone to Sandton City, a muzak-drenched mall on Johannesburg's affluent northern fringes, to withdraw some local currency from an ATM.

The place was bristling with guards in bulletproof vests, clutching pump-action shotguns to their hearts like NRA faithful about to recite the pledge of allegiance.

The security presence was warranted. For months preceding the trip, colleagues, friends and family had warned me of the dangers of travelling through a country where the official murder rate is 58.5 per 100,000 (almost ten times that of the United States).

As John Travolta pointed out to Samuel Jackson by way of a "royale with cheese", it's the little differences between your country and the one you are visiting that are most striking. For example, the South African laxative industry had dispensed with the soothing quasi-medical branding found in Australia in favour of names like "Surge!". The ice-cream trucks blared "Camptown Ladies" instead of "Greensleeves", and a marking on the floor some four metres back from the ATM machines indicated the polite distance that should be maintained by the next in line.

When the elderly gent in front of me had finally figured out which account he wanted to withdraw funds from, I strode confidently towards the ATM, slipped my card into the slot and hesitated for a moment to take in the subtle yet marked differences between this machine and the ones I was used to.

Well, I might as well have shouted, "Hello everyone, I'm a naive tourist!" in all of South Africa's eleven official languages. A deep and friendly voice at my shoulder drew my attention with a polite, "Excuse me". Being one of those phrases one automatically steps aside on hearing, I turned around and a beaming black man in his early twenties and an imported suit brushed past me. With lightning fingers and a quicksilver dexterity born of years of scamming, he hit the cancel button while instructing me to hold down a key on the opposite side of the machine. He then bade me adieu with a dashing smile and responded to my hearty "Thank you" with an equally magnanimous "My pleasure".

I then stared at the screen bearing the instruction "Please insert card" as my brain struggled to make sense of the message my eyes were sending it. My heart raced and my body temperature soared to the point where streams of sweat sprinted down my neck as I realised that I'd been well and truly had. The techno-Fagin vanished quicker than my delusions of being streetwise, and as I searched for the nearest phone so I could call my bank and cancel the card, my eyes came to rest on a poster not half a metre from the cash machine. It bore a depiction of a hulking assailant holding a knife to the throat of a woman at an ATM. It turned out to be a public service announcement bearing the warning, "Don't accept help from anyone".

After sympathetic staff at a nearby bank helped me take the necessary action to ensure Mr Two-Piece wasn't going to take his girlfriend on a coke-fuelled Mauritian getaway thanks to my generosity, I called my sister who lived nearby to tell her what had happened. Her reaction? "Welcome to South Africa."

From its very birth Johannesburg has been a city of scammers, shammers, vagabonds and opportunists looking to make a fast buck. And it was an Australian who started it all.

George Harrison was an itinerant stonemason and prospector who found some casual building work for a widow on

a farm called Langlaagte. It was located about seventy kilometres south of Pretoria, the capital of the independent Zuid
Afrikaanse Republiek which had been founded by the Boers
after they left the Cape to escape British rule. The year was
1886 and I like to think that George was taking a smoko and
casting a lazy gaze around him when a glint on the ground
caught his eye. What he correctly identified as gold was in
fact the tip of a mother lode over 500 kilometres long. A
monumentally important discovery was followed by a
monumentally moronic decision. Having received a free
discoverer's claim, Harrison sold it a few months later for
£10. With that he walked away from a reef so lavish that
within eleven years it was supplying 22.5 per cent of the
world's gold.

Only three years after Harrison disappeared over the horizon in the direction of a no-horse town called Barberton,
Johannesburg was the biggest settlement in South Africa.

The burgeoning mining town was flooded with diggers
from around the world. Most had big dreams and few mor-
als. Working with picks, shovels, hammers and pans, many
made fortunes in months and lost them in weeks or days.
The predictable coterie of hookers, pimps, moonshine bandits and standover men were also drawn to the goldfields like
collagen to a fading starlet. By the time the new century
rolled around, Johannesburg's miners could see it in at one
of ninety-seven brothels in the city – each offering around a
dozen ladies at £1 "a time" or £5 for all night.

So debauched was daily life on the reef that an Australian
journalist who visited the area in 1910 was compelled to
note, "Ancient Nineveh and Babylon have been revived.
Johannesburg is their twentieth century prototype. It is a city
of unbridled squander and unfathomable squalor."

The loose ways of the new city did not sit well with the staunchly Calvinistic government just over the horizon to the north. However, geology soon put paid to their fears of a Sodom next door.

Although the reef delivered consistently spectacular amounts of ore, it was of a particularly low grade and extended ever more deeply underground. This meant that the continued exploitation of the gold seam would require four crucial components: massive investment, vast quantities of cheap labour, technical ability and administrative experience in running an enterprise of this magnitude. Enter the monolithic mining companies that had emerged from the scramble for diamonds begun in the Kimberley area to the west in 1873. Just as they had done in the diamond fields, these Titans flexed their considerable muscle and muscled out the individual diggers.

This suited the government rather nicely – as it would, considering the fact that these Boers were bankrupt. It also corresponded with the recommendations of the chief of the Mines Department, one CJ Joubert, a farmer who by all accounts didn't know his ore from his elbow. After holding numerous meetings with diggers and mining magnates, he set out a plan which was as eerily prophetic as it was far-reaching: "We do not recommend that the fields should be thrown open to individuals as the need for costly machinery calls for a large amount of capital. There is a danger that men who have staked off good claims will be unable to work them, but be forced to leave and, through necessity, take to lawless ways."

And so it remains in the City of Gold. One of the few major world cities located on neither a river nor a coastline, it was founded and sustained by avarice. Sitting at 1500 metres above sea level on a wind-blown plateau, it bakes like a Christmas turkey in summer and is coated with frost most mornings in winter. The only reason people came here and continue to do so is to worship at the altar of cash in the holy house of conspicuous consumption.

Want the money for that BMW (which in the townships stands for Break My Window), luxury apartment or diamond to melt your girl's heart? You have two choices: learn to earn or shoot to loot. In a country where unemployment hovers around the 40 per cent mark and the social welfare system has imploded, fists, blades and bullets are for many the only means of rectifying economic disparity.

In 1998 surveys indicated that 83 per cent of the total South African population believed the police had "zero control of crime". When it came to simply feeling safe, 56 per cent of whites said, "Not me", while 43 per cent of the black population felt the same way. And who could blame them? Between 1994 and 1998 the attempted murder rate climbed by 7.8 per cent, rape increased by 16 per cent (topping the world rankings), assault – and if that's not enough, how do you like this for a qualification – with intent to produce grievous bodily harm shot up by 11 per cent and residential housebreaking soared by 17 per cent. To put this in perspective, for the 3.5 Australians murdered per 100,000 in 1996, 61 South Africans suffered the same fate.

With the staggering amount of relative wealth concentrated in Johannesburg's ritzy northern suburbs, it's hardly surprising that many residents live in a perpetual state of anxiety brought on by the lifestyle they – or, as is often the case, their parents – worked so hard to attain. Homes have become citadels in which every window has bars, each door is double-bolted and the family's bedrooms are sealed off from the rest of the house by an internal gate. On the perimeter, enormous concrete barriers masquerading as fences are topped with razor wire and spikes designed to penetrate bone. High-voltage cabling is another popular deterrent. These houses resemble that middle portion of a mozzie zapper, complete with intermittent blue sparks and a low hum.

Many homes have panic buttons in every room and the cutting-edge electronic surveillance systems normally reserved for embassies. One alarm is all it takes for a private SWAT team bristling with high-calibre hardware to be on your doorstep within seconds. Visit one of these palatial abodes for a traditional Sunday braai (barbecue) by the pool and the topic of immigration will inevitably arise. At which point someone will counter, "But where else in the world could we live like this?" Unable to penetrate the domestic fortification, Johannesburg's bandits lie in wait outside and attack as residents leave or return.

Sentry boxes now stand at the top and bottom of streets I once tore along on my bike. What makes this all the more poxy is that, for all its faults and sins, Johannesburg has some of the world's most beautiful suburban streetscapes and is regarded as a globally significant noncommercial forest. In some places you can't see the security for the trees.

Thanks to the deep pockets and aesthetic whims of the city's founding fathers, the area north of the CBD is one of the most extensively wooded urban areas on the planet. I grew up in the suburbs of Parkwood and Saxonwold on streets that ran beneath a lilac canopy of jacaranda boughs and were lined with verges of soft buffalo grass. As far as vestiges of privilege go, they were bewitchingly beautiful.

Curious to see whether this was still the case, I left Sandton City – one credit card lighter – and returned to my childhood street, Rutland Road. I asked a security guard manning the boom gate if I would be able to wander through for old times' sake. He struck me as the type who had a nickname for his gun – along the lines of Hot Lead Mama or Princess Recoil.

After explaining that I was on a journey of rediscovery which would eventually form a book, and acknowledging that I technically didn't have any business on the street, he picked up his two-way radio to confer with a colleague. An animated conversation in Sotho punctuated by broad smiles and laughter followed.

Having ascertained that the risk of my carjacking a resident was roughly equal to that of Yasser Arafat converting to Judaism, he said he'd let me proceed for R50 ($10).

It was worth every cent. One of the things no one tells you about migration is how many memories stay behind. The big ones – weddings, bar mitzvahs and anything else that demands a buffet – travel with you, but ones like the smells, sounds and even the way the light dripped through the trees on the street where you lived can only be accessed by going back. Of course, as much had changed as remained the same. When I lived there – not in a double or single storey, but split level, thank you very much – it was whites only. Even if a black, coloured or Indian had the means to buy a property here, they would be barred from doing so by the Group Areas Act which forbade such intermingling.

Now the cash bought you the flash, and a broad ethnic mix of residents viewed me with mild concern as I shuffled along the block with the glazed grin that can only be brought on by deep nostalgia or misreading Prozac dosage.

The mores of urban survival are surprisingly easy to acquire and I have felt the suspicion of strangers slipping around my shoulders like a familiar cloak whenever I have returned to Johannesburg.

My on-edge vigilance was aided by the fact that I had been besieged with warnings at home and on arrival. One of the most memorable came from a colleague who instructed me to jump as high as possible on hearing any loud bangs. "That way," she said cheerily, "the bullets will hit you in the legs."

The two most chilling caveats came from separate cousins. The first instructed me: "Never give a taxi driver the bird – they will shoot you for less". The second advised: "If you do have to stop at a robot [a traffic light to you and me], don't pull up right to the white line. I always stop about twenty metres away. It lets me see anyone hiding near the intersection plus gives me room to pick up speed if I have to knock someone over to make my escape."

To the Australian psyche this may sound like paranoia taken to debilitating extremes, but for the thousands of South Africans who have lost not only their sense of security but family and friends as the result of carjackings, it's simply a matter of making it home alive. This form of crime has become a growth sector in Johannesburg as the result of increasingly sophisticated electronic alarms and disabling systems. To steal a car, someone has to be in it.

So prevalent is this crime that central-locking mechanisms only release the driver's door, thus preventing hijackers from leaping into the back seat the moment they hear the alarm being deactivated.

And it's not just the vehicles that are targeted. Many a motorist has felt the cold steel of a gun barrel against their temple along with the demand for a mobile phone, sun-glasses or sex.

Some areas, such as highway on- and off-ramps near townships, are worse than others. Another no-go zone is the central business district. I used to spend a week of every winter school holidays working at my father's company, which was located in the city centre over three sawdust-scented floors of a warehouse on Commissioner Street. The CBD was a thriving centre of commercial activity where crowds of workers bustled between glittering flagship department stores, lunch counters and office buildings. There was a single lock on the premises' door, the frontage was washed each day and the pavement was swept every few hours. Casual good-morning nods had in some cases developed into acquaintanceships and my father knew a number of the merchants whose premises bordered his. It was a community of sorts.

I was advised that going back here on my own would be akin to playing a dyslexic version of Russian roulette in which every chamber bar one contained a bullet. So I secured the services of a guide named Oupa (grandfather) who picked me up in his shiny red Nissan Pulsar. A slight man in his early fifties, with tufts of grey around his temples and eyes which twinkled behind bifocals, Oupa was an avuncular mix of encyclopaedia and softly spoken entertainer. Along with giving out nuggets of information, he took mischievous delight in exposing my naivety and ignorance.

He and I set out towards a CBD that had long been deserted by companies like my father's in favour of safer sub-urbs that were once either exclusively residential or semirural. Even the stock exchange had shifted north and now sits alongside plush hotels and multinational head offices in an enclave where the faces may no longer be white-only but the collars certainly are.

Approaching the CBD from the north, a series of leafy parks slide down rocky ridges and rim the edges of small streams that are probably best viewed and certainly best smelt from a distance. Known as the Braamfontein Spruit Trail, it meanders fifteen kilometres through a handful of the six hundred green spaces which are under the city's adminis-tration by day and witness destitution, degradation and death when darkness falls.

In a city where life is cheap, its value has been slashed even further in Hillbrow. When I was a child, this was the enter-tainment epicentre of the city. On Saturday afternoons my friends and I would catch a (whites-only) bus or even thumb a ride to one of the cinemas in the area. This was followed by waffles that swam in syrup between ice-cream icebergs at one of the nearby eateries with names like the Milky Way and Bimbos Burgers. At night, my older brother and sister would descend on the whites-only area with their mates to *jol* – the local equivalent of raging – at a relatively new form of enter-tainment called discotheques. The suburb's main thorough-fare, Twist Street, was lined with buzzing restaurants, atmospheric oak-panelled pubs and old-fashioned establish-ments which referred to themselves at "Nitespots" and signalled their presence through a neon martini glass that flashed with the promise of alcohol-fuelled romance.

Hillbrow had always hosted its fair share of bloody-knuckled bar brawls but this was tempered by its raffish charms and bohemian sprinkling of galleries and theatres. Neither remain. The suburb has become a clutter of concrete apartment blocks that were hideous to begin with but now have the added aesthetic detriments of decay and filth. Poles festooned with laundry protrude from windowless frames, leaking pipes bleed rust for twenty storeys, and hotel lobby doors have either been smashed or hang limply from their buckled hinges. What is left of paint or plaster has peeled and blistered.

This was once Nana-land, full of residential hotels where elderly folk slipped quietly into elegant decrepitude between hands of bridge and Devonshire teas. My own grandmother had lived nearby in one called the Courtleigh and I vividly recall the typed menus, capacious dining room and bingo evenings in the lounge.

According to the Hillbrow Community Partnership, a local group trying to resurrect the area's fortunes, the bachelor flat my Granny Anne called home is now likely to be inhabited by between seven and twelve people. And thanks to a 1946 decision by the Johannesburg City Council to remove all height restrictions in the area, many of these blocks soar between thirty and forty storeys. With the capacity to accommodate that many people in that many rooms in that many storeys in that many buildings, it's hardly surprising that this area has seen its population explode as the original residents fled in fear or were slaughtered for petty cash on the way to the corner shop.

According to the census, 30,000 people called Hillbrow home in 1996. Five years later that figure topped the 100,000 mark, thanks mainly to an unprecedented influx of illegal immigrants. The highrise apartment blocks and hotels are what Oupa termed "a refuge for the scum of Africa". He pointed out that criminals on the run from authorities in countries as far away as Nigeria and Ghana can disappear for months in Hillbrow until the heat dies down at home.

It's the kind of place where you can lie low because there

will always be someone else attracting the attention of the overburdened police – known as the Flying Squad, apparently for the speed with which they respond to calls for help – who see more carnage on a weekend than many of their colleagues witness in months.

The day before Oupa and I drove through Hillbrow, a toddler was shot dead on the balcony of her cramped unit. She was home alone at the time. The callousness is incomprehensible. As is the fact that on New Year's Eve shootings and stabbings are as traditional as Auld Lang Syne was for the whites that once lived in these blocks, and numerous residents toss bottles and bricks from their balconies as an entertaining diversion.

"Even the cops are scared to come here at night," said Oupa. "The problem is drugs. It's mainly the guys who come in from Nigeria illegally and deal in cocaine, heroin and mandrax. They are fearless, cashed up and give corrupt cops freebies or kickbacks to turn a blind eye."

Those shopfronts that weren't bricked up were swamped by what are known as "informal traders" selling everything from fruit that flies were refusing to touch and telephone calls from lines that disappeared into unseen exchanges to hands-free mobile phone sets and packs of plastic hangers.

And these were the guys just trying to make an honest buck. Glue-sniffers who had barely reached double figures and were unlikely to live through their teens watched our car through jaundiced eyes and made half-hearted hand-to-mouth gestures to indicate they were hungry and wanted money.

"Don't even think about it," Oupa warned. "Most of these guys wouldn't think twice about slicing away a chunk of your hand if it meant you might drop your wallet."

The next three blocks were filled with a sad succession of mostly black, but some white, women in sweat-stained lycra who sold their bodies for hits. They had the haunted, skittish look of those who know what it feels like to be belted as they sleep. Hovering in the background, steel-eyed pimps in Beemers played Jah Rule and made silent threats.

Above this scene on a rocky ridge, Oupa pointed out what is now known as Constitution Hill. Originally the site of a fort that Afrikaner President Paul Kruger constructed between 1892 and 1898 to repel the British, it later became a jail and is now South Africa's new Constitutional Court. Oupa loved the idea. "This place accommodated Ghandi and Mandela because they dared to oppose the South African government's racist policies," he said. "Now instead of symbolising a regime that maintained order through surveillance, intimidation and incarceration, it's going to be the home of what I believe is the most socially progressive government charter in the world."

He had a point and one which is effectively illustrated in the arena of gay and lesbian rights. In the South Africa of my childhood, such relationships – or more specifically, the physical expression thereof – were punishable by laws created specifically with backdoor action in mind. In other words, if you were caught being sodomised by someone you cared for or simply fancied, you would be put in jail where it was likely you would be a far less willing participant in the very same act. Today, men and women can request asylum in South Africa because of their sexual orientation, gays and lesbians can serve in the armed forces, and same-sex partners qualify for immigration rights and their unions are legally recognised.

We rounded a bend in the road and drove alongside a

park, Pullinger Kop, where I used to walk with my grand-mother. The magnificent trees planted in Johannesburg's earliest days had lost none of their impact, but the ornate paling fence now had washing hanging from every post, the toilet had been turned into a squatter's shack, and the man-made brook that had once provided the park with a burbling bisection had been turned off because it was being used as a toilet.

The CBD was marginally less malevolent than Hillbrow. "Since the installation of closed-circuit TV cameras, crime in this area has dropped by 48 per cent," said Oupa, trying to sound both objective and optimistic. It was a statistic I was having trouble computing. Mainly due to the fact that we had pulled up to a traffic light beside which a scrawny shirtless white guy in acid-wash jeans and a Jason Donovan circa '87 mullet was guarding a retail premises with a sawn-off shotgun in one hand and a beer in the other.

The volume of pavement traders quadrupled as we ventured deeper into the CBD. Out the front of my dad's old business premises – now filthy and barricaded behind metal security grates – faded clothes were laid out in makeshift displays on blankets, metal garbage bins served as roadside barbecues, and dozens of barbers sharpened up the appearance of the punters who sat before them on plastic milk crates. Litter choked the gutters and in some cases leapt over them as cars rushed by. There were times when it was difficult to tell where the refuse ended and the goods for sale began.

When I was growing up the best view of the city was always to be had from the Carlton Centre, a fifty-floor statement in architectural mediocrity that stood in the centre of the CBD. Beside it was the Carlton Hotel. This establishment represented the nadir of elegance and luxury in a society where opulence was the norm. It had top-hatted doormen, subdued lighting, a fountain in the lobby and an oh-so-swish restaurant called the Koffiehuis where guests were presented with a chocolate clog in a white gift box as a souvenir of their devils on horseback and chicken à l'orange.

It was now a concrete shell. "Guests were too scared to stay there," said Oupa. "They were mugged every time they went into the shopping mall downstairs. The hotel even arranged for individual security guards to accompany them, but by then it was too late."

And the viewing platform? That was gone too. It was still up there, of course, but only the rats and squatters enjoyed the panorama. The owner couldn't give the place away.

Still, the streets thrummed with vendors, business types and gangstas in low riders looking to easy marks for fast money. This streetscape was set against the aloof Georgian facades of buildings such as the Supreme Court, City Library and Town Hall. Despite obvious neglect, they managed to retain a defiant magnificence and I like to think that each of their columns gave the Third World mise en scène around them a daily Ionic finger.

Most of these grand old dames had been encroached on by rusting shacks and prefab ugliness, but none was more striking than the city's main synagogue in Wolmarans Street. Under its commanding domed roof I had listened to innumerable sermons and copied my father as he slowly beat a clenched fist against his chest on the Day of Atonement. Divided into a downstairs men's section and balcony for women, according to Jewish orthodox custom, it also featured a choir chamber set high above the pulpit from which voices would erupt in earnest harmony to proclaim: "Hear O

Israel. The Lord is God. The Lord is One." It was here that Chief Rabbi Casper – affectionately known as the Holy Ghost – tore the OBE from his chest and hurled it to the ground when it came to light that Britain had refused safe harbour to a group of Jews fleeing the Nazis. Now there was a Chicken Licken out the back and the inside had been gutted to be installed in an exact replica of the building which had been erected in a safer suburb.

I was crestfallen. Sensing my disappointment, Oupa offered to end our day with a walk through "one of Johannesburg's oldest alternative medical centres". At the southern end of the CBD was a street my trusty guide referred to as "witchdoctor alley".

The place was a ramshackle strip of peeling single-storey shops with the odd remnant of a deco flourish; each establishment had a sloping tin awning from which hung a sign proclaiming the proprietor's skills. Some were *sangomas* (those who divined directly by reading bones and channels), others were *inyangas* (*sangomas* who were also traditional healers dispensing minerals, animal products and herbs) and an intriguing few were multigenerational practitioners who called themselves Doctor.

One of the latter worked in conjunction with his grandmother and promised not only to relieve one of money and relationship problems – in that order – but to extend a customer's genitals to more satisfactory proportions. ("Hey Nan, how does the uncircumcised girth chant start again?") And all within fourteen days.

The competition next-door raised the stakes even higher. Dr Macsuid and his Rock of Gibraltar Herbs could naturally enhance the night tool's dimension as well as clearing up impotence, premature ejaculation, stroke, epilepsy, arthritis, diabetes, all STDs and a mysterious ailment known as sexual weakness. He could also supply winning Lotto numbers and exorcise demons.

Aside from having hyperbolic claims in common, these stores all had a certain look about them. Dark beaded curtains were mandatory, as were armfuls of dried brown herbs and yellowing grasses displayed in metal bowls or hung from the ceiling. Behind the mahogany-stained counters that dominated each space were shelves containing rows of jars filled to the brim with roots, leaves and what were unmistakably animal bones. These stores smelt like a hippie share-house and usually featured a couple of treatment rooms down a dim corridor, beyond which lay a courtyard in which nervous poultry tried not to attract attention. However, their undeniable air of tantalising exoticism was markedly undercut by the fact they accepted Visa and were uniformly tuned to a radio station celebrating Celine Week.

To better understand the nature of the city, Oupa suggested I spend the next day delving further into its seamy origins at a recreated mining village called Gold Reef City.

Driving out there the following morning, I had to take a concrete flyover under whose shadow the witchdoctors from the previous day counselled the gullible, the faithful and the curious. On my left, the smart new Nelson Mandela Bridge, a vibrantly coloured meccano set, was being raised near the crumbling Main Station which the ANC had targeted in one of its more successful bomb campaigns during the days of the Struggle. Moments later an innocuous grey building loomed over the highway.

Known as John Vorster Square, it was a typical government affair: all grey spackle, fluoro lighting and with a swathe of blue tiles added late and ineffectually to counter the dreariness of the structure. It had been the headquarters of the Johannesburg police, and numerous apartheid activists went in handcuffed only to leave in body bags or through windows. In the basement cells, deeds were committed in the name of the law that would chill a war crimes court. Soles were beaten and spirits crushed. Genitals had electrodes attached, skulls were pulped so the brains therein swelled to bursting, and residents whose arms had been broken somehow managed to hang themselves with bedsheets. Now the building was covered with an enormous poster featuring beaming children of all races welcoming the globe to the cricket world cup.

In the distance lay some of the 400 mine dumps which ring the city like the yellow stains on a smoker's fingers. The biggest is at Randfontein and forms a 42-million-tonne white-headed pimple on the landscape which rises to a height of 111 metres.

A few weeks before my arrival in Johannesburg, the city parks department put forward a plan to utilise these disused mine shafts as burial grounds. Crime and a rampant AIDS toll sees 20,000 Johannesburgers popping their clogs every year; the figure is set to rise to 70,000 by 2010 and the city is rapidly running out of space to bury them.

Mulling over the inescapable conclusion that a number of the workers who now toiled in the mines would likely end up spending a vertical – much more space-efficient – eternity there should this plan come to fruition, I pulled into the car park of Gold Reef City.

Just as I locked my door, a black man with a smart uniform and wide grin materialised by my window. He issued me with a ticket on which he scribbled my registration number and explained that I would be allowed to drive my car out the lot only if I could produce this ticket at the exit gate. "That way," he beamed, "you and Corolla always go home together."

I had been to Gold Reef City shortly before emigrating. Not to discover more about the city in which I had lived all my life, but because there was a pseudo-saloon where the can-can girls were reputed to possess a penchant for revealing their nipples between high kicks. It turned out that only one did, but when you're eighteen, an areolic glimpse plus an elaborate backstage fantasy can sustain one through a surprising number of lonely nights.

Much had changed at Gold Reef City. For a start, I don't recall being subjected to a frisk and metal-detector search before being allowed in. The place had also traded in much of its interactive museum emphasis in favour of amusement park rides and tawdry trinkets. Mouse pads covered with airbrushed depictions of big game jostled for shelf space with wooden salad servers whose handles resembled zebra heads, pencil holders shaped like crocodile mouths and miniature tribal shields covered in calfskin. Behind these stood a forest of knee-high "trees" featuring gilt limbs and trunks plus leaves made of tiger's eyes, agates and hematite. They were enough to have converted Liberace to minimalism.

I wandered around a nearby hall filled with the kind of interactive scientific curiosities for which I have an undeniable fondness – something I suspect I inherited from my father. One of the items on display was a floor piano on which I played a swinging version of "When the Saints Go Marching In" and was rewarded with spontaneous ambivalence from those around me. There was also a human jigsaw, comprised of a hollowed-out mannequin and a collection of plastic innards. "If you put the organs back in the right order," declared a notice beside the exhibit, "you won't need to force them."

Beyond this lay a mining museum in a draughty hangar which I had to myself. This was mainly due to the fact that the majority of visitors to Gold Reef City are drawn by a series of rides that promise to spin, dip, twirl, drop and flip you like a rag doll in a tumble dryer. Its slogan should have been "Five types of nausea for one low price! Kids under twelve chuck free."

While it should be acknowledged that the mines' unquenchable demand for labour tore asunder the fabric of South Africa's indigenous rural communities, the undertaking also produced feats of astounding mechanical and technical innovation. Necessity may be the mother of invention, but greed gives birth to ingenuity.

The main hoist of the disused mine on which the theme park stands could draw on 8250 kw of power – you'd have to combine 150 average hatchbacks to be in the same ballpark. Down the road a mine was using a fifteen-kilometre steel rope to haul humans and ore to the surface, while the headgear of the nearby President Steyn shaft stood at ninety-nine metres – we're talking Big Ben plus one. The fervour with which the engineering challenges were overcome becomes clear when you consider that one local mine, West Driefontein, produced around 2 per cent of all the gold ever accumulated by humanity.

To best get a handle on the reality of the experience, you had to head underground. Equipped with a miner's helmet and tiny lamp powered by a weighty battery pack, I joined a tour group exploring shaft 14 of Crown Mines. When the facility was in full operation there were fifty-seven working levels and those who toiled at the lowest of these often faced a two-hour trip to the face. The place had since been flooded to the fifth level, where we were to wander.

I left daylight and my stomach on the surface as the cage in which the half-dozen tour members and myself free-fell 220 metres at thirty kilometres per hour – your average office building variety clocks up about five. Our guide, a rotund black woman, explained that the lift had been slowed down from the forty-five kilometres per hour at which it operated when the mine was fully functional. Apparently, there had been "incidents".

It was like Times Square on New Year's Eve down there as tour groups squeezed past one another and guides battled to make themselves heard. Imagine the scene: a guide not working in her mother tongue explaining mining technology and folklore to a group who had only two things in common: their location and English as a third language. This resulted in our guide's every sentence being followed with a sequence of translations accompanied by vigorous nodding.

The miners themselves once faced similar problems as many spoke their own tribal language and their white bosses knew only English or Afrikaans. The response to this Babel was Fanakalo, a language that evolved underground and became the universal mine parlance. Comprising 80 per cent Zulu words and the remainder English, Afrikaans and Xhosa, it featured a vocabulary of 2000 items – 500 of which were profanities.

For the first thirteen years of the mine's existence it was not electrified and workers chipped away at rock faces with chisels and hammers by candlelight. With electricity came hydraulic power and drills were introduced. This necessitated a change in the way miners were remunerated and they were now expected to remove a set number of inches from the rock face to be deemed as having completed a day's work.

Before the drilling demonstration took place, we were asked to cover our ears. It was a timely warning. As its tungsten tip made contact with the face, the drill bucked and shuddered like an epileptic at a strobe factory. The noise they produced was a closely interspersed staccato burst akin to someone rapidly banging metal garbage-can lids together an inch from one's head.

Unfortunately for those in her tour group, one translator had fallen behind the mine guide and the instruction to block the Germans' middle-aged ears was issued way too late. The net result was twenty-five Berliners in miner's helmets leaping in simultaneous fright and emitting a chorus of "Gott in Himils" which echoed through the shafts.

In the industry's nascent period, the men behind the drills had it relatively easy. Their colleagues assigned to move the fully loaded pans along rail tracks from the face to sorting points were expected to shift a tonne of rock at a time. They were eventually replaced by donkeys that could pull six pans. These pack mules were originally kept underground for months on end, but not only did their health suffer, they were instantly blinded by sunlight when they came to the surface. As a result, vast pens were maintained by the mines and the animals were rotated through the shafts. Many historians have suggested that the donkeys were treated better than their human counterparts.

In addition to the respiratory ailments that used to plague miners, the working environment was made all the more dangerous by the constant presence of dynamite, which was extensively used to blast new tunnels. Stored in bright red wooden boxes, the dynamite could only remain underground for forty-eight hours. After this it became so unstable that the heat of a miner's palms had been known cause an explosion.

Shaft collapses were common. Buttressing was an obvious solution but no native trees could be found to reliably produce straight, strong timber that would not be compromised by moisture. The land that produced the man who discovered the reef also provided the solution to this quandary. A variety of eucalypt timbers were imported from Australia to support mine shafts, and plantations were established in South Africa that still thrive today.

The eucalypts were not the only imports on the goldfields. Cornwall, Cumberland and Lancashire supplied a trickle then a flood of skilled miners and machine operators. Low on the social scale of their motherland, their new home split its people not according to class but colour. Their experience was in short supply and they were able to protect their income via trade unions that struck deals for better pay and conditions. Earning well, free from the oppressive nature of the English class system and attended to by servants, these men soon imported their wives and children to settle into a relatively comfortable family life.

The same could not be said of the African worker.

Although they were not allowed to own land in the province where the goldfields were located, thousands were employed as worker-tenants by wealthy Boer pastoralists. It was a win-win situation as these indigenous farmers could not only generate enough produce to give the white landowners remuneration or a share of the crops, they could also feed themselves and many of the early prospectors.

The Boers of more meagre means who regularly complained to government about the "insolence" of the Africans in the marketplace (who were clearly more skilled farmers) found a ready ally in the labour-hungry mine owners. The government appeased both by passing a law limiting to five the number of tenants that could set up shop on a white farm.

Deprived of a subsistence income, Africans had to seek wage labour and an instant work force was born. Touts from the mines conveniently appeared as the ink on the legislation was drying. Working on a commission for each man they signed up, these flim-flammers lied shamelessly about the conditions and wages. It was only when these workers arrived at the mines, often having had marginal success evading the white swindlers who posed as policemen and demanded shillings at bogus tolls, that they discovered they would be on year-long contracts with no vacation and no guarantee of renewal. They also found out that they would be housed in sterile, violent compounds from which they could not come and go as they pleased and where a pass system would prevent family visits.

As each passing year revealed further mineral riches, the initial system devised to supply labour soon proved to be hopelessly inadequate. In 1913, three years after the disparate South African states were united as a Commonwealth nation, a law was passed that provided all the manpower the mines could ever use, and then some. Known as the Natives Land Act, it prohibited Africans from purchasing or leasing land outside set reserves. These reserves initially comprised a bare 7 per cent of the country and was only increased to 11 per cent in 1939.

The concentration of people and livestock on the reserves saw the quality of soil plummet, waterholes run dry and vegetation disappear. Subsistence farming became a contradiction in terms, malnutrition ran rife and over 20 per cent of children died in their first year of life.

As difficult as it may be to believe, the government then found a way to make life even more difficult: taxes. Societies which had prospered for thousands of years using a barter system now had to generate cash to sate the demands of various municipal, provincial and central authorities. In 1925 a poll tax of £1 per African man aged eighteen or more and a local tax of ten shillings per dwelling in a reserve was instituted.

I grew up believing that Africans worked on the mines because it offered a stable way to support their families. It never dawned on us that these men never had a choice. Their wages were barely sufficient to maintain themselves and few were able to send money home to their families, who in turn struggled to eke a living from shrinking holdings. For the next three generations the life of a mine worker bore all the hallmarks of penal servitude: abysmal working conditions, zero freedom of movement and negligible pay. But all these men were guilty of was being black and poor.

When our tour was over, we took a lift to the surface. I stepped into sunshine that reduced my irises to pinpricks and a world that many of the men who once toiled here would have thought impossible. Groups of teenagers of all races and similar awkwardness roamed the park smoking and trying to look disinterested. Afrikaner staff addressed all customers as "Sir" and "Ma'am" and Buppies (Black Urban Professionals) strolled by with one hand in their partner's and the other SMS-ing a mate about that night's activities.

There was a good chance those plans would have centred on Melville, a suburb with a long history of bohemianism and a lusty sprinkling of welcoming venues. I headed to the

area that evening with a cousin who still lives in Johannesburg and encountered a striking change since my previous
fleeting visit four years earlier.

It was a Thursday evening and Melville was up for a big
night. In cosy cocktail bars couples flushed with one-part
inebriation and one-part infatuation swapped compliments
over candlelight and margaritas. Crowds of caramel-
coloured coquettes in Gucci and muscled men still young
enough to have faith in their charisma spilled onto the pavement from crowded pubs. The *nts-nts-nts* of African drum
and bass shared the air with the lemongrass and coriander
wafting from the restaurants and sidewalk cafes. But the
most striking aspect of all was that people were actually out.
On previous visits to Johannesburg, crime had impacted so
severely on the city's inhabitants that they had socialised
primarily at piazza-style shopping malls where their person
and vehicles were watched over by armed men. Here the
streets had been noisily and joyfully reclaimed.

The topics of dinner conversation had also moved on. A
few years earlier no gathering would have been complete
without tales of an acquaintance who had been beaten,
hacked or blasted to death for their car or wallet. On the one
hand all this talk was undoubtedly a coping mechanism, but
on the other it was like listening to the morbid fascination
some elderly folk develop with the maladies affecting their
contemporaries. Now these tales no longer surfaced with
such bloody regularity. It seemed that a collective decision
had been taken to accept the reality of the situation, do what
could be done to minimise its impact and get on with life.

Not that this was a new attitude in these parts. The next
day I was heading to where it had practically been patented:
Soweto.

Chapter 3

Struggle Town

To understand Soweto you have to understand the system that created it. To understand this beast, you head to the Apartheid Museum. I was repeatedly advised that travelling to Soweto alone and white was tantamount to waking Mike Tyson by punching his testicles. So warned, I once again enlisted the aid of Oupa, who collected me in his immaculate sedan.

On the way we stopped at a set of traffic lights which functioned as a drive-through mall. At most major intersections in South African cities, pavement entrepreneurs have set up shop selling everything from neatly packaged garbage bags, cool drinks and hangers to mobile phone rechargers and hands-free sets. Previously the men and women who worked these streets would tap on your window with a pathetic expression, point to their stomachs to indicate hunger and clinch the deal by accessorising the image with a child in rags. And don't assume that they were all black.

"You'll like this," said Oupa as he fished some change from his pocket and waved one of the nearby men over. The merchant exchanged the shrapnel for a pamphlet printed in red ink that stained his fingers. It was entitled "Jokes 4

Change" and contained a series of satirical poems, cartoons and topical quotes from comics. What a marvellous grass-roots scheme this was. It put money in the pockets of the seller while making the buyers seem wittier and better read than they actually were.

The Apartheid Museum, on the other hand, was anything but a chuckle hutch.

Appropriately located in the no-man's-land between Soweto and Johannesburg, the museum has a penal austerity about it. It is made of white concrete blocks, black metal sidings and eight-metre-high walls of yellow rubble from the goldmines encased in mesh. These materials were chosen to contrast and are separated by the harshest of angles. It is bereft of softness.

The building manages to be both a practical museum space and a metaphor for a social system that divided by colour. At the entrance stand seven concrete columns, each engraved with a cornerstone of the constitution written after the 1994 transition to majority rule: democracy, equality, reconciliation, diversity, responsibility, respect, freedom.

In their shadow is a row of faded green wooden benches with the words "whites only" stencilled on them. They face a shallow pool of reflection above which a quote from Nelson Mandela is etched onto a granite slab. "To be free is not merely to cast off one's chains, but to live in a way that respects and enhances the freedom of others." It is the first surface on which black and white appear together.

After buying our tickets, Oupa put them behind his back and said, "Choose." I tapped his left hand and he produced a card that read "nonwhite". Not black, Indian or coloured.

"I'm 'white'," he beamed as he flashed his card and ushered me towards the steel gate allocated to me by race.

The corridors diverged and Oupa disappeared with a wry "Have fun". We were separated by floor-to-ceiling steel grates and he was obscured by enlarged identity documents that hung from the roof. Referred to by authorities as a reference book and known as a "dompass" (dumb pass) to blacks, every South African was issued with one of these ninety-six-page passport-style documents.

If you were white, this generally accumulated dust on a wardrobe shelf and was only hauled out at election time to prove you had the right to participate by virtue of your melanin.

If you were black, your very life could depend on it. Failure to produce this pass on demand was an offence punishable by imprisonment. Police who viewed you as "an idle or undesirable native" could cancel the pass at will, which meant you had to leave an urban area within seventy-two hours.

I clearly recall various pass dramas with our even more various maids – it's so difficult to find someone who'll clean, wash and cook for a pittance, retain a pleasant demeanour, refrain from pocketing the silverware and not drink herself into a stupor on the one day a week she has off. Having one of my parents' signatures on this document was literally a "get out of jail" card.

From the other side of the steel bars, Oupa remarked, "There were times when policemen barged into my house at three or four in the morning on the chance that I might have had visitors staying over whose passes may or may not have been in order. The pass system was one of the factors that made blacks support international sanctions against South Africa. There were some well-meaning but misguided whites who believed that blacks would be the only ones to feel the brunt, while the rich would remain unaffected. That may have been the case, but we were used to suffering and starvation, so we figured we might as well do it for a good cause."

I scoured his tone and eyes for bitterness but could find none. Unwilling to accept his demeanour as genuine, I tried to push a button by asking if he still had his pass. "Of course," he said with the smirk of a man who had seen through an obvious ploy. "I used it as ID when I voted for the first time."

Although most visitors to the museum are familiar with the basic premise of apartheid, many, myself included, do not know how it was instituted, applied and enforced. This is where things took a turn for the didactic.

Aside from featuring a photograph and mandatory details such as a name and address, the dompass included a box marked "race". The entry assigned to you under one of the primary pieces of apartheid legislation – the Population Registration Act of 1950 – would shape your life for much better or far worse.

If you were deemed to be on the dark side of the colour bar, you were legally denied access to museums, galleries, zoos, sporting facilities, pools, beaches and employment prospects beyond unskilled labour. The top of the career tree for blacks in apartheid South Africa was as a nurse, teacher or policeman and these only came about because the posts were located in areas where few whites were willing to work.

This act was also the cornerstone of a policy that mandated who you were allowed to have sex with or marry. Civic organisations were compelled to become racially exclusive to the point that the apartheid government instructed the National Ornithological Society to expel its only nonwhite member or cease to be. Needless to say, birds of a feather ...

The devil was in the detail. One of the most notorious early classification procedures was the pencil test. If an HB was inserted into your hair and remained there, it signified frizzy strands, and therefore classification as black or coloured.

This legislation remained in place until well into the 1990s and since racial categorisation had such a bearing on your life prospects, it was frequently appealed. In 1985, for example, 702 coloureds became white; 19 whites became coloured; one Indian became white; 20 coloureds became black; 249 blacks became coloureds; 50 Indians became coloureds; and 11 coloureds became – of all things – Chinese. No blacks became whites. No whites became black.

Once the government had slotted the population into genetic categories, step two of apartheid involved dividing the nation between them with a piece of legislation called the Group Areas Act. Residential segregation had been part of South African life since the early nineteenth century but this principle was now extended and implemented with vicious efficiency. The idea was to split each town and city into regions where a single race would live and trade. This was accomplished by controlling the purchase of homes or rentals on racial lines.

In hundreds of suburbs this involved the violent dissolution of neighbourhoods where numerous races had lived in harmony for decades. One of the best known was Sofiatown, a jumping neck of the Joburg woods where black gangsters who modelled themselves on Capone's boys mingled with Jewish clarinet players, Indian artists and torch-song chanteuses whose racial backgrounds were exotically indistinct. The National Party government, which introduced these acts and ruled from 1948 to 1994, viewed areas like Sofiatown as "the deathbeds of the European race".

If the one-two delivered by the Population Registration Act and Group Areas Act left the country's hopes of racial parity teetering like a punch-drunk fighter, a piece of legislation called the Bantu Authorities Act delivered the knockout strike, then got in a few cheap shots as its opponent fell to the canvas.

Designed to rid the African population of their last scraps of rights, it created a number of tribal reserves – or homelands – where these people could apparently enjoy the constitutional privileges so recently ripped from their grasp. The government spin likened this process to the decolonisation of European empires in tropical Africa. Although the South African economy flourished in the 1950s and 1960s, the nominally independent homelands were destitute. Nearly all consisted of up to nineteen fragments of land separated by white-owned farms and investing directly into these areas was a punishable offence under corporate law. With the often substandard land unable to support ever higher concentrations of people and stock, the inhabitants had no choice but to leave as migrant workers seeking employment in major industrial centres.

These three ideas – racial classification, dividing of urban areas according to skin colour and creating new territories that provided cheap labour without any social obligation – were the foundations of one of the most insidious attempts at social engineering the world has seen.

In my twelve years of history studies at whites-only government schools, the mechanics of the system that delivered my classmates and I such privileged lifestyles were only hinted at. And curiosity had its consequences. For example, when a schoolmate expressed an interest in writing a paper on influx control – the government term for ensuring black labourers didn't hang around white cities any longer than necessary – she was stripped of her prefectship and talk of expulsion filled the quadrangle.

The Apartheid Museum experience is designed to provoke alienation, discomfort and shame in people like me. It succeeded on all counts.

It tells two distinct tales and I'd heard neither growing up in South Africa. Not only does it detail the system of legislated racism, it also covers the resistance it engendered.

One such event took place on 26 June 1952 and was known as the Day of Defiance. Throughout the Witwatersrand, Cape and Natal, cheering crowds watched groups of protesters deliberately break unjust laws. Entrances marked "Europeans only" were brazenly strode through, curfews were ignored with cavalier disdain and lunch menus were demanded at counters reserved for whites only.

When the government picked up its collective jaw from the parliament floor at the gumption of these uppity "Bantus", legislation was rushed through parliament ensuring dire retribution against the organisers of such campaigns. Key resistance personnel were arrested daily. By October 1952, nearly 6000 protesters had been jailed. During the same period ANC membership exploded from 7000 to over 100,000. For every person jailed, seventeen volunteered to take their place.

Speeches delivered by a young lawyer named Nelson Mandela, who had worked on the mines as a security guard, rebounded off the museum's concrete ceiling. As did the words of activist Steven Biko – Malcolm X to Mandela's

Martin Luther King Jr – who died naked in the back of a police van after interrogation.

These utterances jarred with those of the gimlet-eyed Afrikaans politicians who beamed from a jumble of TV sets in a barbed-wire maze and whose speeches were peppered with the smug phrase "separate but equal".

On one monitor flicked grainy footage of ANC leaders being lead to court for treason. On another a girl no older than fifteen lay face down on the street, her heart still rhythmically pumping blood from the hole in her head made by a rubber bullet. These images were interspersed with documentary evidence of the effect of apartheid on individuals: a letter from a pining mine worker to his wife far away; a photograph of a black maid carrying a silver-service tea set to the pool while her white madam reclined on a chaise longue; court orders declaring activists of all races banned, which meant forced deportation.

The museum is not a place of subtlety and its message is bluntly reinforced. Above the exhibits, spotlights, wailing sirens and surveillance equipment stand guard. Cages on all sides prevent visitors from wandering off the designated path. There are no seats.

Taking up the bulk of a wall ten metres wide and eight high is a billboard detailing every act that was passed over fifty years to reinforce apartheid. The degree to which the policy impacted on the minutiae of daily life was brought home by something called the Bantu Beer Act. The state decreed when, how and where you could sink a frosty.

Oupa's path and mine finally converged in the next room, which was occupied by a yellow armoured carrier known as a Caspir. Riddled with bullet holes, it was like being inside a giant colander. Equipped with bullet-proof slits for gun barrels and an interior made entirely of grey steel cladding, these bright yellow vehicles were the first to respond to township violence and frequently left a smattering of corpses in their wake.

They took heroic pride of place in news bulletins where commentary praised their occupants for protecting us from what was known as the "swart gevaar" – the black danger. These brave boys faced mobs so we didn't have to.

Inside the Caspir was a monitor spooling surveillance footage of township demonstrations taken from these very vehicles. Unlike the plodding "What do we want? When do we want it?" affairs common in many other nations, these South African protests featured heaving crowds, often brandishing tribal shields and spears, which fell into a rhythmic shuffle somewhere between a dance and a canter. Shot from the side of a road at the base of a small rise, the footage showed a tumultuous black cascade cresting the hill and tumbling towards the police line. The odd white face is also apparent and draws the camera's zoom lens. There is a curious energy about the gathering – part predatory, part celebratory. Although smiles are abundant and a curious sense of liberation is palpable, I was left in no doubt that it was only a matter of time before the sky was raining Molotov cocktails and hailing rocks.

The museum's most chilling exhibit is a room painted black and from whose ceiling hang 121 pristine nooses. This macabre chandelier represents each of the South Africans executed between 1962 and 1986 for their political beliefs alone.

For all its fastidious detailing of the pain and suffering wrought by apartheid, the museum chronicles its downfall without gloating. Equal reverence is given to both Nelson

Mandela and FW de Klerk, the protagonists in a revolution that was bloodless despite the scale and savagery of the oppression which prompted it. The simple black and white sketch of the agreement for the nation's first democratic elections is on display alongside aerial photographs of serpentine black queues at polling stations. Photos of a beaming Madiba sharing a joke with the Afrikaner he replaced as the country's leader sit alongside ballot sheets stacked with parties once banned.

Despite a stomach-churning sense of guilt that my family and I had participated in this system by not opposing it, the sense of joy and justice created by the museum's commemoration of the transition to majority rule is infectious. Formulated to be a cathartic experience for all who visit, its motto is Walk Away Free. Which I might have been able to do were I not Jewish. Having suffered through scores of racial persecution campaigns, did it not make us doubly guilty that we not only remained silent but reaped the privileges of this one?

Oupa interrupted my self-indulgent hypothesising by declaring that I was "now ready for Soweto". In the apartheid era, you didn't see it until you were in it. From a distance the city was a vast smudge of smoke created by hundreds of thousands of oil lamps, kerosene stoves and cooking fires. Soweto wasn't electrified until 1988 and then only through the efforts of Mayor David Tebehadi who had to travel to the United States to privately secure the necessary loans.

Soweto came into being as the result of two distinct factors. Firstly, in the lead-up to World War II, African labourer–tenants were evicted from rapidly mechanising white farms and driven from overcrowded, drought-stricken reserves in search of work and a better life in the city. Secondly, at the same time, coalmining and the manufacturing industries expanded rapidly to stand alongside gold as a major employer. So rampant was the growth that between 1938 and 1945 the number of employees in the coal industry increased by 50 per cent, while the ranks of those in manufacturing swelled by 60 per cent. By the end of 1946, Johannesburg's black population had risen by 100 per cent in a decade.

While industry was glad to harvest the labour that this influx provided, it paid little regard to the housing needs it prompted. The city authorities shared the apathy. The solution they came up with to deal with this crisis involved issuing innumerable licences permitting householders to take in subtenants.

This was to prove as effective as a rice-paper condom. Areas such as Pimville – today a suburb of Soweto – became so overpopulated that sixty-three water taps were used by fifteen thousand people and one in five children did not live to see their fifth birthday.

So deplorable were conditions in these slums that many Africans moved out and began setting up homes on any vacant piece of land they could find. The thought of burgeoning black communities living where they chose under their own rules appalled municipal authorities and prompted the belated implementation of low-cost housing programs. Uptake was initially slow as squatting was cheaper than living in one of the council-built dwellings and camps could be set up nearer to places of employment, which in turn cut down on transport costs.

Eventually, however, the state succeeded in crushing the squatter communities by force and pushed them into vast estates where they could be more effectively subjugated. And

so the loose conglomerate of shanty suburbs, native locations and council bungalows became a city.

This process was hastened by mining magnate Ernest
Oppenheimer who in 1954 arranged a R6 million loan to
build 24,000 houses in five years. Some say his generosity
was inspired by sympathy for the poverty which haunted the
township like an emaciated ghost. Detractors believe he was
simply prolonging the lifespan and yield of his workers.

Still, at scores of depots and railway stations, ticket windows were besieged daily by throngs of hungry Africans with
just enough cash for a one-way fare to Egoli, the City of Gold.

As far as concepts go, Soweto seemed like a corker. Corral
the black population in a location close to the city, but out of
sight, where they could be monitored and utilised as workers
for the mining and manufacturing concerns that transformed Johannesburg into the country's commercial capital.
While our white homes were situated in suburbs dripping
with elegant Anglo nomenclature, such as Sandhurst and
Hyde Park, this Brobdingnagian experiment was merely
lumped with a contraction of its geographical location:
South Western Townships became Soweto.

Very soon Soweto spilled over its boundaries like a fearsome gut running roughshod over an elasticised waistband.
The last time such matters were calculated, the city squatted
over a sixty-five-square-kilometre collage of tin shacks, litter-
strewn wasteland and bungalows designed by architects who
would have done a far better job if there was the remotest
possibility that they would ever have to live in these brick
boxes. Three million call the place home.

And it's not all poverty and despair. In a city of this size in
a country where race is no longer an impediment to prosperity, there are always going to be some haves and plenty of

have-nots. By Oupa's reckoning, at least half-a-dozen millionaires have resisted packing up and heading to suburbs that were once reserved for whites only. The luxury end of Soweto is Diepkloof Extension where a handful of mock Tuscan villas look across rolling lawns to Tudor piles next door. These are few and far between and the wealth in Soweto is made all the more conspicuous by its surroundings.

Referred to as "informal housing settlements", patches of urban wasteland have been swallowed by clutters of shacks that ripple off in every direction like a corrugated-iron ocean. Stones hold their roofs in place and plastic sheeting prevents the rain turning the floor to mud.

Oupa had arranged for me to view one of these dwellings but I was rather uncomfortable with the prospect of taking an up-close gawk at a stranger's poverty. "It's okay," he reassured me as we parked the car and made our way along a dirt road towards an elderly woman who waved us in her direction. "This is the way Maria makes her living. And besides, *Wallpaper* were here last week."

"The decor magazine?" I asked, having trouble blending the world of ergonomically designed toilet seats and thousand-dollar scatter cushions with the lean-to Maria inhabited.

"The one and only," beamed Oupa, taking obvious delight in my discombobulation. "She made enough money out of the shoot to cover almost six months living expenses."

On stepping into the single room that Maria shared with her two grandchildren, I could immediately understand why some art director had swooned in her Pradas. Depressed at the prospect of being surrounded by rusting iron, Maria had decided to add some colour to her home. She carefully peeled the labels from cans of pilchards – a township staple on account of its affordability and nutritious value – and began creating a mosaic. Three years later, every wall was covered in thousands of fish dancing against a background of fire-engine red and sunflower yellow. Had Maria done the same thing in a gallery, she would have undoubtedly been hailed as a tongue-in-chic installation artist. It was mesmerisingly vibrant and Maria was justifiably proud.

Up until a few years ago Maria had been a domestic worker. That all changed when her former employers decamped to Toronto after a smash-and-grab attack in which a spark plug was hurled through their car window and a handbag plus all sense of security was extracted. Maria informed me that she now makes more money showing her home to tourists than she ever did "cooking for that bitch".

It was only when I was asked for an entrance fee that I was able to wrench my retinas from the wall. "It's R20 or $2," said Maria in a tone which suggested that some visitors actually tried to bargain her down. If it was a ploy it worked and I doubled her asking price.

Maria's spotless home was dominated by a Sony television set which her previous bosses "couldn't be bothered schlepping". An American soapie was on and I got the distinct impression that, before another troupe of tourists arrived to stare agog at the wall, Maria was anxious to catch up on whether Dakota would recover from her coma before Montana married Phoenix only to discover that Alabama was in fact her sister. I asked Maria how long she planned on staying. "It's been almost four years now," she sighed, "but any day now Nelson is going to give me a house."

How do you solve a problem like Maria's? Her faith is founded on the fact that every working day since the democratically elected government took power in 1994, 500 homes have been built for South Africa's poor. However, as yet the supply has barely dented demand. Clusters of these freshly built dwellings have sprung up on the road between Soweto and Johannesburg. Many have shiny cars in the driveways, a patch of lawn, satellite dishes and views of the shantyland their occupants may once have called home.

Like any city of Soweto's size, there are areas that are better off, those that are worse for wear and others where one might venture if euthanasia was unavailable in your home town.

For the most part, the older bungalows I saw were not occupied by the same upwardly mobile middle class moving into the new developments. However, what they lacked in conspicuous indicators of financial liquidity, they more than made up for in house pride. Many streets seemed as though they were in the midst of an anal-retention pageant with house after pristine house set behind a modest yet lovingly tended sprinkling of flowering plants. Neighbours gossiped over fences and kids kicked footballs on the pavement. I was expecting a ghetto but instead encountered a neighbourhood which residents obviously and affectionately considered home.

The northeastern skyline of Soweto is dominated by a pair of cooling towers which in recent years have been painted with psychedelic swirls and acid-trip lashes of tangerine and lime. Not that these ever provided juice for the city in which they stood. Instead they exclusively served the Johannesburg CBD and were a daily reminder to Sowetans of who possessed the power.

Tours of the township have become big business, but only a small percentage of white South Africans have ever ventured into this particular conglomeration of thirty-nine suburbs. Soweto has a habit of slapping visitors around the head with their expectations and assumptions. First off, they are more likely to be greeted with smiles and waves than weapons and intimidating demands.

"It's safer in Soweto than in Johannesburg city," said Oupa in the fraying tone of a man who made his living shattering stereotypes about his home town. Enthusiasm began to percolate within him once again as he pointed out a squat cream building with a flat tin roof and a cramped gravel car park.

"That, my friend, is the Pelican Nightclub," he grinned.

We pulled over to the shoulder and he gazed at the faded signage with the almost imperceptible head shakes that come with reminiscing about wild nights long gone. "When I used to come here to listen to kwela [a raucous form of idiosyncratic South African jazz] in the 70s, I had beers with white boys from the suburbs like you. The bands that played there weren't allowed to perform in Johannesburg, but they were the best in town. So the white kids who wanted to experience it often put shoe polish on their faces and pretended to be black to get in. This wasn't because they would have been badly received by the regular clients, it was actually to avoid being targeted as political activists by police who raided the place from time to time."

This city thumbs its nose in delight at the simplistic notions that tourists bring with their dollars. From the smart campus of the Vista University, you can make out aloe-lined fairways of the eighteen-hole Soweto golf course. There are bowls clubs, tennis courts and SPCA offices with paddocks for injured horses and a patient line of locals nursing cats down to their last life.

Ingenuity runs rampant and local entrepreneurs have set up shop around busy intersections with a staggering array of goods and services on offer. One tried to tempt me and Oupa with "the freshest barbecue chicken in town". This involved selecting the unfortunate live fowl from an overcrowded cage beside an oil drum whose lip was licked by flames from within. Sensing our hesitation, the proprietor attempted to convince us with a poultry liver appetiser. Overcome by a sudden bout of vegetarianism, I politely declined.

Beside Giblet Joe was a carburettor specialist, and across the road was the Soweto equivalent of a shopping mall. This consisted of a line of freight containers which served as premises housing everything from mobile phone dealerships to hair salons and boutiques. With doors and even display shopfronts cut into the metal walls, many of them were branded with handpainted logos and slogans. Affordable, transportable and impervious to the elements, a number also functioned as cafes and bars.

Our next stop was a patch of red dirt known as Kliptown Square. Today it is the backdrop for a ragtag street butchery where rusted trestle tables are piled high with flyblown meat and purple entrails. In 1956, however, it drew 2884 delegates from around the country to witness the drawing of the ANC Freedom Charter, the document which forms the basis of South Africa's new constitution. With police strictly enforcing pass laws and monitoring travel between provinces, reaching Kliptown was a feat in itself. In one notorious incident a group of Indian delegates who did not have the necessary permits to enter the Transvaal bluffed their way out of custody by pretending to be musicians on their way to a wedding. Taking the better than average odds that your average white cop wouldn't know talentless sitar playing and howling Hindi showtunes from the masterful varieties, they belted out number after number until the cops ushered them along, grateful for the silence.

When the police eventually swooped late on 26 June 1955, officers painstakingly recorded the details of every delegate. One hundred and fifty-six of the leading activists were arrested and charged with treason. Held in two large cages at Johannesburg's Fort Prison, they came to represent the democratic doppelgangers of the 159 members of the all-white South African parliament. This mass incarceration proved to be a boon for the resistance leaders as it gave them their first opportunity to openly discuss the Struggle en masse. It was a situation the government had been trying to prevent for years and founding ANC leader Albert Luthuli later reminisced, "The frequent meetings that distance, other occupations, lack of funds and political interference had made difficult, the government now made possible".

The trial drew international attention and funds were channelled from around the globe for the plaintiffs' legal fees, food and clothing. The charges were eventually dismissed and the detainees were released to jubilant scenes. The Freedom Charter had claimed its first victory.

In 1960 another group of protesters assembled to voice their objections to the pass laws. Their assembly point was the Sharpeville police station near Soweto. The protest was organised by the Pan-African Congress, a splinter group of the ANC headed by the charismatic Robert Sobukwe who advocated a purely Africanist philosophy and rejected the idea of working with whites.

A crowd of between 3000 and 5000 assembled for a peaceful protest, buoyed by the news that similar gatherings were taking place at nearby settlements. After a scuffle in which one of the police station's perimeter fences was pushed over and a section of the crowd surged forward to have a sticky, the police panicked.

"Then the shooting started," recalled journalist Humphrey Tyler. "We heard the chatter of a machine gun, then another, then another. Hundreds of kids were running too. One little boy had on an old blanket coat which he held up behind his head thinking perhaps that it might save him from the bullets. Some of the children, hardly as tall as the grass, were leaping like rabbits. Some were shot."

Tyler described a policeman who had taken up a position on top of a Saracen vehicle and was firing his machine gun into the retreating crowd in a 180-degree arc "from his hip as though he was panning a movie camera".

When the ricochets of bullet on bone eventually dimmed and the corpses on the road stopped twitching, sixty-nine protesters were dead. Almost 200 were rushed to nearby Baragwanath Hospital.

On duty that night was a medical intern named Desmond Miller. He had left the tiny country town of Vredefort a few years earlier to study in Johannesburg and nothing could have prepared him for the carnage he was about to encounter.

"We got word that dozens of casualties were en route," he told me, "and had to clear the wards of people whose conditions weren't life-threatening. We assessed and dismissed as quickly as we could, then spent what felt like days picking bullets out of people."

Miller, who subsequently migrated to Sydney shortly after Soweto erupted in the infamous riots of 1976 and had the good sense to marry my mother some years after my father died, recalled: "Every single one had been shot in the back. These people were running for their lives, but still the police kept on firing."

* *

Oupa was palpably proud to live in Soweto and as we skirted an area he termed the Wild West – a trio of suburbs bitterly and bloodily disputed by at least five gangs – half-a-dozen shots rang out from the cemetery on a hill nearby.

"Gangstas," spat Oupa. "To show their respect for the friend who died, they shoot the coffin as it is being lowered into the ground. I don't understand these young guys – they just want to be like Americans with their rap music, guns and crack. Because many of them have grown up in Soweto, they have no connection to their tribal culture and its sense of right and wrong. Their parents were the ones who suffered under apartheid but these young guys have a sense of entitle-ment. They know nothing about their heritage. They're not interested in the fact that people struggled so they could have the opportunities and freedoms on offer. They just want it easy."

The air was soon filled with the frenetic sound of *kwaito,* a local amalgam of boyz in da hood rap, African street slang and the odd Afrikaans glottal.

"Here come the Beemers," sighed Oupa. Sure enough a quartet of top-of-the-line Z3s driven by scowling mourners in Ali G ensembles slid past, daring us to make eye contact.

Not that gangs hadn't long been part of township life. Back in the 50s one of the most prominent had been the Hazels. Seriously, if you were naming a batch of hoods with no good on their minds and knuckledusters in their pockets, wouldn't you steer towards a name that inspired fear? Amid thoughts of whether the Hazels ever mixed it up with the Veras or rumbled against the Ethels, I couldn't help but notice how busy the graveyard was for a Tuesday afternoon. Not that I had any legitimate basis of comparison, mind.

There were four funerals on the go, each attended by at least 200 mourners. These were not the quiet sniffling-into-a-hanky affairs I was used to. There was diaphragm-shaking wailing going on; bosoms were heaving and coffins were being clung to.

I asked Oupa if this was a particularly hectic day in tombtown. He shook his head sadly and replied, "Not since AIDS arrived in Soweto".

A death in the family is a lavish affair in black cultures. The send-off reflects the esteem in which the metabolically-challenged was held and many families take on fat slabs of debt to ensure the last hurrah is appropriate. Others spend years contributing to funeral funds which operate on a similar principle to life-insurance policies.

We left the heaving hordes to their grief and drove on past handpainted mural advertisements on concrete walls and gunmetal-grey streetlights to which posters advertising cheap abortions were tied. From time to time we'd stop at an intersection where a mate of Oupa's would pull up beside us or rib him from the sidewalk as he made his daily circuit of Soweto with the obligatory wide-eyed whitey in tow.

The roads were dominated by the 10,000 minibuses which ferry Soweto's residents to and from work. This massive industry arose in response to the apartheid government's lack of adequate public transport and there isn't a town or city in South Africa which wouldn't come to a swift commercial halt if the local taxidrivers went on strike. A ride from Soweto to Jozi, as it is known by township residents, will set you back a dollar.

Passengers motion in the direction of an approaching cab, which will frequently lay down an inch or so of rubber as the driver crunches the brake pedal as one would a roach on the kitchen floor. This invariably causes the cars behind him to swerve like sidestepping ruckmen. Unlike many other cities where such behaviour would generally by greeted by the rolling down of windows, expletive medleys and the casting of aspersions on another's parentage, most taxidrivers in South Africa are merely fixed with an admonishing shake of the head or the briefest of glares.

This is because they generally carry a fearsome reputation for responding to a minor fracas with extreme violence. Their vehicles are prime targets for the carjackers who service a network of chop shops where taxis can be disassembled and unrecognisably reconfigured within hours. As a result the overwhelming majority, most of whom are regular joes trying to make an honest buck, have been forced to arm themselves with hot pieces, which also come in handy when turf wars break out between the taxi companies vying for a chunk of this multimillion-dollar game.

The Orlando West section of Soweto lays claim to the only street in the world that two Nobel laureates have called home. From this neatly nondescript patch of middle-class Soweto came two men whose humanity and lack of vengeful bitterness was made all the more remarkable by the brutality of the regime determined to deprive them of their rights. Desmond Tutu lived on the corner in a modest whitewashed home shaded by trees and bounded by a metre-high concrete wall. A block up the road was the compact brick bungalow that lawyer Nelson Mandela came home to after a day at his Johannesburg office. It was from this light-drenched living room that he plotted revolution in the 1960s with his comrades and second wife, Winnie.

Now divorced from Nelson – who is happily married to the

widow of a political mate, the old fox – Winnie no longer lives here. She resides in a flashy palace behind three-metre walls which was built through donations from such luminaries as Moamar Gaddafi, Jane Fonda and Clint Eastwood. The old house has become a museum of deplorable tackiness which hardly befits the man whose life it purports to celebrate. After the carefully crafted detachment of the Apartheid Museum, this exercise in merchandising was as disheartening as it was blatant. T-shirts proclaiming Winnie – who could be bothered showing up for only three sitting days of parliament in 2002 – as "The Mother of the Nation" were on sale alongside perspex jars filled with dirt "direct from the Mandela backyard". In the garage was a virtual shrine to the woman, composed of framed tributes and an airbrushed poster of her punching the air before an adoring crowd.

Long before she walked hand in hand with her husband through the gates of Victor Verster Prison, Winnie had achieved a measure of notoriety through a series of scandals, inappropriate comments and the kind of fashion sense that made Dame Edna Everage look like Coco Chanel. First, her coterie of henchmen was implicated in the kidnap and assault of a boy barely into his teens. Then she addressed a political rally at which she incited supporters to liberate South Africa through necklacing suspected police informers with a burning tyre filled with petrol. Her latest embarrassment involved allegations of embezzlement and the forged signatures of ANC Women's League members. This was responded to with her now well-practised denials and predictable retorts of a witch-hunt.

None of this was even hinted at amid the ramshackle displays, the highlight of which was a gown reputed to have been worn by Mandela at the time of the treason trial.

The monumental crappiness of the experience was all but obliterated at the next venue we visited. Two gargantuan blades of steel come together like hands in prayer to form the roof of the Regina Mundi Church. Beneath its vaulted recesses and bathed in the subdued sheen of lemon stained-glass windows, Bishop Desmond Tutu took the pulpit with firebrand oratory advocating sanctions against the apartheid government. The church also provided sanctuary for protesters with sjambok- and shotgun-wielding police in pursuit. Bullet holes bear testament to the sieges that it witnessed. A statue of Christ that once stood outside until a messianic hand was removed courtesy of law-enforcement shrapnel today stood sentinel over a neighbourhood choir practice.

A group of fifty girls in smart uniforms, a dozen potential supermodels among them, had shuffled into the front pews, followed by an equal number of boys. It was obviously the low point of a school day that had plumbed new depths in tedium. The only thing both groups shared were discreet admiring glances in one another's direction and a mutual desire for time to switch to turbo mode. Then they began to sing.

It was the kind of hymn that had me looking around the hall for a dog-collared type who would sign me up to Christianity. The girls' voices blended into a singular symphony of the sweetest soprano given delicious depth by the bulbous bass of the boys singing the same lyrics a few phrases behind. The result was a traditional call-and-response gospel tune that filled my chest with joy and had my eyes brimming. I didn't understand a word, it stemmed from a doctrine that was not my own, and yet it stirred within me a sense of elation for which I was wholly unprepared. I guess they don't call 'em spirituals for nothing.

Oupa was anxious to hit the road but I begged for one more song like a mosh-pit groupie braying for an encore. He looked at me with the blend of mild exasperation and tangible pity I used to dish out to my mother when she got misty in Hallmark commercials, but eventually acceded.

Oupa waited outside and I eventually found him chatting to a white woman beside a shed where a mosaic workshop was being held. "Is she teaching the congregants," I asked as we clambered back into the car. "No," replied Oupa. "They're teaching her."

Our route took us past the Hector Pietersen Museum which opened on 16 June 2002, twenty-six years to the day after the blood-spattered riots ignited by the regime's insistence that black students be taught in Afrikaans, the language of oppression. Although the museum commemorates the Soweto uprising which drew the world's attention to the plight of South Africa's oppressed majority and resulted in the international boycotts and sanctions which precipated the end of apartheid, it is named after the day's most famous martyr. The thirteen-year-old featured in an iconic photograph that distilled the rage of the rioters and the brutality with which it was extinguished. From the screaming confusion of tear gas and hurled rocks emerges Mbuysia Makhubu in denim dungarees, his face contorted by grief, the dying body of Hector Pietersen in his arms. Besides him runs Hector's sister Antoinette, her hand extended as if trying to halt the horror unfolding before her or at least stem the blood gushing from her brother's mouth.

A memorial stone close to where he fell lies beneath the entrance to the museum and bears both his name and witness to an uprising in which 555 others died. Most were protesters shot in the back as they scurried for safety. Others were so enraged by the slaughter that nothing could restrain them from attempting to take vengeance on the police who were armed with automatic weapons and stirred on by their secret nightmare of black rebellion fomenting before them.

As I pondered the memorial to dead children who deserved a better future sluggish rain began to leak from a contused and incontinent sky. Oupa noticed the degree to which I was moved and in a single sentence crystallised the fundamental similarities of all men: "Fancy a beer then?"

We wound up at Wandie's, a popular lunch stop for the tourist buses that wheeze diesel through Soweto most days. It was late afternoon and the sharpness of the light had only just begun to soften. Burnished and backlit, the city took its foot off the accelerator. Commuters leapt lazily from minicab taxis, flicking smiling jibes and laughing farewells over their shoulders. The tempo had dropped from samba to slow groove and ambling in the twilight was the order of the day.

Across a rush-choked stream lay a football field we had passed earlier in the day. A sun-roasted slab of rectangular desolation, it sported the agricultural equivalent of a comb-over, with modest patches of jaundiced grass vainly clinging to a bald pate. Now, though, it was redolent with cries of "man on" and the leather-cushioned thud of perfectly executed volleys.

It was the soundtrack to my childhood and struggling to see a ball in the remnants of light leaking below the horizon was one of few experiences I shared with black boys growing up in the townships. The sports club where I played junior football was the first in the country to become multiracial. In

1978 the Wanderers Club displayed remarkable courage by instituting this policy which skirted dangerously close to being illegal. Not that we realised the enormity of the situation at the time. We just turned up to training one day to find a new centre back named Jacob in the squad. The novelty of his colour had dissipated by the end of the warm-up and the rest of us were impressed by his defensive instincts, aerial skills and willingness to dish out the odd elbow to the team pratt, a malicious turd of a child called Steven Hess with an overbite and a delicious sister called Terry who stood me up on a date some years later.

Jacob became the rock to which our defence was anchored and he and I played together for five seasons. He was my first black mate and the team formed a fiercely protective barrier around him when we toured regional centres where racism often surfaced. He came over to my house a couple of times, but I never went to his. The closest I came was when my visibly apprehensive father dropped him off on the outskirts of Alexandra after a game one night. We crunched to a halt on a rutted gravel road, the Merc's light refracting through a bottle graveyard by the kerb before dissolving into a darkness flecked by a sprinkling of distant coal fires. The township had no streetlights at the time, yet my father wore the unmistakable pallor of a person standing directly beneath one. It was the first time I had seen him jittery.

"This is fine," said Jacob, perceptive enough to lie. "My house is not far away. Thanks for the lift, Mr Smiedt." With that he broke into a megawatt grin, leapt from the car with his kit bag slung coolly over his shoulder and was absorbed into the night as if by osmosis.

At the time sport was strictly defined along racial lines, of course. Rugby was a white game whereas soccer was predominantly played and watched by the black population, with Soweto clubs such as Kaizer Chiefs and Orlando Pirates generating a rivalry on a par with Liverpool and Manchester United, Barcelona and Real Madrid, Britney Spears and Christina Aguilera. The inclusion of players like Jacob led to white boys like me being invited to play curtain-raisers for national soccer league games. As a result I found myself among eleven excited under-12s making our way down the players' tunnel of Soweto's Orlando Stadium on a handful of occasions. Someone once told me that when you die, the journey involves travelling a dark corridor towards a welcoming light – if that is true, I found heaven in Soweto.

Orlando Stadium is a seething bowl of rivalry and expectation on match day. Comprised of wooden benches that accommodate far more spectators than modern plastic seating, the stands rise at impossibly sharp angles from the turf, giving spectators the appearance of being stacked one upon another like a chanting human pyramid. Being a goalkeeper I was closer to the fans than most. Aside from my coach and some team-mates, there was not a white face in the 50,000-strong gathering but we cared not a jot – we were playing before a packed stadium on turf so luxurious I even had a few practice dives. Much to the delight of those behind the goals.

At one point a wily striker suppurating chicanery and arrogance razored our defence and deftly lobbed the ball over my head, resulting in squeals of delight from the fans a few steps to my rear. In a moment of athleticism so rare in my subsequent sporting endeavours that I sadly still cling to it today, I flung myself backwards like a diver off a high board, threw a hand toward the ball and tipped it over the crossbar.

The crowd roared their approval and I turned around to

see tens of thousands of football aficionados nudging their mates with "Did you see that?" expressions plastered on their beaming faces. They continued to shout encouragement throughout the game and even applauded me off at full-time with "Good boy, keeper". It was once-in-a-lifetime glory and I have Soweto to thank for it.

Oupa snapped me out my liniment-scented reverie with a coldie and the news that the dinner buffet was on. We made our way through a cosy terrace where a group of African-Americans were posing with Wandile Ndaba, proprietor, raconteur and Soweto bon vivant. "Welcome," he declared to the group who I later learned were IT consultants from Detroit. "Welcome home." Oupa rolled his eyes but the Yanks beamed like returning soldiers who'd just set foot on Mom and Pop's doorstep in Encephalitis, Arkansas.

The buffet was comprised of a dozen three-legged cast-iron pots arranged in two rows of six. Since prime cuts were usually beyond the budget of your average township chef, many perfected the art of slow cooking the gristled goat flesh and sinewy steak purchased at street-side slaughter spots until it didn't so much fall off the bone as leap from it. Pepper-scented chicken curries inveigled beside tomato-laced mutton stews and bubbling birianis. This fare was accompanied by pap, a white maize meal staple that is cooked with water until it reaches a consistency thick enough to mop up gravy flotsam.

I could hear my arteries hardening as dish after dish streaked with pearls of glistening oil was piled onto the mound in the centre of the plate.

Oupa joined me at the table clutching another pair of frost-kissed Castle Lager longnecks which played consort supreme to the meal by taking a crisp blade to the sauce-soaked meat.

By the time he suggested it was time to head back into Johannesburg, an obscene tally of carnivorous indulgence had left my face coated in a happy sheen, my fingers bearing the saffron stains of the tandoori junkie and my stomach groaning the painful symphony of distension.

Over the course of a single day my heart had been stolen, broken, melted and coated with cholesterol by South Africa's blackest city. My next meal would be in its whitest.

Chapter 4

Postoria

Heading north from Johannesburg, a gentle sense of anticipation settled on me as I realised that from this point in the
journey onwards, I would be experiencing destinations I had
not lived in but only visited. The first was Pretoria. Located
just seventy kilometres north of Johannesburg, it might well
have been another planet when I was growing up.

The two cities could not be more different. Johannesburg
was a pulsating commercial harlot founded on profit over
principles where English was the language of choice. Pretoria
was a staid and graceful administrative centre which formed
the capital of a republic founded by Afrikaners fleeing British
rule.

It was in Pretoria that my brother Richard underwent
basic training as part of his two-year compulsory military service and we made the journey to visit him at the air force
base most weekends. Between mouthfuls of Jewish comfort
food such as fried fish and chopped herring, he would regale
us with tales of 4 am inspections, beds whose corners could
only be cajoled into the required right angle by slipping in a
metal food tray, and the virulent anti-Semitism displayed by
some in his barracks. Although he had never been fitter or

stronger, I'd never seen him look so miserable as he did trudging back to his dormitory clutching some home-made fudge with which he would vainly try to soften the suspicions and stereotypes his cohorts held about Jews.

The base was a spirit-sapping paean to the philosophy of breaking down recruits in order to build them up again. However, the most noticeable attribute of Valhalla was that there was no irony in its name. It was the plushest, plumbest posting you could get for basic training and Richard was only stationed there through the intercession of a family friend who was well connected in the defence hierarchy.

In the early 80s, countryside of mild undulation and grassy hue separated Johannesburg and Pretoria to the extent that the halfway point was marked by a solitary oak by the side of the highway. Today the green belt has shrunk to a shoelace as business parks and factories flee ever northwards from Johannesburg's CBD and industrial suburbs. At the same time Pretoria is expanding southwards with fresh-out- of-the-box suburbs like Centurion.

Naming a posh new enclave after a Roman commander chosen to lead one hundred men into battle struck me as an odd choice for a capital city trying to shed its reputation as the spiritual home of apartheid. I mean, if you go to all the trouble of building a lake as the suburb's centrepiece, surely Greenbanks, Waterview or even Lapland might have been more appropriate.

However, the gladiatorial mores of locals was underlined just before the turn-off to Centurion – where the world champion one-day cricket team was to kick off its defence of the title – with a billboard that read "Die Aussies Die". And a warm welcome to you too.

I obviously wasn't the only one who believed this simply

wasn't cricket because the billboard was removed some weeks later amid justifications from a tanty-tossing art director who believed it was nothing more than an innocent jibe in the context of good-natured sporting rivalry.

Pretoria has always had an air of quiet prosperity about it. The streets are wide, neat and lined with stately jacarandas that wrap a lilac pashmina around the city's shoulders every spring. Through my childhood and teen years it was decried as a larger regional centre which was to urban sophistication what rhinestones are to denim. Those who had ventured there for business trips entertained us with stories such as the time so-and-so ordered a cappuccino and was told, "Sorry, we've run out. Do you mind if I serve it in a mug?" There were also myriad hilarities regarding English-speakers from Johannesburg trying to make it through working lunches with Afrikaners from Pretoria. My favourite involved a cousin who had sailed through one such meal impressing his clients with his bilingual capabilities. Things went downhill rapidly, however, when he meant to order *aarbaie* (strawberries) for dessert but instead requested *ambaie* (piles).

I checked into my hotel in the Hatfield district then took a stroll. As I walked I discovered that the city had undergone a radical metamorphosis. Home to three universities, as well as the University of South Africa, the world's largest correspondence institution, Pretoria feels like a casting call for *Dawson's Creek*.

Hatfield's streets were lined with pubs, cafes, clubs and restaurants between which flitted packs of three-sheets engineering faculty lads and cliques of mocha-skinned nymphs wearing gravity-defying hipsters and "yes but not with you" expressions.

Then there were the Afrikaners. How could a race with

such ugly ideas produce such beautiful women? I followed a group of these celestial creatures into a square bounded by four pubs whose patrons were all watching South Africa take on the West Indies in the opening match of the World Cup. Regardless of whether they were in the German, Irish or ultraviolet-suffused Cheeky Monkey bar, punters had draped themselves in flags and cheered every boundary while their bored girlfriends silently wished the overs away.

Nursing an amber, I occupied a stool in the corner of the Red Wolf bar and was immediately struck by the relaxed nature of the city's inhabitants. Unlike their counterparts in Johannesburg who clutched their bags to their chests like fullbacks taking a Gary Owen, the women in Pretoria were entirely comfortable leaving their totes on pub tables while ordering a drink at the bar.

As the game progressed, the home team's fortunes sank. With defeat looming, you could cut the testosterone with a knife. It soared even higher when a few stultified girlfriends decided they'd had enough of this shared experience and wanted to call it a night.

There are two things I cannot look away from: one is traffic accidents and the other is a couple arguing in public. Invasive? Perhaps. Intriguing? Certainly. I was entertained by unresolved issues being raised from relationship limbo on three fronts. It was a veritable cavalcade of confrontation as phrases that began with "You never ...", "Well, you always ..." and "How was I supposed to know?" ricocheted around me like emotional ammunition.

Suitably entertained, I made my way to a steakhouse where I spent the meal trying to figure out whether the cowhide motif was horribly inappropriate or merely brutally honest.

Energised by Pretoria's vibrancy and the party-till-you-puke philosophy of the locals in this area, I pooh-poohed the idea of returning to the hotel and took to the streets for a stroll, my hands thrust deep in my pockets as I am wont to do in moments of simple contentment.

I chanced upon a gloriously glitzy pool hall where I played the kind of immaculate stick you do when alone in a foreign country after several stubbies. The table beside mine was being used by a pair of local women in their early twenties who struck up a conversation by asking if I was practising for a tournament. Spoken for though I am, it was the most flattering opening line I'd ever received. I asked them if my perception that Pretoria was far more laid-back than its stressed southern neighbour was accurate.

"Sure," replied a freckle-flecked blonde of tousled allure named Marli. Pausing to mentally translate from her first language of Afrikaans into English for my benefit, she continued, "But we still have a high crime rate here. My car has been broken into so many times that now I just leave the electrical cords exposed under the steering wheel so thieves think someone else has got there first and couldn't start the thing." Call me crazy, but there's something pretty cute about a woman who can hotwire her own car.

I woke up the next morning with a companion I hadn't counted on: a hangover that carpeted my tongue with shag pile and made my skull feel as if it was being tattooed from the inside. This was exacerbated by the fact that it had barely gone 6 am and I had been roused by a piano accordion. With a mouth foul in more ways than one, I peered out of the window to see a solitary jive merchant alternating between singing and whistling as he cajoled a melody from the cumbersome instrument. Unlike the Bavarian Brunnhildes one usually sees playing the piano accordion with graceful wrist movements, caressing fingers and the kind of anguished expression that suggests either infinite melancholy, polka-induced psychosis or chronic constipation, this musician brought a different energy to the instrument.

He played it more like a percussion instrument, pumping bellows with the urgent rhythm of a conjugal visit. The combination of his voice, the accordion's joyful wheeze and his uncle-dancing-at-a-wedding shuffle stopped a commuter exiting the station. Then another. And another. The music went from being infectious to sparking a full-blown epidemic of exuberance as a twenty-strong crowd of toe-tappers gathered in minutes. Just as quickly, however, they dissipated amid glances at wristwatches and the arrival of buses. No hat had been placed on the floor as a shrapnel receptacle and not a cent had been solicited. It had been music for the pleasure of its sharing and I couldn't have asked for a better start to the day.

Nursing a stream of cappuccinos in the hotel restaurant, I mused on the idea that the drink had been named after the Capuchin monks who came up with the idea of diluting black coffee with warm milk. As caffeine and my bloodstream renewed their happy acquaintance, my mind began idly to contemplate various other useful articles that had been named after the folk who had presumably inspired or invented them. You had your Stanley knife, your Phillips head, and my personal favourite, your Lazy Susan.

It was peak hour by the time I joined the traffic and crawled through the stately suburb of Arcadia, which boasts a hundred embassies in a five-kilometre radius. Heading away from the CBD, my route took me past a series of gushing fountains fed by the natural springs that prompted the city's forefathers to settle here.

My destination was the Voortrekker Monument. Commanding views across the city, the monument is a granite cube as high as the statue of Christ over Rio, forty metres wide and forty metres long. Designed by Gerard Moerdijk, it was reputedly inspired by the ruins of an African civilisation in what is present day Zimbabwe. Which is an odd twist for a structure that for both devotees and critics was apartheid's holy tabernacle.

Its original raison d'êtremental was to commemorate the Great Trek, a flight to freedom undertaken by thousands of Afrikaners who left the Cape in the 1830s. Under various leaders along different routes, the Voortrekkers, as they were known, shared a common motivation: the desire to be free of British rule and the abolitionist philosophies that were gaining political clout in London.

This seminal migration was to form the cornerstone of Afrikaner identity and shared numerous parallels with the settlement of the American West which took place at roughly the same time.

It was a journey Homer would have written off as improbable. Over the course of six years, 15,000 Afrikaners dragged their wagons, families and dreams of autonomy over mountains that shattered axles like toothpicks, interminable deserts and swamps swarming with malarial mosquitos gagging to go Dutch. These calamities were compounded by battles with hostile tribes prepared to kill to protect their ancestral lands. With Bibles in one hand and muskets in the other, the Voortrekkers inflicted and suffered horrific casualties.

The monument commemorates their sacrifices and ethos.

It is ringed by a fence made of black steel spears which represents the ocean of assegai-wielding warriors the Voortrekkers had to navigate. Beyond this lies an encircling wall carved with sixty-four ox wagons replicating the laagers into which the settler would manoeuvre their convoy in preparation for battle. Every corner of the building is redolent with symbolism. The busts of slain leaders squint out over the countryside they died to call home. Above the entrance a menacing granite buffalo head – the most dangerous wild animal in the land – dares would-be assailants to have a go if they reckon they're hard enough.

I struck up a conversation with a guide named Conrad, whose tour group had descended on the souvenir shop with the giddy lack of discrimination that comes with being armed with pound sterling in Africa.

A proud Afrikaner, Conrad said, "When I was growing up, this place was like a church to us".

Inside, it is more mausoleum than cathedral. One of the walls is taken up entirely by mosaic windows of a shade presumably intended to have been golden but which instead bestows upon the few sombre visitors an unflattering jaundice. The remaining walls are occupied by the world's largest marble friezes depicting a series of crucial moments during the Great Trek. Because the craftsfolk and facilities for creating a work of this size were not available in South Africa when the monument was constructed, sketches were made and dispatched to Italy. As a result, your average Zulu depicted in the frieze possesses a nose so Roman it might as well be diagonally parked across a laneway pavement in the shadow of St Peters.

The most brutal and detailed of these friezes commemorates the Battle of Blood River where 10,000 Zulus were routed by Boer leader Andries Pretorius, after whom the city was named, and his band of 470 commandos. The story goes on that Pretorians vowed to God that if they were victorious by His hard, the day would be forever commemorated.

Nowhere is the import of this battle and the implications victory carried for the Afrikaners more dramatically displayed than on a granite tomb that forms the museum's altar. Located a floor below the entrance and best viewed through a balustraded oval hole cut into the marble floor, it is made of black granite into which is chiselled the words *"Ons Vir Jou Suid Afrika"* (We For You South Africa). The entire monument structure is crafted around this cenotaph and every year at 12pm on December 16 (the day of the battle of Blood River) a ray of sunlight passes over the inscription confirming Afrikaaners' divinely mandated rights to the land.

For reasons best known to themselves, the initial administrators were so concerned that black visitors would throng this monument to their subjugation that they instituted a policy whereby visitors of colour would only be permitted on the premises on Tuesdays. From the 1950s, however, they were banned altogether. It was a policy that stood firm for half a century and the dozen black teenagers who were dragging themselves around the place on the day I visited seemed somewhat underwhelmed by it all.

I was beginning to feel the same way and decided to top up my personality with a cappuccino and *koeksister*. Despite the fact that it appeared on the menu, the definitive constituents of the former were a mystery to the cafe staff who topped a cup of Nescafé instant with two tablespoons of cold double cream. However, they were clearly at home with the latter. A twist of deep-fried pastry injected with, soaked in and sweating golden syrup, *koeksisters* are one the Afrikaners' gifts to humanity.

Gazing across the 341 hectares of grassland surrounding the monument, I tried to picture them filled with the crowd of 250,000 (ten times the population of Pretoria at the time) that gathered here with traditional costumes, songs, wagons and attitudes to celebrate the centenary of the Great Trek in 1938.

The assembly gave crucial weight to the burgeoning Afrikaner nationalism that would eventually sweep the architects of apartheid to power a decade later. Many of those present at the foot of the monument in 1938 had been forced off the land a decade earlier by the worst drought since settlement, only to be slugged by the unemployment and degradation that accompanied the Great Depression.

Staunchly Afrikaans political parties and cultural organisations seized on the discontent with promises to uplift what they termed "poor whites" by providing improved housing and social conditions. They also undermined trade unions by seizing on corruption amid their English-speaking hierarchy to illustrate that they would never have the interests of Afrikaner workers at heart. The English domination of business was portrayed in heartless, anti-Semitic terms with an alternative being provided in the form of compassionate new banks and financial institutions which were founded by Afrikaners for Afrikaners. The us-against-them line was hammered home by Afrikaner newspapers, and paramilitary organisations modelled on the Nazis clashed with government troops in the streets.

When World War II rolled around and South Africa fulfilled its Commonwealth obligations, even more Afrikaners turned their back on the government because they believed this was not their conflict. By the 1948 general election, the Purified National Party had added to the weight of Afrikaner nationalism with a propaganda campaign which played on fears that the nation's cities were soon to be overrun by black migrants. The government was split on the issue and dilly-dallied like a game-show contestant trying to decide between the foot spa and the sheet set. What's more, Jan Smuts was seen as an ageing prime minister more interested in playing the role of international statesmen and writing the preamble to the fledgling United Nations than address-ing the suffering of his people.

On promises of rigid segregation and job protection for whites, the government that would administer apartheid for the better part of half a century snuck into power with a minority of the vote but a higher number of rural constituen-cies. And all from a picnic in a paddock.

Up close the Voortrekker Monument is so imposing that I didn't adequately take in the view it afforded of the city until I was driving away. Ensconced in a jacaranda-canopied bowl bordered by gentle slopes, Pretoria's other most notable architectural landmark threw seductive glances my way from a ridge on the other side of town. The Union Buildings were designed by Herbert Baker in 1910 as a trial run for New Delhi's government buildings. As prototypes go, it isn't half bad. Inspired by the Acropolis, it presides over the city from the acme of a magnificent tiered garden. Its facade is the hue of a hangover-strength latte, sapiently teamed with a bur-nished red Italianate roof. A Renaissance extravaganza of fluid arches and shaded colonnades set behind Doric col-umns, it appears to be the happy beneficiary of an explosion in a nearby cupola factory. Stately, graceful and more entrancing the closer you get, it was everything a seat of government should be. Perhaps except transparent.

The complex spreads across the top of a lawn exploding in marigold pyrotechnics and converges on a central lily pond flanked by fountains and potted palms against a backdrop of domes upon which the figures of Atlas and Mercury look towards the Voortrekker Monument. It's an aspect that is unlikely to alter as building laws restrict the height of any new developments that may obscure the view. Apparently the omnipresent sight of the monument would remind the trekboers' parliamentary descendents of the struggles of their forefathers and their divine mandate to rule the land. *Ons Vir Jou Suid Afrika.*

It was time to explore the city, so I dumped the car at the hotel and set out on foot. Church Square was once the CBD's architectural showcase. Bounded by the French and German baroque Ou Raadsaal (Old Government House), the century-old Palace of Justice, the South African Supreme Court and the imposing Reserve Bank, the square was in sore need of a high-pressure hosing. In these buildings brutal injustices were carried out in the name of the law and policies were drafted to deny the majority of the population the opportunity to earn a fair day's wage. Judging by the decrepitude and neglect on display, it seemed the current government viewed the space as a tainted reminder of a bleak history. In the first of many instances in which my guidebook sank into ludicrous euphemism, it described the square as being "mellowed by a wide grassy expanse, where Pretorians may be found enjoying an afternoon nap".

Mostly in their own vomit it turned out. Hustlers with suspicious trouser bulges eyed me from park benches as though they were calculating how much one of my kidneys would fetch on the black market. Metho-scented vagrants lay strewn across park benches and weed-choked beds. Fruit peels and food splotches decayed into pungent pavement collages and all that moved with any sense of purpose were the intermittent whirlwinds of litter.

There are certain phrases guaranteed to deliver a dose of fleeting arrhythmia to any man. Right up there with "as long as we remain monogamous and on medication, the burning should eventually die down" is "Get in the van! Now!" So naturally when I heard this being hissed in my ear I did what anyone would do and panicked. Much to my embarrassment it was only Conrad, the guide I'd chatted to at the Voortrekker Monument; he had spotted me from across the square and, having safely locked away a vanload of Belgian tourists, had decided to save me from a visit to one of the city's casualty wards.

"This is a very dangerous place," he said, ushering me in the direction of the tour bus. "I don't even allow my tours to get out here – they just take pictures through the windows. This used to be the safest place in the city, now it's the worst. A lady had her finger cut off for the ring on it last month."

I hitched a ride with Conrad to the home of Paul Kruger, the first president of the independent Boer Republic. This was a remarkable man on many counts. Not least of which was the fact that he instructed Johannesburg's city planners to shrink the size of the blocks to accommodate an increased number of corner sites, which attracted higher rent.

Born in the Cape Province to strict followers of the Dutch Reform faith, his family joined Voortrekker leader Andries Potgieter in fleeing British rule. Kruger's empire enmity would last a lifetime and flared in response to Britain's annexation of the Boer Republic north of the Vaal River in

1880. After his initial attempts at diplomacy fell on deaf Westminster ears, he proved an adept resistance leader who frequently defeated the disciplined British troops through a combination of guerrilla tactics and the fact that the former's bright red tunics made them stand out like a vegetarian at a spit roast. Elected president no less than four times, Kruger was a negotiator of note who secured the republic's independence from Britain and constructed a railway line between Pretoria and Maputo in what was the Portuguese territory of Mozambique. This was a masterstroke as his independent republic was now no longer dependent on British ports to the south; he even appeased his more resistant constituents with free trips to the sea on the shiny black choo-choo. A man of the people before the term equated to donning the jumper of a local football team in a marginal electorate, he would frequently take up a position on his verandah, a signal to passers-by that the president was available to hear any concerns they might have.

His accomplishments become all the more remarkable when you consider that he rooted like a rabbit. In the entrance hall of the single-storey tin-roofed house in which he lived for the last sixteen years of the nineteenth century hangs a photograph of his second wife, Gezina du Plessis, who bore him no less than sixteen children and wears the understandable grimace of a woman with a birth canal that was more of shipping lane.

In a shed out the back is Kruger's trophy room. Feted by the leadership of every nation or territory who had a bone to pick with Britain and her "shift over, old chap, you're about to become a colony" proclivities, he was viewed as hero by more than just Afrikaners. The shed walls are adorned with sumptuous messages of congratulation from the nascent

American government and a cover of the French magazine *Le Petit Journal* showing a wild-eyed Boer bull impaling the startled Lion of Empire date-first on a jagged horn.

A shower and change of clothes later, I found myself seated before a frosty long-neck and a steak that didn't quite touch the sides – something which was more than made up for by the puerile thrill of being able to order "a lady's rump" slightly louder than was strictly necessary.

The bedside radio jolted me awake with a mouthful of vowels the next morning. It seemed that the previous occupant had not only settled on one of those "nonstop block chock full of rock" stations, but wanted to sing along to Limp Bizkit in the shower and had adjusted the volume accordingly. As I scanned the dial, a current affairs station emerged from the static in crisp stereo, atwitter with a story that would grip the nation for the better part of the week.

By all accounts it had been your standard bashers, smashers and slashers Monday morning at the Bronkhorstspruit police station until a blond-haired, blue-eyed teen fronted up to the constable on duty and addressed him in the Ndebele language. According to the eighteen-year-old he had been kidnapped twelve years previously by his family's black maid and kept as a slave in a remote village. Beaten, threatened with poisoning and forbidden from watching television after he saw his picture "sometime between 1994 and 1999", he went by the name his new family had given him: Happy. Turns out that Happy Sindane was most likely Jannie Botha, whose 1992 disappearance sparked a heartbreakingly fruitless search.

My final destination in Pretoria was the National Botanic Garden. Truth be told, I've never been the type to detour for flora and on the occasions I have found myself wandering such establishments have routinely passed the time by swapping the names of plant species with diseases or body parts in a mildly amusing manner. "Can't come in today, boss, I've got an inflamed gypsophila." "Next thing I know he's standing on the doorstep with a contrite expression on his face and a bunch of chlamydia in his hands."

What had in fact drawn me to the garden was a single statistic: 75 per cent of all the plant species in Southern Africa occur only in this area.

It was a crisp, clear Monday morning in late summer and it felt as though I had the place to myself. Divided into a formal garden and nature trail separated by a squat rocky ridge, the garden was not merely manicured but had undergone a cosmetic surgery overhaul. The result was beguilingly contrived and undeniably fetching. Thick shafts of opalescent sunlight lasered through the trees, throwing stone pathways into chequered relief. A few of the thoughtfully placed benches were occupied by retired couples who wore the soft smiles of those who have realised that life doesn't get much better than an unhurried cuppa with the love of your life by a sea of perfumed roses.

It was like stepping into a Hallmark card. Flanked by stands of trees drizzled with the first blushings of autumnal scarlet, a gentle slope of lawn tumbled away from a thatched bandstand from which the sounds of Porter, Gershwin and Basie drifted every Sunday.

A section of the park is given over to traditional healing herbs of the Ndebele tribe and with a tuneless whistle of contentment on my lips, I wandered through the most fragrant pharmacy I have ever visited. In one bed lay pelargoniums whose crushed leaves release scents from rose and peppermint to pine and spice and are used as a remedy for diarrhoea, dysentery, fever and colds. In another were rangy helichrysum stems which support the universal curative powers of a good lie-down by being used as both bedding and a fever remedy.

From syphilis (pineapple flower) to sinus (wild garlic), one's every ailment could be cured; but for sheer flexibility, you can't go past the marula tree.

This botanic equivalent of a Swiss Army knife boasts a coarse outer bark which is used for haemorrhoids (although whether the remedy is applied externally or internally remains unspecified); the inner bark is an effective antihistamine for insect bites; the oil from its nuts – oh grow up – makes a fine preservative; its fruit produces a potent moonshine and the peel of the fruit can be burned and ground into a coffee. But what about the gum? I hear you cry. Mix it with soot and you have pretty decent ink for cave art. Finally, if you're into cruising, why not take your lead from Namibian tribes who have been making boats from marula wood for centuries.

The gradient had sharpened by now and soon I found myself atop the ridge, face to face with an animal whose nearest living relative is the elephant. Cross a rabbit with a guinea pig then yank it by the arms and legs until it sinks a tooth clear through your thumb and you've got one remarkable little creature called a dassie. Aside from the fact that they do not drink water, instead preferring to source it through grass, roots and bulbs, they have the endearing habit of standing on their hind legs to view oncoming predators or wheezing, sweat-stained authors, whichever manifest first. And so it was that I was greeted by a dozen curious heads that popped up simultaneously from behind a boulder in much the same manner as the inhabitants of an open-plan office when voices are raised by the water cooler.

As enchanted as I had been by the immaculate garden section, I much preferred the nature trail which was marked out with rough-hewn stone slabs from which sprung petite purple and white buds. Ducking and weaving the velvet bushwillows that overhung the pathway, I felt as though I was inspecting the estate of a reclusive tycoon who'd let the grounds dwindle to a vegetative state as he did the same. Descending through knotty trees covered by chocolate bark speckled with mint-green moss, I made my way into a small valley where the trunks grew thicker, the leaves became more expansive and the sound of running water burbled in a glade unseen.

It was like walking through Disney's *Jungle Book* and as the path brought a ten-metre high waterfall into view, I half expected to see Baloo gambolling about beneath it singing "The Bare Necessities". Ensconced in a blanket of banana trees with leaves you could wrap a child in and ferns whose tendrils spoke of chameleon tongues, the falls emptied into a shallow pool rendered amber by stray dollops of sunlight. Lusher than Robert Downey Jr the day before checking into Betty Ford, it instantly leapt to the top of my list of places I'd like to buried.

It turned out that the locals viewed it more as a location for beginnings than endings. Declarations of undying love accompanied by princess-cut diamonds were apparently almost a daily event on these sylvan banks and many couples chose to take their vows at a nearby thatched pavilion. A fact attested to by a noticeboard from which taffeta brides and mulleted grooms beamed.

Beyond the pond was a whitewashed tearoom and a series of paved terraces sporting wooden chairs and tables. At least half-a-dozen were occupied by near Mrs feverishly consulting bloated lever arch files as they planned their weddings. The others were taken up by women of a certain age who it seemed gathered here regularly for Devonshire teas and the character assassination of anyone who couldn't attend.

Amid eavesdropped gems such as "Well, if Merle won't wear an off-the-shoulder dress, she can't be a bridesmaid" and "Poor Vera, she honestly thinks hormone replacement therapy will stop her husband sleeping with the maid", I gorged on gossip, Earl Grey and buttery scones.

With insistences to the waitress such as, "Don't you take her money, dear; you know it's Tuesday, Gladys, and I always pay on Tuesday" wafting over the marigolds, I reluctantly left the gardens to drive a couple of hours west to the high court of the Sun King.

Sun City was the brainchild of Sol Kerzner, the fiercely ambitious and freakishly shrewd son of Russian migrants, who grew up in a tough Johannesburg suburb where he worked in his parents' milk bar. Already a hospitality magnate with a string of luxe properties and a Miss South Africa trophy wife, he exploited the policies of the apartheid government to launch an empire which at last count spanned thirty casinos across the Caribbean, southern Africa and the Indian Ocean islands.

The idea was ingeniously simple: legally provide moneyed South Africans with all the illicit pleasures banned by the straitlaced Calvinist regime. These irresistible temples of sin would only succeed if they were located reasonably close to white population centres. Enter Bophutotswana, the nominally independent homeland established by the South African government, which functioned under its own malleable constitution and was less than three hours drive from Johannesburg.

Sun City wasn't the first of Kerzner's casinos to blossom under this strategy, it merely expanded the cornucopia of forbidden delights. Aside from gambling, there were Vegas-style revues called Extravaganzas where showgirls shimmied in extravagant headdresses and not much else. For those who preferred their titillation bluer and lived in a society where *Playboy* was banned, there were strip shows and soft-core porn films. So novel was the concept that I recall groups of my parents' contemporaries lined up outside the Sun City cinemas to catch a late-night flesh flick.

Second to gaming, Sun City's prime attraction was musical entertainment. Offering enough cash to anaesthetise many an artistic conscience, Kerzner secured a string of international talent to play his venue. Which wasn't technically in South Africa and therefore dubiously rationalised as in no way condoning apartheid. Thus it came to pass that audiences – which comprised 99.9 per cent white South Africans – starved of internationally recognised live acts would stampede out of Johannesburg to the resort. Between 1979 and 1986 I saw Frank Sinatra, Liza Minnelli, Jack Jones, Ben Vereen, Elton John, Queen, Rod Stewart and The Village People (the last with my mother as a birthday gift – for me).

I had fond memories of the four separate hotels, two golf courses, acres of swimming pools and composite paradise gardens that made up the Sun City sprawl. In our first genuine taste of independence, my mates and I, aged sixteen or thereabouts, would pile into buses at the central Johannesburg railway station for the three-hour journey through the serene Magaliesberg mountain range and the town of Rustenburg to the rock concert venue.

Aside from the fact that I wasn't trying to look down the top of the girl seated in front of me, the current journey was much as I remembered it. Sun City, however, was not.

The monorail that took excited punters from the mammoth car park to the hotel was no longer in operation, leaving a suspended superfluous iron ribbon above proceedings. The lobby which was once an octagon of futuristic hedonism had been papered over in an Indiana Jones theme in which cardboard macaws held spotlights in their beaks, lurid artificial three-metre leaves were affixed to the walls and a rope bridge dangled above a waterfall which gushed over a precipice of gold coins and oversize gambling chips. The once exclusive black and chrome salon privé had dated no better and the gold fabric and chandeliers that had been added in a half-hearted attempt to drag the space into this millennium only resulted in a look that Imelda Marcos might have favoured for a guest toilet.

Although casinos are now legal in South Africa, 25,000 visitors a day still come to Sun City, whose most recent addition is the Lost City, a mythical African utopia that has supposedly been rediscovered. One of the world's few six-star hotel, it is a cornucopia of domed towers, vaulted archways and bronze big-cat fountains. All of which overlook a mosaic of swimming pools, cascades, lakes, streams and a man-made beach complete with waves and waterslides that require the surgical retrieval of one's Speedos. According to the PR blurb, it's the kind of place that doesn't have an entrance, but a "grand porte chochere". As opposed to those modest porte chocheres you're always running into.

The Lost City is approached via the Bridge of Time which

is flanked by tusked sculptured elephants, presided over by a huge carved leopard resting on a pillared pergola, and which shakes every hour on the hour as a reminder of the volcanic eruption that reduced the Lost City to ruins so many centuries ago.

The interior confirmed my suspicions that the Lost City was not my cup of twee. Beneath a twenty-five-metre frescoed dome in the Baroque style, zebra-print furniture sat atop a floor made of 300,000 fragments of polished marble and granite in thirty-eight shades. Animal motifs abounded with jade monkeys adorning a pillar, lions rendered in semi-precious stones featuring in wall mosaics and a life-size bronze elephant dominating the courtyard. His name was Shawu, which I believe is an ancient Sotho term for "horribly ostentatious".

The odd thing was that everywhere my eye wandered it was greeted by elegant craftsmanship – an intricately carved balustrade, a delicate mosaic border on a marble floor, a blurred detail in a woven rug depicting a cheetah in full flight – but instead of these touches complementing one another, it was rather a case of gauche almighty.

I made my way back across the Bridge of Time, pausing to look out over the golf course where thirty-five Nile crocodiles are the water hazard at hole thirteen. Then it was on through the gaming hall where row upon row of blinking, whirring machines were being fed by row upon row of equally automated but rather less animated punters, some of whom had children curled up at their feet. It was a timely reality check on just how the Sun King's palace came to be, and, like they say, casinos aren't built on winners. The high-octane glamour with which Sun City once beckoned me had faded to a tawdry facsimile of its former self. I was glad I'd come but felt the same way about leaving. Besides, my next destination was to prove equally surreal. As you would expect from a mineral springs resort where the majority of clientele can soak for hours yet appear no more wrinkled than when they were dry.

Chapter 5

Soak Opera

The road to Warmbaths is bounded by a parched landscape that can only aspire to undulation. Were it not for the odd clump of lugubrious acacia trees bearing thorns like drag-queen nails, I could have been driving across a nutmeg-dusted pancake. Beneath a gargantuan liquid sky across which flat-bottomed clouds lumbered, the fringes of the tarmac liquefied in the heat and yellow lines were rendered serpentine by the wheels of semitrailers.

It was at this point that I first encountered the curse of rural travel in South Africa: Jacaranda FM, which billed itself as "the soothing alternative". This turned out to be a blatant lie on both counts as a Bryan Adams lunch hour was as serene as vigorous sandpapering of the scrotum and no other station seemed to broadcast on either the AM or FM frequencies in the area.

Throughout the 60s and 70s, Warmbaths had been a resort where couples could spend what would later become known as quality time. Unfortunately, as was the case with my own parents, the tensions leading to the need for such an interlude were not often left at home. As a result, the chalets frequently resounded to the airing of grievances rather than the rhythmic beat of headboard against gyprock.

The Warmbaths resort is spread around a series of shallow free-form pools fed by thermal springs which ejaculate a staggering 22,000 litres per hour from hideous chrome and perspex fountains mounted on granite blocks. Having clearly seen better days, the main accommodation block was being half-heartedly refurbished. The process was being carried out in the manner of a middle-aged divorcee who buys a wardrobe of low-cut tops so prospective paramours won't immediately notice her crow's legs. But try as I might, I couldn't ignore the carpet layer who had decided to take a break from his duties and curl up for a nap by the lift doors.

It also seemed that a kleptomaniac convention had been through the previous week and I was accompanied to my lodgings by a porter who skipped over the recumbent tradesman and proceeded to read out an inventory of the room's contents. He paused after each item so that I could acknowledge the presence of the two bath towels, one drinking glass, duo of pillows and so on. Once he had completed the extensive list, I was informed that the process would be repeated before checking out to ensure that no items had "vanished".

When I asked where the remote control for the TV was, he said that a R100 deposit was required.

At every turn, evidence mounted that I had checked into the modern-day equivalent of one of those Victorian sanatoriums where one might secrete a three-eared cousin born out of wedlock. The resort guide which I mistakenly assumed was to inform visitors of the varied spa delights on offer was instead a chilling catalogue of the dangers lurking in the mineral-rich waters.

Those with heart conditions were forbidden from a

certain pool; another was unsuitable for anyone over sixty, and one was described as having the potential "to cause respiratory problems for children after twenty minutes ..." Clearly believing that young guests and parents alike would flout this warning with cavalier contempt, the management saw fit to end the sentence with "and possible death".

Suitably enthused I slipped into my boardies and made my way to the spa complex which had once been the resort's pièce de résistance but was now, as the French say, monumentally crappy. It was arranged around a large indoor pool beneath a two-storey ceiling made up of the white prefab panels most frequently found in government offices and sheltered accommodation. Aside from the fact that several of these were missing, affording a view of rust-weeping pipes, the atmosphere was made all the more clinical by walls covered in fluted concrete. The top floor, which was once given over to treatment rooms that resounded with the cracks of stubborn vertebrae, shiatsu-triggered groans of delight and the yelps that provide the soundtrack to the art of waxing now lay dormant. Outside each of these locked cubicles stood dusty receptacles which resembled oversized cricketers' boxes. Once attached to humidifiers, guests awaiting their 3pm back, sack and crack depilation would shove their faces into these contraptions for a shot of sinus-stripping eucalyptus.

Despite being hemmed by cracked tiles and festooned with posters either prohibiting jumping or once again informing patrons in graphic terms of the dangers that accompany soaking for more than twenty minutes at a time, the pool was an inviting prospect. Pale blue and quilted with patches of sunshine from prodigiously placed skylights, it was dominated by a dozen jets arranged in a circle which shot water five metres towards the ceiling. Here they were met by a suspended abstract chrome sculpture that looked as if it might have been scavenged from a bin outside the Alessi factory.

Dotted around the place on creaky chaises longues was an equally creaky handful of octogenarians in load-bearing one-pieces and Nancy Reagan memorial hairdos. They were accompanied by likeable sun-withered husbands in faded Speedos who felt compelled to greet you no matter how many times your paths crossed during the day. These saluta-tions would inevitably start out with a crisp "Morning" before moving into the activity-focused realm, as in "Off for a dip are we?", and settling on a game-show host wink with the inevitable cheek-cluck noise.

After a stint in the main pool I made my way to the hydro spa which was decked out in lurid orange tiles and acres of that wood panelling the Bradys had on the side of their car. At 37°C and possessing a mineral cocktail said to open a can of whupass on rheumatism, it lulled me into the kind of drowsy stupor that required two hours of prostrate recovery on a sun lounge by a fragrant jasmine hedge.

At that point a curious turn of events occurred. Perhaps it was the combination of dehydration and a midday beer but the place began to grow on me. Yes, it was faded and tatty. Yes, there was a likelihood that somewhere in the depths of the complex lay a fully equipped S&M dungeon where guests could be flagellated senseless under the pretext of therapy. However, despite its numerous faults, the place had an air of relaxed egalitarianism about it that must have approximated a Black Sea resort circa 1975.

For children on school holidays it surely offered the self-contained universe that characterise many of my fondest vacation memories. When substantially occupied, it was the kind of place where you could assemble a gang of prepubescent contemporaries quick time. A place where it felt like the summers were endless. A place where first kisses and lines like "Mary told me to tell you that you're dropped" were doled out in equal measure. Decrepit as it was, there was also a sense of sedate innocence about it.

This bonhomie was heightened by the fact that those whose budget would not stretch to a room could camp on a verdant stretch of lawn by the tennis courts. Had a spa with exclusive access to this multitude of natural springs been located in close proximity to Sydney, Stuttgart or Sante Fe, it would have been the A-list playground of twerps called Serge and Anastasia who program their enema appointments into Palm Pilots and address staff as "honey".

After dinner at the on-site rib restaurant – that's my kind of health spa – I retired to my room to sample the local televisual fare.

Television only arrived in South Africa in 1976 and for its first two decades was entirely government controlled. Until then, radio had been the primary entertainment medium and we used to rush home to crowd around the stereo for shows like "Squad Cars" and "Jet Jungle" – a superhero powered by oats. Like everything else in the country at the time, the radio stations were divided by race. Those for English-speaking whites played pop music of the Chris De Burgh and Bread ilk. Those for Afrikaners had their own country music which still does big business, while the black population had to share a series of stations where air time was divided across half-a-dozen or so languages.

Many of the most popular programs, however, appeared across the radio spectrum in several tongues. Fleeting attempts to make these shows more multicultural were abandoned after participants with the most basic of educations were asked to answer questions in what was obviously their second language. The incident which prompted this retreat – and stakes out the shadowy ground between urban myth and "my brother heard it live" – took place on a show called *Check Your Mate*, where couples found out how well they really knew one another. "Where is the strangest place you've ever made love to your wife?" was the question posed to a man, who replied with something along the lines of, "In the carpark outside a casino". After responding with a lame "talk about a winning hand" single entendre, the host then instructed the man's wife to be escorted out of the sound-proof booth and asked, "Where is the strangest place your husband has ever made love to you?" After taking a moment to consider her options, she replied, "In the bottom".

Television confined our radio listening to the car and even though broadcasts in its nascent years were limited to two hours in the evening and two in the morning, the box provided us with a variety of entertainment we could barely fathom. Previously, yearnings for talking pictures meant a trip to either the local cinema or film shop. Most everyone we knew owned a small projector and reels of film in metal canisters would be lugged home with feverish anticipation on movie nights. After a few such evenings were marred by the choice of a pastel green wall as the projection surface, thus rendering all the stars slightly bilious, my dad soon mastered the art of stringing up white linen bed sheets.

Irrespective of what was happening between the sheets on screen, these nights were invariably filled with romance as Mum and Dad snuggled on the couch beneath a flickering beam of light, only to be disturbed when the celluloid snagged and snapped, causing us kids to glare at my father as if he had purposely misfed the projector. Sometimes there was even a fair whack of drama. The most notable of these instances was when a young maid named Maria who was new to the city and had recently begun working for us (everyone under our roof was always invited to movie night) was confronted with her first moving image. Seated beside me on the couch, she looked at the sheet not three metres away from her to see a steam train barrelling in her direction with a trail of gun-toting cowboys in pursuit. With a wide-eyed squeal of fear, she was over the sofa like an Olympic hurdler and halfway down the block before my dad caught up with her.

When our first TV – an enormous Telefunken with faux mahogany panelling – was delivered, the projector was unceremoniously relegated to a musty cupboard in the storeroom. As difficult as this may be to believe, my family and I actually watched the test pattern for a good hour after the set was initially tuned. The excitement during the build-up to the first broadcast was palpable in schoolyards, offices and beauty salons across the land.

And what was the first show we ever saw? It was a tutorial on how to tune in your TV. As we elbowed one another in glee, it didn't dawn on us that what we were in fact viewing was the quintessence of redundancy. We were viewing and that was all that mattered.

Aside from the restrictions placed on news services by a state-run broadcasting authority, the insidious presence of the apartheid regime manifested itself in myriad small-screen ways. Until a pair of dedicated channels was introduced in the early 1980s, the only black people you saw on

TV were playing servants, rioting over something or other on the 6pm bulletin or dazzling spectators on the soccer field.

Even the notion of racial equality was a no-no. For example, I recall watching the simpering host of a show called *Pop Shop* announce the "Ebony & Ivory" video with the words, "Who'd have thought you could write a song about the keys of a piano?"

Things have come a long way and the racial make-up of South Africa is now reflected on television. From cap-toothed presenters, product-hocking guests and collagen-friendly soapie stars to dreadlocked game-show hosts and sexy weatherwomen, most everyone is black, multilingual and working it Oprah-style.

The ads also now feature groups of upwardly mobile black women perving on waiters at cafes with oh-so-hilarious orders for coffee – "Hot, dark and strong – like my men". As opposed to sweet, white and weak perhaps.

The saving grace of the block of advertising I saw was the most heart-warmingly honest slogan I have ever encountered from a public utility. "Travel South African Rail," went the pitch. "It's a pleasant experience." Not great. Not marvellous. Just the best you could hope for.

South African television is mercifully behind the times in that its definition of current affairs has not yet been broadened to include the secret filming of compo cheats, extensively tattooed bickering neighbours and exposés of what really goes into your margarine. That evening's episode of a show called *Carte Blanche* had me scrambling for my notebook as it chronicled a rural hospital crisis that would depose any First World government.

So traumatic are the working conditions in overcrowded, under-resourced South African hospitals that staff would rather be unemployed than face what awaits them over the course of a shift. Rural health authorities argue that the infrastructure has crumbled in the wake of apartheid's demise, leading to such a lack of training that nurses do not have the diagnostic skills to prioritise between chest pains and haemorrhoids, a maintenance program so underfunded that gastrointestinal wards have no working toilets, and compromises such as "a drunk radiologist is better than none at all".

Definition of a crisis? When a black doctor working in a far-flung location stares wearily down the barrel of a camera and says, "I'm glad the old system is gone but I saved more patients' lives under it". The show ended with the shattering tale of a young family who had gone to visit their father after a minor operation to find him dead in bed with a still-hot meal by his side.

After passing the room inspection the next morning, as well as a brief pat-down to ensure I hadn't secreted a tumbler in an orifice, I made my way to reception to check out.

"Have you heard?" asked the woman behind the counter as she handed over my remote control deposit. It's a fairly open-ended question, especially when put to a person prone to bouts of morning sarcasm. Stifling the urge to respond with "on numerous occasions", I was intrigued by the combined tone of glee and gravity that accompanied the question. "About what?" I replied.

"Shane," she clucked earnestly.

Sensing my confusion, she added a helpful, "The sheik of tweak". It seemed the boy who had been missing for twelve years and had lobbed into a police station sprouting allegations of slavery had been bumped to page two in the wake of a certain Australian spinner testing positive to a banned diuretic on the eve of his team's first World Cup match. Unable to conceal their glee at the prospect of Australia's strike weapon being sent home in disgrace, the staff took a smirk break as I threw my gear into the car and my car into gear.

Continuing northwards, I cruised by endless paddocks used for the cultivation of maize, wheat and the crop that sounds more like a dental complaint than anything else: sorghum. At this time of year, however, they lay fallow. The area was known as Springbok Flats, named after the rivers of gazelle which crisscrossed this plain before the settlers began blasting the bejesus out of them for land clearance, but were still so numerous that they continued to attract the odd lion with a venison hankering up until the 1930s.

Beyond the bucolic blandness to my left lay the Marakele National Park, home to cycads older than Zsa-Zsa Gabor and 800 breeding pairs of Cape vultures, a species which has been observed to glide the currents for over twenty minutes at a time with a single wing flap.

My destination was the town of Nylstroom. I wasn't hoping for much and this dreary hamlet delivered in spades – as you might expect from a town whose welcome sign is sponsored by the local liquor outlet. The town's main drag was a wide affair bounded by single-storey discount furniture outlets, feed stores and the kind of clothing shops favoured by menopausal women who attend a lot of funerals.

The town offered precisely two highlights. The first was its name. According to a group of devoutly religious Voortrekkers, this region was the Promised Land of the Southern Hemisphere. Known as the Jerusalem Travellers, they fled the Cape in the 1860s in search of a Holy Land unblighted by Brits. When they eventually reached this region, they put two and two together and got three.

Encountering a stream flowing north through fertile land at the eastern tip of the Waterberg plateau, the parched settlers thought it appropriate to give this source of fresh water a name. Searching about for inspiration, their eyes were drawn to a nearby hill referred to by the local tribe as Modimolle (Place of the Spirits). Dominating the landscape and vaguely conical, the trekkers concluded that what they were in fact staring at was a pyramid. Which naturally meant that they couldn't be anywhere but Egypt. Therefore the stream already had a name – the Nile. Hence they christened the new settlement Nylstroom and have pretty much been embarrassed ever since.

The second of Nylstroom's delights was that it was the location of my first Afrikaans conversation in fifteen years.

While refuelling the car, I was accosted by a man weighed down by an overstuffed plastic laundry bag slung over his shoulder who asked if I would be interested in buying a leather jacket. At which point I surprised myself by wrenching a coherent declination from a lexicon that had not been utilised since George Michael was a heterosexual sex symbol.

He then proceeded to yank from the bag the kind of double-breasted number most frequently sported by the underlings of *Miami Vice* drug lords. An impassioned sales pitch followed in which he countered my every point with a slick retort. I'm one of those types for whom haggling carries all the fun of a barium meal, but although I had zero intention of purchasing, the fact that I was conducting the negotiation in Afrikaans led to it lasting longer than it should have.

Having ascertained his chances of making a sale were slimmer than that of a Beatles reunion, the mobile boutique was eventually hoisted onto the salesman's back and he trudged off in the direction of the main street.

A dozen of years of mandatory Afrikaans study has guaranteed most white South Africans a degree of bilingualism. However, besides making Dutch street signs somewhat easier to decipher – a handy skill in the wee hours having extensively sampled Amsterdam's finest diversions – the language is of no use outside the nation's borders. However, despite being synonymous with a regime of soul-sapping discrimination and possessing such an abundance of gutturals that fluency makes one appear to be trying to dislodge a moth from the windpipe, Afrikaans is a language with its fair share of soul and beauty. It has spawned poetry of rare insight and depth, authors such as Herman Charles Bosman who mastered the twist-in-the-tale short story half a century before Roald Dahl published *Tales of the Unexpected*, and a vocabulary with an idiosyncratic charm all of its own. An accident, for example, literally translates as an "unlucky". A cemetery is a "burial farm".

The road north to Potgietersrus gently arcs its way through vine-wreathed paddocks and fragrant melon farms along a valley floor with the watercolour grey Waterberg Mountains on the left and the charcoal Strydpoort range on the right.

Where Nylstroom was slipping into a coma from which it didn't look likely to recover, Potgietersrus had an air of quiet languidness about its wide streets overhung with tropical bowers. Apart from a nearby cave network from which has emerged everything from the bones of extinct sabre-toothed predators to a hearth system indicating that between 50,000 and 100,000 years ago the controlled use of fire was a sophisticated endeavour, the town's primary tourist attraction was the Arend Dieperink Museum.

Upon my arrival I was greeted by a rotund Afrikaans woman in a floral smock and Crystal Carrington do who was just about to lock up for her lunch break. Having convinced her that doing so would deprive an international visitor of a unique cultural experience, she wanly introduced herself to me as Hendrina, rolling her r's extravagantly as she did so.

"I'll be back in an hour. If you need to know something before then, ask one of the ladies," said Hendrrrrrina with a wave in the direction of two elderly black women. "I don't know if they'll be able to answer your questions, but they've been here for fifteen years, so they must have picked up something."

The driveway was littered with the decaying carcasses of tractors, hoes and ox wagons. One building was given over to the formidable archaeological heritage of the area. Another focused on the domestic environment endured by the early settlers. Between 1903 and 1910 the typical house in the area was either made from stone, clay and sods or baked bricks. The walls were washed with lime, the roofs were pitched and the floors were smeared with dung, which must have proved pretty useful when someone baked an air biscuit over dinner and there was no dog to blame.

It was the start of a faecal theme that culminated in the following room where there was an exhibit of the bush remedies developed by the settlers. Apparently bee stings were best treated with "warm faeces". Note the temperature specification. I could only imagine some poor farmer enjoying his morning constitutional in the outhouse only to be disturbed by his wife beating on the door and yelling, "Push, Harry, push – the kids are swelling up like balloons".

When I finally caught up with Hendrrrrrrina, she got me tanked and came over a touch Mrs Robinson.

In a stroke of genius that museums around the world would do well to emulate, the Arend Dieperink had installed a distillery out the back in which the South African equivalent of moonshine was manufactured. Utilising the most gloriously tenuous of pretexts, Hendrina justified the sideline by pointing out that the still used was an original nineteenth-century artefact. With that she ushered me into her office, shut the door and proceeded to clear a space on her desk which was piled with yellowing photographs from the 1950s and dusty manilla folders. She then fished a pair of shot glasses from her top drawer and plonked them down one-handed.

"First," she said, "we'll try the *witblits*."

Literally translated as white lightning, this is not so much a top-shelf spirit as an under-the-counter one. Seems the Voortrekkers were less than impressed with wine's measly 13 or 14 per cent alcohol content and decided to turn things up a notch by producing a drink from grapes that was to be slugged not sipped and could kick you into next Tuesday.

Boasting a 75 per cent proof rating, the shot of *witblits* I threw back under Hendrina's watchful eye singed my sinuses, transformed my gullet into a fire trail and had my brain bobbing around my skull like an olive in a martini.

"That was what you might call an entree," purred Hendrina as she edged her chair closer to mine. "Now for the main course."

This turned out to be three shots of a drink known as *mampoer*. Made from seasonal fruit and proudly proclaiming an alcohol rating of 60 per cent proof, Hendrina joined me in accounting for a tot of orange *mampoer* followed by one of peach. Sweet without straying into the sickly stickiness of ouzo or sambuca, the *mampoer* was magnificent in a vowels-overpowering-my-consonants way. However, the piss de resistance was marula *mampoer*. Made from a native berry that tastes like the result of an untethered geneticist's attempt to create a guanana, it had the spin rooming and brought out in Hendrina a coquettishness I was unprepared for.

With each slam of drained shot glass on mahogany, she had inched further towards me so that our knees were now separated by no more than a layer of denim and the thinnest of surgical hose. I'll let you guess who belonged to what.

"Do you want to taste the fruit?" she asked with a hint of slur and a disturbing tone which suggested a foray into metaphor.

"Okay," I responded, my intended air of politeness hijacked by a tentativeness which manifested itself in an upward octave change between syllables.

Hendrina reached into a plastic bag behind her and retrieved a cumquat-sized berry with a lime-green tinge. Not content with simply handing it to me, she manoeuvred her hand towards my mouth in a motion so agonisingly slow that the full horror of its implications was not merely played out but ticked over one frame at a time.

"You have to bite gently to get the juice," she continued with an expression that screamed, "Boy, I'm gonna curate you senseless." Clumsily intercepting her fingers with mine, I fed myself the fruit and overcompensated for the awkwardness of the moment by asking what other alcoholic treats Hendrina had in store.

Cue the liqueurs. One was the kind of creamy coffee number most often favoured by teenage boys for getting prom dates out of their shot taffeta and onto a back seat. The other was a sweet diversion delicately flavoured with a tart local tea called *rooibos*.

Combined with the *mampoer* and *witblits* shots, these tipped Hendrina from mischievous to maudlin.

"You know," she said, her eyes suddenly far away, "we whites did many things wrong in the past, but why does that have to mean our culture should be allowed to die? I have had a black boss for six months and, aside from the archaeology, he can't see the value in this museum. Since apartheid ended, my budget has been ripped apart, I have had to let most of my staff go, and important historical items are rusting in the front garden because there is simply no covered space left."

It was at this point that Hendrina's train of thought was derailed by the alcohol bandits. Betraying the suspect attitudes of anyone who feels compelled to start their sentences with "I'm not a racialist, but", Hendrina continued, "Blacks just don't value white culture, which developed hand in hand with the Bible. They don't believe in a God that will punish them.

"It's not only me," she said. "Hundreds of small museums around the country will disappear over the next few years. It's a part of our history the new government feels is no longer relevant and should be done away with. But how can I convince a victim of apartheid that it's as much a part of South Africa as his culture?

"Even the names of places are changing because the government feels they have associations with the Great Trek, which lead to the deaths of hundreds of thousands of blacks."

Summoning a trio of her staff, Hendrina then named a

number of towns to which they replied with the new govern-ment-approved appellations and shared small smiles as she attempted the pronunciations. Pretoria became Tswane. Warmbaths became Bela Bela. Nylstroom became Modimolle.

Hendrina's logic couldn't be faulted on this count. It was an utter crock. The exercise had cost millions of rands, which could have been far better spent trying to reduce the dispar-ity between rich and poor that a decade after the fall of apart-heid is only trumped by Botswana and Brazil.

After a slurred excuse pertaining to a fictitious interview and two strong coffees on the main road, I bade Potgietersrus and its coy curator farewell. I had lingered longer than I had intended and by the time I reached my overnight destina-tion of Pietersburg (Polokwane), all that remained of the sun-light was a razor cut on the horizon bleeding orange.

Nursing a 6pm hangover, I checked into a motel located so close to the highway that I could overhear truck-drivers' CB radio conversations as they whizzed past. I made short work of a pizza so greasy that the bottom of the box had become transparent by the time the delivery arrived, and then did what I could to steel myself for the next day's first destination: a concentration camp.

At the end of the nineteenth century Britain's once invul-nerable economic might was being eviscerated by the par-venu across the Atlantic and Germany. The extent of her empire meant that Britain had become the centre of world finance and banking, but the status quo could only be main-tained if more – lots more – gold could be found to bolster the thinning ingot quota that was held in the Bank of England's vaults and which underpinned the value of the pound. Brit-ish eyes turned northwards towards the independent

Transvaal republic and acquired the unmistakable lust for acquisition.

Having fled the Queen's rule in the Cape, Paul Kruger's renegade republicans were hardly likely to be seduced by diplomatic efforts to be brought back into the fold. A bloody and bitter conflict flared up in 1880–1881 and erupted into full-scale war from 1899 to 1902.

Adhering to the fervent – and not entirely unfounded – belief that the Brits were advancing on a homeland they had fled to long before any traces of gold were found, the Boers immediately put paid to any thoughts of gentlemanly conduct in the field of battle. They obeyed commands only when they agreed with them, thought nothing of galloping away to resume the fray under circumstances where the odds weren't so drastically stacked against them, and had a penchant for picking off British infantry from concealed positions as they marched in tight formations along the veldt.

The Brits responded to the subterfuge of the Boers' guerrilla tactics with a scorched-earth policy. Between 1900 and 1902, 30,000 farmsteads were razed and crops torched as they attempted to starve the Boers into surrendering.

Many did just that and were placed in what were termed "refugee camps" to protect them from other Boers who viewed their actions as treacherous. Later, the suddenly homeless wives and children of Boer combatants were also concentrated at designated areas around railway lines and water sources. And lo, the concentration camp entered the pantheon of British invention.

Little thought had been given to how the refugees would be accommodated and managed once they had been contained in these camps. Overwhelmed by the sheer number of women and children they had forced to abandon their burning homes, the British military continued to cram thousands into tent cities. Their ranks were soon thinned. Pneumonia, chicken pox, dysentery and measles ran rife, and by the end of the war 28,000 Boers had died in these camps.

Located in a light industrial area on the fringes of town, Pietersburg's concentration camp was appropriately solemn and utterly disrespected. The size of a modest suburban cricket oval, it had been home to over 4000 people. Of the 657 who never left, 523 were children.

Beyond a black metal gate savaged by decay and expletive-laden graffiti lay row upon row of half-buried stone coffins, many no longer than my forearm. Save for a few streaks of sickly grass and the odd knotted acacia, it was a litter-strewn dustbowl. So extensively vandalised was this graveyard that what few fragmented tombstones were left were haphazardly affixed to a nearby shrine of remembrance. There was also a plaque that once bore some solemn sentiment. Or at least I think it was as a plaque. Now nothing but a silhouette remained and the engraved face had been ripped from its bolts for a few rand from a scrap-metal dealer.

Scanning the perimeter from a nearby wall that had been veneered with granite slabs bearing the names of those who died here, it struck me that after all these years this place was still bounded by razor wire.

Where there were fifty-five of these camps for whites, sixty-six were established for blacks. If the Afrikaans inmates did it tough, those of darker hue lived in conditions vomited up from the depths of purgatory.

A chill wind from Buchenwald seemed to have dropped the temperature by ten degrees. Aside from what those who lived and died here suffered, what moved me most was how their memory was being allowed to wither with neglect.

Disconsolate and hungry, I ventured into the centre of Pietersburg which had all the charm you might expect from an administrative and economic regional centre whose population almost doubles during the workday but is swiftly decimated come quitting time. It's one of those places people *have* to come to as opposed to *want* to.

Heading northwest, the landscape erupted in outcrops of boulders that sat like pumpkins in a thick soup of green foliage and flourishes of aptly named candelabra trees leapt from the undergrowth. These soon gave way to leafy hillocks that pierced the plain.

They turned out to be appetisers for the sumptuous main course that was the Soutpansberg range, a 130-kilometre arc of sandstone magnificence that straddles the Tropic of Capricorn. Ruggedly mesmerising from through a car window, it was the kind of terrain that could break resolve by sundown at ground level. Yet it played host to Stone Age rock art from the San people, and the nearby Limpopo River was once routinely plied by dhows with Arab and Indian traders at the helm, who bartered beads and ceramics for the gold and ivory – sounds fair – of the ancient African kingdoms.

By the time I rolled into the town of Louis Trichardt, I was thoroughly smitten. Set against wine-bottle-green hills, it looked out over a sporadically wooded grassland that shimmered into liquid on contact with the horizon. It boasted the ubiquitous white church cheerily embellished with blazing beds of pansies and was populated by locals with the easy familiarity that comes with having either slept, gone to school or prayed with everyone in town.

In what was once a staunch bastion of Afrikaaner pride, the townsfolk were now getting on with life in the new South Africa.

Where there were previously separate stores for separate races, consumers were now being presented with goods they might never have seen before as they appealed to the other group's vanities.

Nowhere was this more evident than in the field of hair care. Beside one another on the desegregated shelves of the Louis Trichardt chemist lay the usual array of shampoos, conditioners and gels making outrageously lustrous promises, as well as products formulated specifically for African locks.

Packet after packet featured cocksure models sporting Lionel Richie circa '85 'fros and bore branding such as American Look Two-Step Shampoo. Another unguent was titled Dark & Lovely, beneath which was the slogan "now with even more cholesterol". Perhaps the idea was to bloat your tresses to such a degree that cowlicks or haphazard parts inevitably collapsed never to be revived again. The most intriguing potion was a "hair relaxer" called Special Feeling, which I was sorely tempted to purchase.

This is because I have Jewish hair, which is neither straight nor curly and sits perilously close to the steel wool end of the fine–coarse spectrum.

"Thousands of years of religious persecution and you're bitching about the hair?" I hear you cry. Actually, I hear my mother cry, so we'll pause for the inevitable. "You know there are children in Russia who don't have hair?"

Yes, but they didn't grow up in an era where no girl would look twice at you without Kevin Bacon (in *Footloose*) hair and some fancy dance moves to go with it. Not even the combination of half a pot of gel that hardened to bullet-deflecting strength could help and to this day a part of me still yearns for the kind of fine stray locks that fall seductively over the bronzed foreheads of men with one-syllable names and star-ring roles. Instead, I got hair that falls upwards, is receding like the Zimbabwean economy and a surname that has a silent d.

The hair relaxer was making me tense, so I headed out of town to the Ultimate Guesthouse.

I'd found the listing in an accommodation guide in town and, thoroughly sick of cheap motel chains where the bed-spreads were suspiciously crusty and the bars were filled with regional reps who divided their commission between Johnny Walker and their children's orthodontia, I prepared myself for an establishment that couldn't possibly live up to its name. I couldn't have been more wrong had I answered the question "What's the square root of nine?" with "Cara-cas".

After proceeding in fits and stops between two of those enormous petrol tankers you see making sedan sandwiches on the news, I turned onto a rocky dirt road that pounded out a samba on the car's undercarriage. Flanked by broad rib-bons of corn under a pale sky, the track was intermittently broken by the odd driveway and a sign alerting anyone who'd like to know that they were passing by the residence of Paul and Hettie Labuschagne. One of these notices directed me down a dappled driveway to the guesthouse and, call me an old Semite, but from the time I saw the word "shalom" above the front door, flanked by bloated gilded cherubs no less, I felt immediately at home.

The place was run by Mona Du Plessis, who had only recently fled from Zimbabwe with her husband and two chil-dren. Diminutive as she was warm, and radiating the kind of hospitality no hotel school could ever teach, she instantly called to mind that cool older sister of a friend who would scrape together our combined pocket money and buy us a bottle of Southern Comfort before disappearing into the night in a veil of Impulse Body Spray and a Datsun 120B.

Hacked into a subtropical hillside, the Ultimate looked across a valley bisected by a willow-laced stream. Beyond this stood an imposing hill. Anchored by a raft of blue gums, above which rose a belt of granite, it was crowned by a dusting of leopard trees festooned with sulphur buds. I'm sure that the flora was not all native and that telephone cables lurked amid the gum trunks, but from a distance it appeared unmolested by humanity. It was one of those views that are best shared and Mona arrived on cue with a beer and self-deprecating "Not a bad backyard, is it?"

The recipe for contentment was completed by three things. A distant radio reporting the frequent fall of Pakistani wickets in the face of the Australian pace attack. The intermittent spray of palm-size butterflies with wings of Rorschach amber splotches against a midnight blue sheen. And a black labrador who would drop by every few minutes for a scratch.

In light that flared then faded, I was joined on the verandah by a friend of Mona's. Clinton Baes was a gruff, fortysomething engineer who serviced jets at a nearby air force base and was clearly fond of three things in life: his family, his stubby holder and the expression "as slippery as snot".

After a series of the perfunctory sheep-shagging jokes that Australians tend to make about New Zealanders, I asked what had drawn Clinton to Louis Trichardt.

"I was born here and it's my place as much as anyone else's," he said. "I'm not going anywhere." The last sentence was delivered with a trace of the traitorous contempt I hadn't heard since making the mistake of sharing our emigration plans with my year 12 maths teacher. After which she lectured the class about how "people were turning their backs on a country that had given them so much".

Clinton's tone softened as he took a slug of beer and declared, "I'm a white kaffir and proud resident of Makhado, which is what the town is now called. I quite like the fact that it has been renamed in honour of a VhaVenda chief who rained down fives types of hell on some white ivory hunters – not some Calvinistic Voortrekker who lived here for ten minutes then died on the way somewhere else. But do you have any idea how much it costs to change every street sign, government letterhead, map and so on in a town that was settled in 1898?

"See that guy over there?" he said, flinging his eyebrows in the direction of the affable and obliging waiter who had been plying me with amber. "His name is Ronnie, helluva nice guy. When the new government came to power, he got his own land. No running water, no sewerage, no electricity for the first few years – just a plot. I helped him build his three by three metre house from corrugated iron. With R1000 he could have bought 4000 bricks, but the government decided that this kind of grant was extravagant. Ask him if he'd prefer to live in Louis Trichardt surrounded by bricks and mortar or in Makhado under a roof that rusts.

"I have no problem with a majority government or even paying higher tax rates because I have benefited financially from apartheid, but I get the hell in when they screw their own people."

Like many South Africans I met, Clinton did not merely view the process of change as inevitable but welcomed the shift to a more just society. He even seemed resigned to his redundancy.

At forty he had five years left on his contract with the defence force, after which new jets were being procured and he didn't qualify for maintenance training. "That's affirmative action for you," he sighed. "The government has mandated a quota system designed to give more blacks access to senior jobs and better pay. We weren't even given the opportunity to apply for renewal. I'm the wrong colour and the wrong age. In fact the only thing that most white South Africans get for free these day is piles."

It was at that point that I called it a night. I was lulled into REM by Clinton's bravado and flagrant non sequiturs drifting in from the patio. I dreamt of balletic gazelle, cats that could outrun the ram-raiders' sports car du jour and troupes of blue-arsed baboons.

Chapter 6

Where the Wild Things Are

Travelling west from Louis Trichardt, the mango, avocado and banana plantations, and the vendors selling these fragrant delights from plastic buckets by the side of the road, capitulated to grey eucalypt forests. These in turn became scrubby farmland on soil that curious shade of orange which characterised the early efforts of the fake-tan industry.

The road itself could have been the expert level in a video game. So narrow that two sedans could not approach each other without exchanging licks of duco from their side mirrors, it was pockmarked with chassis-scraping potholes. These were frequently followed hard upon by unheralded chicanes in the middle of which sauntered a herd of cattle that only screeching brakes prevented from becoming meat on my grille.

At the end of this perilous road lay the Kruger National Park. The Punda Maria gate marks the entrance to the park's most northern camp. It was late afternoon by the time I paid my modest entrance fee at the stone hut and proceeded through the boom gate towards the settlement. Excited by the prospect of a game drive I had booked for that evening – dusk and dawn are the prime viewing times – I was also glad to have some company in the form of Sam, who worked as a chef at the camp and needed a lift from the gate.

Sam, however, wasn't what you'd call the chatty type. But the one piece of information I did eke out of him was a beauty. After responding to a stream of questions with either "I'm not sure", "I don't know" or "You do realise I'm not a ranger", we drove the nine kilometres between gate and camp in silence. That was until he sprang to life with, "You see that clearing? One of the women I work with saw a man being squashed by an elephant there last week." And that was his story. He didn't know whether the guy lived or died. Ditto where he had come from, where he was headed or if he was a poacher.

The camp was founded in 1919 and consisted of a series of eighteen whitewashed mud-walled huts with pitched thatched roofs which extend to shade verandahs. Captain JJ Coetser was the first ranger to be posted to the area and was therefore given the honour of naming the camp. Much like the joke that ends with the line "Why you do ask, Two Dogs Rooting?", he christened the outpost after the first animal he encountered, a zebra. Using what he believed to be the Swahili term for striped donkey, he declared that the settlement be known as Punda Maria. It was only some months later that it was pointed out that Punda Malia is, in fact, the correct Swahili term for a zebra. For reasons never quite uncovered, JJ didn't correct the error but stuck with the original name on the grounds that his wife's name was Maria and she was awfully fond of striped frocks.

Because the region's dense vegetation is not as conducive to game viewing as the vast grasslands to the south, Punda Maria is one of the least popular camps in Kruger. Yet only ninety minutes north is Thulamela, a series of stacked stones on the edge of a plateau bordering the forested Luvuvhu River. Accidentally discovered in 1983 by a ranger on patrol, it turned out be a settlement that had been occupied as early as 1200AD and whose occupants were clearly a wealthy, sophisticated society that mined gold and manufactured jewellery. They also fostered expansive trade ties as glass beads from India and pieces of Ming dynasty porcelain have been recovered from the site.

The temperature dropped along with the sun as I made my way to the assembly point to meet the tour guide, who introduced himself thus: "My name is Ezekiel. I'll be your leader and protector. I have a gun."

A jovial Xhosa, Ezekiel possessed an easygoing charm, encyclopaedic knowledge and a wry wit that put the tour group at ease. With myself and four Nebraskans – whose names I can't recall but were distinctly of the verb oeuvre: Chip, Chuck, Biff, Rip – all stowed in the elevated viewing vehicle, Ezekiel piloted us into the crepuscule down dirt tracks tantalisingly marked with no-entry signs.

Turned out Zeke was something of a botanist on a crusade to make visitors understand that without the flora, the park's fauna would be a contradiction in terms. Over here was a row of towering evergreen nyalas. Over there was a clump of russets whose clusters of silver foliage drooped to the soil and indicated the presence of underwater streams. In the distance stood a lanky cathedral of guarris, whose branches are used as divining sticks by witchdoctors.

Zeke and I were the only ones on board who found these facts remotely interesting; Biff and Biff Junior launched into their own conversation while Mrs Biff shielded her embarrassment by staring into the bush, the still air filled only with the grinding of her unnaturally pristine caps.

"Did you know," said Zeke, embarking on a more main-stream subject, "that the heart of a giraffe is bigger than that of an elephant?"

"Crikey!" cried Biff Junior in a lame Steve Irwin impression. Whereupon I reached across Zeke, grasped his rifle and emptied two tranquilliser darts the size of frankfurts into Biff Junior's thigh. Actually, Zeke just caught me staring at the rifle and gently shook his head with a "It wouldn't be worth the paperwork" look in his eye.

What floated my safari companions' collective boat was not the bachelor herds of grazing impala whose skin was glazed mocha by a waning sun. Nor was it the grey kudus that glided silently through the bush like antlered spirits. They had come for Punda Maria's renowned birdlife, a fact which became startlingly clear when Mrs Biff hissed, "Paradise white at ten o'clock". This was followed by a perfectly synchronised donning of infrared binoculars avec swivel. It couldn't have been more precisely choreographed if Martha Graham had been crouched on the bumper bar yelling, "Lift, two three, now turn two three."

Like a seasoned nightclub comic working the room, Zeke obligingly tailored his observations to the feathered domain and pointed out European rollers, helmeted guinea fowl, green pigeons and black-shouldered kites.

Armed with searchlights whose beams would illuminate the animals' retinas like rubies set against black velvet, Zeke and I scoured the ground while the troupe in the back peered into the trees. Every now and then one would stage-whisper something like "Inflamed perineum at six o'clock", "Scarlet-nobbed dowager at 3pm", or "Schizophrenic shrike at two, no four, no eight ..."

The tedium was broken when Zeke suddenly stiffened, cut

the engine and brought the four-wheel drive to the gentlest of halts. "Leopard!" he breathed in an excited whisper. "And she's pregnant!"

I heard her before I saw her; my guidebook's at first seemingly incongruous description of the call "sounding like a plank of wood being cut by a coarse saw" proving a masterpiece of simile. I could only faintly make out her lustrous flanks of gold and black as she skulked slowly towards the grassy shoulder with her laden belly scraping the tarmac.

Of the prized sightings in the African wild, no cats are rarer than the leopard. They hunt alone and operate under cover of darkness. To view one without bars between you is at once a blessing and a threat. They rarely attack humans, but of the 152 recorded man-eaters, 94 per cent were male. In my guidebook this stat was swiftly followed by the fact that most leopards are so agile that they can squirm through an average lavatory window with relatively little effort. Can you imagine the incident that prompted this detail?

Kruger is one of the last places on earth where wild animals can be seen in anything close to their natural state, and when one so rare crosses your path, all the *National Geographic* close-ups in the world can't adequately prepare you for the adrenaline rush.

What sets the leopard apart from the rest of the feline family is its appetite for destruction. Where cheetahs have to be taught that hunting is necessary to survival and lions kill primarily for the purpose of sating their hunger, the leopard is the only cat that kills for sport and would rather chew its own leg off than be caught in a trap.

Without warning, she took off into the bush in response to some movement on the road. Zeke spotted it before we did. It was a pair of the hundreds of refugees from civil-war ravaged Mozambique who flee across the park each year in search of a better life in South Africa. Many, however, are torn to shreds en route by a leopard with some time to kill or a pride with a hankering for rump and ribs.

Zeke floored it to the spot where they'd disappeared into the bush and called out in a trio of languages for them to come out. He assured them that they'd be safe and warned them there was a leopard nearby. There was no response.

"These guys follow the power lines in the park because they know they lead to South Africa," he said. "Lots of them don't make it and it's not good for the ecosystem."

We returned to the camp in time for dinner. It happened to be Valentine's Day and the staff had gone all out in cranking up the romance factor in the tiny bistro. Air Supply was playing on the stereo, candles in wine bottles were burning on the formica tables and the whiteboard on which the menu was printed bore a sprinkling of love hearts. The scene struck me with a pang of longing for my girlfriend Jennie, which gradually gave way to a flush of anticipation, as she was meeting me in Cape Town towards the end of the journey and there was a diamond in my backpack with her name on it. The dining room was empty bar a Teutonic couple that passed the evening whispering sweet gutturals in one another's ears and peering at my Birkenstocks while swapping condescending "can you believe he's wearing them without socks?" smirks. The camp store had closed thus cancelling out any possibility of buying some meat and charcoal for the barbecue by my bungalow. Which kinda sounds like a country and western song if you don't think about it too deeply and refrain from trying to rhyme anything with bungalow.

Greeted with the invariable cocktail of two parts veiled

suspicion to one part utter pity that accompanied my request for "a table for one", I was ushered to a spot in the corner. There are few activities that underline the otherwise agreeable solitude of being a lone traveller than dining. Especially when there's a mandatory tealight policy in place and all you have for a company is a newspaper and the Schadenfreude wafting over from the only other occupied table in the place.

On my way back to the room, the urge for chocolate struck. I retrieved a Mars bar from my rucksack, plonked myself on a verandah chair and took a bite. With my attention distracted by a glistening multitude of stars that can only be viewed away from city lights and smog, a furry flash hurdled the table, wrapped its nimble fingers around the chocolate bar and wrenched it from my grasp. I had met my first vervet monkey – the artful dodgers of the animal kingdom.

Nuisances in camps throughout the Kruger Park, they are nicknamed "thieves" by the local Shangaan tribe. The adults stand at no more than half a metre high and are predominantly grey but have faces covered in white fur, which gives their plaintive eyes a hyperexpressiveness. These remarkable creatures have also developed a vocabulary of thirty-six distinct calls, half-a-dozen of which relate to specific predators. They also boast some uncanny similarities to certain *Homo sapiens* in that their friendly greeting is a kiss with pursed lips and that the dominant male in a group signals status by displaying his scarlet penis at any given opportunity.

Given that I wouldn't get out of bed at 4.30am for a pelvic massage by Claudia Schiffer, it was with no small measure of self-congratulation that I joined the small group of vehicles that had lined up by the camp gate in anticipation of the five o'clock opening. The best viewing time in the park is undoubtedly the hour following dawn when nocturnal predators are feasting on the night's spoils and animals of all description are drawn from the frost-crusted grass to the tarmac which slowly heats as the sun climbs.

No matter how many geographical comparisons you hear – it's bigger than at least three nations: Wales, Taiwan and Israel – the vastness of the park cannot be adequately comprehended until you start driving. After the vehicles at the camp had peeled off down various side roads, it wasn't until 9am – that's four solid hours at forty clicks through a park that attracts one million visitors a year – that I encountered another car.

Although Kruger is flanked by mountains on its eastern and southwestern fringes, ridged with sandstone hills in the north and crisscrossed by riverine precincts and their attendant alluvial plains, it is for the most part dry savanna bushveld, a craggy carpet of rolling plains.

It is a landscape of illusions. Like one of those computer-rendered 3D paintings, you can stare at a stretch of bush for what feels like hours seeing little more than the odd scarlet-nobbed dowager. Then as if by some curious process of reverse osmosis, the foliage will produce a glimmer of warthog tusk, a two-tone burst of zebra rump or the muddy wag of a wild dog's tail. Your eyes become accustomed to searching for the faintest flickers of movement, and the seemingly empty landscape begins to teem.

The first animals I encountered were a nursery herd of gazelle, presided over by a lone male who would retain his position until a successful challenger emerged from the bachelor herd that kept a discreet distance. This early in the morning, the African sun is twenty-four-carat and rendered their backs caramel, their ribs weak latte and their underbellies pristine white. It was like staring at three dozen Rothko paintings. Except with the aaaw factor cranked to max as the infants tottered unsteadily after their mothers like debutantes in their first heels.

The scene was made all the more splendorous since it was set against pale bush willows, overhung by an olive marula canopy and punctuated by burn-outs. A common sight in Kruger, these are trees that have succumbed to thirst, resulting in cadavers set in bleached rigor mortis as they reach heavenward in a final futile plea for rain. Eventually they collapse under the weight of tortured metaphors or are devoured by termites.

The fact that Kruger exists at all can be attributed to two very different factors: the dreaded tsetse fly and an ivory-hungry president. Some sources list Portuguese navigators as having landed on the Mozambiquan coast in 1497, launched an expedition to the interior then prudently turned tail once it became clear that the area was awash with malaria, a fly that could condemn you to the delirious hell that is sleeping sickness and less than welcoming nomadic tribes that had settled there 800 years previously. Others assert it was a Dutchman by the name of Francios De Cuiper. Either way, the result was the same. Neither hung around. When the first stream of white hunters came along shortly before the dawn of the twentieth century, they discovered a landscape in which you could fire a shotgun in practically any direction and be guaranteed a pelt, tusk or trophy that would fetch a handsome price in the civilised world.

Having made a fortune from tusks himself, Paul Kruger – mad rooter and president of the Transvaal Republic – decided to curb the slaughter by proclaiming a game reserve in the southern part of the current park. Whether he was spurred by guilt or simply wanted to keep some ivory stock on hand should he need it in the future is a matter of some debate. Two things, however, are clear. His 1898 proclamation marked him as one of the world's first ecologists and it was accomplished despite strenuous opposition.

Originally known as the Sabie Game Reserve, the park was bordered by the Crocodile River in the south, the Sabie River in the north, the Lebombo mountains in the east and the Drakensberg range in the west. If the entire Kruger Park is an Aladdin's cave of natural treasures, this original slab is still the equivalent of a vault where only the most precious jewels are kept.

On its western fringes lies a cluster of what were once drought-stricken farms but are now private game parks which in the last decade have removed their boundary fences with the park so that wildlife moves unimpeded across the region. Obscenely luxurious and beyond the reach of all but the wealthiest of South Africans, their aircondi-tioned tents and individual fresh-water plunge pools are most often filled by either EU industrial barons whose fathers made their fortunes by dubious means in World War II or honeymooning orthodontists from Boca whose green-back tips alone substantially outweigh most of the hospital-ity workers' annual salaries.

Some also come to fulfil their Hemingway-esque big-game-hunter fantasies. Conservation is a costly business and many parks welcome guests willing to shell out wads of cash for items that will later be stuffed. Permits to dispatch popu-lous species are exchanged for funds which become wardens' salaries, concrete watering holes, poacher-patrol vehicles and so on. Even the odd Big Five species falls to a bullet, the theory being that the substantial fee – tens of thousands of

US dollars – garnered to assassinate an ageing leopard or elephant that was likely to die or be killed within a short time anyway will better serve the next generation. One is sacrificed so that many will endure – the way of the wild.

A significant number of the guests at these resorts are lacerated and bruised during their stay. From Harley Street to Hollywood, canny South African medicos have established consulting rooms where they flog packages which put the rhino into rhinoplasty. What makes these deals so enticing is that for less than what it would cost the hook-nosed, weak-chinned or amply-buttocked to be operated on at home, they also receive a safari that does not merely sit in luxury's lap but is clutched to her velvety bosom. One can only imagine the excitement that beats in the chest of a cashed-up A-cup at the prospect of having seen the Big Five and coming home with the Big Two.

A century before the Botox-for-lunch set began flocking to the park's western rim, Paul Kruger's plans for the sanctuary had been put on the backburner in the wake of the Anglo–Boer war. Although little remained of Kruger's troops or the man for that matter – he died (some say of a broken heart, but don't they always) in exile in Switzerland in 1904 – his vision for the park was enthusiastically taken up by the powers that defeated him.

The man chosen to be the park's first warden was Major James Hamilton-Stevenson, a short-tempered Scot. Despite referring to the park in its early days as a "pathetic and dust-covered little wench", over the next forty years he acquired an additional 10,000 acres and in so doing ensured the survival of one of the world's last wild kingdoms.

In what I like to think was a manner reminiscent of Yul Brynner in the *Magnificent Seven*, he also acquired a band of rangers who responded to a job ad that must have read something like: "Wanted: single men proficient with firearms to protect vast tract of malarial bush from trigger-happy poachers. Previous experience with ravenous wild felines and bouts of fever-induced delirium essential."

One of those who thought this sounded like the cut of his jib was Major AA Fraser, a whiskey-swilling behemoth for whom the most cursory of record-keeping was anathema and who was known to deal with the frosty Kruger nights by dozing off beneath his twenty-five dogs. Another was Harry Wolhuter, who in 1904 literally fell from his horse into a lion's mouth and vanquished the cat with the combination of three fortuitous strikes from a six-inch blade and primal screaming.

Characters like Fraser and Wolhuter have of course been replaced by rangers with hospitality training programs under their belts but, as I was soon to discover, the lions ain't goin' nowhere.

As the temperature bounded effortlessly into the low thirties, the animals retreated from the road in search of shade. What made the searing stillness even more exciting – in an odd kind of way – was the unmistakably pungent evidence that I'd just missed a large herd of elephants.

As is the custom in Kruger, cars frequently stop as they approach one another to share information on recent sightings. It's a convivial affair that frequently leaps language barriers through clumsy mime. There was no need for such malarky with the occupants of the first vehicle I encountered. The pair of bull-necked Afrikaans lads in the ute were atwitter with excitement and throwing feline plurals in my direction.

I followed their prescribed route over a bridge marked as a

safe spot for passengers to get out of their vehicles and stretch or snap, then turned onto a dirt track 500 metres away. Beneath a gnarled thorn tree lay a blood-flecked lioness gnawing on a giraffe leg the length of her body. The carcass had been dragged beneath a tree to avoid detection from the air and its entrails covered with dirt to mask the scent.

Standing a metre high and easily tipping the scales at 150 kilograms, the lioness moved with a languid fluidity. Even as she ate, the bulbous muscles in her neck and chest shimmied beneath the skin. From a crouching start she could have covered the five metres between us in less than a second, but ascertaining that I was merely an ardent fan, she went back to her cartilage tartare.

After a few minutes she was joined by another female. And another. And another. And another. From every direction they prowled out of the undergrowth until nine converged on the carcass, each met with teeth-baring hisses and the flashing slashes of claws like meat hooks. Most were likely entitled to a share of the spoils as lionesses have mastered the art of hunting in packs.

With the hard work done, the male strutted into the picture. Incidentally, your average male lion can put away thirty-five kilos of meat – around 15 per cent of their body weight – in a single sitting and mates four times an hour for less than a minute over a two-day period. It's good to be the king.

What had been a flicker in the rear-view mirror turned out to be the man of the pride. He made the mistake of loping a little too close to my car's exhaust pipe and emitted a roar that caught the attention of my sphincter way before my ears. Which is to be expected when a low-frequency rumble that can carry up to eight kilometres through the bush emanates from a metre behind you.

Sporting extravagant pectorals and crowned with a coarse faux-fro, the lion reminded me of David Hasselhoff in *Baywatch*. Until he began to eat, at which point the resemblance took a turn for the Orson Welles at a seafood buffet.

A transfixing hour later I drove back to the main road and within ten minutes was putting away a cheeseburger in the Shingwedzi camp restaurant. Considering the view it afforded, it seemed absurd that I had the tennis-court-sized thatched pavilion to myself.

The support cast of the spectacle before me was airborne. Midnight-blue birds washed opalescent by the sun were trailed by tangerine African monarch butterflies and a variety in a yellow I'd only seen previously deep in lemon-delicious puddings. The main players were a wallow of hippos (I'm not sure if this is the appropriate collective noun, but it damn well should be), a smattering of waterbuck bearing perhaps the most unfortunate marking in the animal kingdom – a ring of white fur on the rump which looks uncannily like a target – and a thirty-strong troupe of chacma baboons.

With 109 kilometres between me and the evening's camp, I reluctantly pulled myself away and continued south. Kruger spoils you for choice, and the grazing zebra, loping giraffe and nyala buck – one speaks of them in the singular apparently – that had me pulling over to gawp in wonder earlier in the day now warranted a mere deceleration as I scanned the grassland for the more spectacular.

My first elephant appeared at a drinking hole 150 metres from the road. Even from this distance the sheer bulk of the animal had me opting for idling in case a swift getaway was required. A full-grown male stands as high as the guttering on a double-storey house and easily accounts for five tonnes.

You do not want to piss them off. As I found out after turning onto a concealed dirt loop far faster than I should have. Whereupon my windscreen was filled with a wall of dusty brown elephant vagina. Stomping on the brake, the car fishtailed off the powdery sand track as the tyres vainly battled for traction. The elephant spun through 180, flapped her ears forward to make herself look even bigger and tucked her trunk under her body in the classic preparation for a charge. With a piercing trumpet of aggro, she bolted towards the car, then pulled up abruptly as it became clear that I was not merely beating a swift retreat but disembowelling one.

By the time I reached the Letaba camp, my heart rate had dropped to mere panic. Arced along the foreshore of the river after which it is named, this is one of the park's bigger camps and includes dozens of rondavels, a general store, elephant museum, auditorium and restaurant.

Letaba is an oasis of shaded lawn and curved stone paths beneath clusters of chocolate-bark mopani trees. It is immaculately neat in the pseudo-military manner that only government-owned enterprises can muster. My double room with private patio and river view – cue gambolling hippo – set me back the grand total of $40 for the night. There was even a resident herd of bush buck, the species that inspired *Bambi*. I could see paradise by the dashboard light.

On the way to the general store, I was halted by a notice alerting visitors to the reptilian dangers that routinely slip through the barbed wire of the compound perimeter. The first venomous suspect to watch out for is the puff adder. Responsible for 60 per cent of the fatal bites in the region, this piece of slithering death is thick, yellow-brown with pale-edged black chevrons on its back and produces a cytotoxic venom. Which means swelling, necrosis and eventually the shuffling off one's mortal coil. It lies in wait and its preferred strike zone is the shin.

Not that you want to remain vigilant only for what's lurking in the grass. Curled around mopani limbs, the boomslang is the acme of disguise. Comprised of a mahogany-brown body, yellow throat and algae-green eyes, it is rarely discernible in the tree in which it lives. However, when it wants to get your attention, 1 mg of its poison acts as high-octane haemotoxin which prevents the victim's blood from clotting, resulting in a haemorrhage of epic proportions.

The final member of the trio of local agony is the black mamba. Easily sliding into the five deadliest snakes on the planet list, it can grow four metres in length and raise up to one-third of its body length when getting ready to rumble. Two drops of its venom will kill a man but it usually doubles the dose as a matter of course. By the time even the speediest medic has sliced a chunk from your recently punctured flesh to suck out the poison, your throat would be throbbing, your bowels would be prompting the nausea of a thousand congealed kormas and your muscles would be in the grip of seizures that would make you feel as though you were being ripped into bite-size chunks.

Mindful of these lunging venomous dangers, I hotfooted it to the airconditioned sanctuary of the general store, a large portion of which was given over to souvenirs that made Disneyland look like Orrefors. Should one come over peckish, the very animals that had filled you with awe in the bush could do likewise in the stomach department via kudu, impala and springbok pates. And if you were searching for a gift for that person with everything bar taste, look no further than the vacuum-packed canisters of genuine elephant dung.

Outside, dusk was falling in pastel smudges and a mauve cumulonimbus levitated above green hills in the distance. Cormorants waded amid buck by the water's edge; tree squirrels darted across the grass at my feet, and a lone elephant lumbered over to the meandering Letaba for a drink.

With another 4am rise scheduled for the next day, I turned in early and elated.

For those to whom dawn is a rare experience, it feels pristine to the power of ten when you're in the wild. The air was as crisp as starched linen and alive with birdsong. The neon bar of orange that hovered just below the horizon gradually flushed the sky peach. The dark bush began to yield forms and movement. My third and final day in the park would be spent travelling to the Phalaborwa gate, located roughly halfway along its north-south axis. The first animals that clip-clopped across the road were a herd a gnus, named after the high-pitched sound they emit.

A couple of kilometres down the track, half-a-dozen giraffe loped across the road. Improbably long-legged with tapering necks and lithe torsos, their gait has an effortless elegance made all the more beguiling by their mottled complexion. In Afrikaans they are called *kameelperd*, which literally and rather succinctly translates to camel horse.

These seemingly passive giants can make life hell for a hunting cat. Because of their height, the usual feline tactic of leaping onto a prey's hindquarters to knock it to the ground is foolhardy. One well-directed kick can shatter a lion's jaw, thus condemning it to starvation. Instead, the highest degree of pride work is called for. Using stealth and surprise, their tactic is to give the giraffe such a fright that it loses its footing and life in quick succession.

A roadside sign informed me that the exit gate was twenty kilometres away and I was promptly suffused with the same sort of feeling that schoolkids are burdened by on Sunday evenings. I didn't want the experience to end. So rather impulsively I swung the car in the direction from which I had come and made it back to Letaba in time to join a guided bushwalk.

A dozen participants piled into a Land Rover truck and in twenty minutes we were standing by a ramshackle building in the bush which was once used by soldiers running insurgency raids into Mozambique. At ground level Kruger offers a world beyond that which can be viewed from a car. The baked soil seeped heat through my soles as our twentysomething rifle-toting guide Edgar, bearing the understandable smile of a man with the world's best office, lead us across a flood plain. The air buzzed with cicadas; the sharp blades of knee-high grass sliced at my shins, and the ground tremored as a dozen zebra took off in a dust storm after spotting us. They were the only animals we saw before stopping for a lunch of fruit juice and cheese sandwiches – with a side serve of mopani worms. A staple for local tribesfolk, these plump buggers are harvested off the tree that gives them their name, piled into hessian sacks, then dried before being fried with onions and tomatoes. For all intents and purposes, they taste and look like gnocchi.

The second half of the walk delivered more zebra, a smattering of kudu and an up-close view of an animal that has not changed in twenty million years. The white rhino Edgar spotted thirty metres to our left had no clue we were there.

Despite assurances that this breed is far more chilled out than its darker, smaller counterpart, it is still a creature of rare menace. It's built like a Humvee complete with armour plating and sports a spike that looks far larger and deadlier in the flesh than it ever could on a TV screen. It is also not white at all – the name stems from a mistranslation of the German word for "wide" which was used to distinguish the shape of its mouth from that of the black rhino. When sufficiently motivated, these animals can hit forty kilometres an hour. No mean feat when you tip the scales at 2300 kilograms.

Shifting his rifle from shoulder to hand, Edgar instructed us to follow as he inched towards the rhino. We had travelled about fifteen metres, roughly one-third the distance between our original viewing point and the animal, when the dweeby Belgian in front of me trod on a twig that snapped with a crack. The rhino swivelled in our direction; his mouthful of grass might have bestowed an almost comical moustache effect were it not for the fact he was wondering whether he should amble away or puree us camera-toting interlopers. The stand-off was as brief as it was thrilling and he lumbered off in the direction of a dry riverbed.

My Kruger experience was now complete. I had seen four of the Big Five (one at ground level), watched the sun rise over multitudinous herds of leaping springbok. My work here was done. Besides, I had a conjurer of storms to track down.

Chapter 7

Long May She Rain

The road northwest to Tzaneen was a grey ribbon that rose and fell gently as if being flicked by the skilled wrist of a rhythmic gymnast. On either side lay dense mopani forest, randomly interrupted by hills comprised of bus-sized boulders that appeared precariously stacked and resembled the Jenga set of the gods.

Troupes of chacma baboons congregated by the side of the road; vervet monkeys leapt between tree limbs, and the low olive hillocks that rose from the savanna grasslands ceded to lusher gradients as I climbed towards the ancestral realm of Modjadji VI, Rain Queen of the Lobedu. Securing an audience with the only female tribal ruler in modern-day South Africa is fraught with challenges. Tribal lore mandates that she dwell deep in a mist-swirled forest on a mountain, ensconced behind foreboding barriers of powerful juju.

The tale of the Modjadji is one of bloodshed, magic and a double dose of incest. The line is descended from the powerful royal house of Monomotapa, which ruled over the Kalanga people in Zimbabwe in the fifteenth and sixteenth centuries. Back on a lazy 1589 afternoon when the Internet was down and the cricket had been rained out leaving nothing to watch on TV, one of the tribe's princesses got jiggy with her brother, eventually delivering a child whose father was her uncle. The new dad's half-brothers wanted to kill the baby to stop him from becoming king one day. Wary of having a civil war on his hands, old man Monomotapa gave the child's mother, Dzugundini, a magic horn for making rain and advised her to take the child plus some loyal followers further south to establish a kingdom.

Over the next 200 years the Dzugundini became a substantial tribe. In around 1800 their chief, Mugodo, was warned by the ancestral spirits that his sons were plotting to overthrow him. He killed them all and promptly impregnated his daughter, saying it had been supernaturally decreed that a dynasty of women would be founded as a result.

When she gave birth to a son, the baby was quickly strangled. Her second child, however, was a girl who signalled the inception of the female line. When Mugodo popped his incestuous clogs, the grand-daughter Modjadji became queen.

Modjadji's life was spent in seclusion in the forest where she performed precipitation rituals which were famous throughout Southern Africa. She was called the Rain Queen and supplicants came from far and wide to beg for her moist blessing.

For traditional African societies that based their wealth on cattle, rain was the most precious of commodities, so in a land where storms were sporadic, unpredictable and varied wildly in terms of duration, anyone who could make the sky cry at will wasn't worth getting offside. Even if she was merely a meteorological prodigy who could predict rainfall with sopping accuracy, you wanted her on your team.

The rain queens' powers faded with age and the first few obligingly took their final bow with a poisonous cocktail extracted from the brain and spinal cord of a crocodile. After which their decaying bodies were stored for weeks and water poured over them to create a rain-making potion. As you do.

Practically every chief in the southern half of the continent, including those with an insatiable lust for conquest such as supreme Zulu warrior Shaka, attempted to ingratiate themselves with the early Modjadjis. In times of drought, caravans of gifts were sent up to her village, also called Modjadji. This seat of power undoubtedly appeared all the more mystical thanks to the fact that it is a climatic anomaly. Set on dry slopes above a drier plain, it squeezes enough rain from the clouds blown off the Indian Ocean to maintain a predictable fertility in the midst of barren surroundings.

Interviews with the Rain Queen, which cost around $50 a pop with a further $50 fee tacked on for photographs, could apparently be arranged via a tourist office in Tzaneen. Despite my enthusiasm for a brush with royalty, I took the long way into town through the cool silence of the pine forests of Magoebaskloof which soared towards swathes of cyan sky like tent poles supporting a white-flecked canopy.

The conifer canyons were eventually usurped by mango and peach farms where the trees clung to steep-sided hills and drooped under the weight of pendulous purple fruit.

Tzaneen itself was equally picturesque. Located along a latitude that lent the entire town the kind of lush tropical lustre resorts frequently sport, it gleefully gave the conventional notion of grid town planning the old chuck you farlie by cuddling into the jade hills from which it rose.

At the best of times, wandering into the local tourist office in Tzaneen and requesting an audience with the local regal climate controller was tantamount to tapping a Swiss guard on the puffy shoulder and asking whether JPII was in. What made my timing even worse was that the Lobedu were apparently between queens.

When Modjadji V died of renal failure in 2001, the royal family was faced with a succession crisis the likes of which it had never seen. Only two days earlier her daughter Princess Maria Modjadji had also passed away, with the next in line being twenty-three-year-old grand-daughter Makobo Modjadji. Unseasonable rains fell hard and heavy for days.

It was only after three years of intense tutelage that Queen Modjadji VI's coronation date was announced – roughly a month away from my requested interview date, rendering said chat all but impossible. I was, however, welcome to drive to the royal compound nearby.

The Rain Queen's home was fifty kilometres away down single-lane tracks that skirted the banks of the Molototsi River and climbed into foreboding hills cloaked in vegetation so dark it looked black from a distance. Asphalt yielded to red dust as the road meandered by villages of mud huts topped with corrugated-iron roofs. The sound of my approaching vehicle prompted scatterings of scuff-kneed children who would wave cheerily then put out their hands for coins, yet did little to deter the goats who would blithely wander into the road, oblivious to the fact that I could turn them rapidly into cashmere.

The entrance to the compound was marked by one of those council-built blocks that could be anything from a public toilet to a library. I was told to follow a path up the hill to an information centre. Here the previous queen's coronation throne – a high-backed wooden affair emblazoned with a bush-pig carving – was displayed along with the leopard skin that signified her divine position.

"Any chance of meeting the queen-in-training?" I asked after rousing the woman on duty from a deep desk-draped slumber. She gave me that "I'm afraid not, son" look most frequently seen on parents' faces in response to the question "Is Scamp coming back from dog heaven?" then added I might be interested in wandering around the village.

It was much like any other rural South African shtetl: some brick bungalows, a handful of thatch-crowned rondavels, a series of baked-earth pathways, outcrops of flourishing corn and citrus trees, and locals who grinned as they threw a "*Kunjani baba*?" – the local equivalent "Howyagoin mate?" – my way. What set it apart, however, were two rows of wooden staves that formed a columned walkway to the royal compound.

I was about to enter the square from which a power was wielded that brought Africa's fiercest warriors barefoot and on bended knee, clapping their hands in deference and toting gifts so lavish that the Modjadji's domain became known as Lo Bedu, the land of offerings. For a zenith of mysticism, it was thoroughly underwhelming – not least for the fact that most of the villagers seemed to be crowded into an adjoining building watching the local version of *Big Brother*.

I struck up a conversation with a teenager in a New York Yankees baseball cap who'd come out for a smoke break and my day brightened dramatically when he offered to introduce me to the lady herself. "You must take a gift," he added. "R100 will do fine."

Just as I was retrieving the note from my wallet, an older woman popped her head around a door and unleashed a tirade of venom on my would-be guide that sent him slouching off to the opposite side of the square.

"That boy is a *tsotsi* [thief]," she bellowed, apparently as angry at me for falling for his ruse as she was at him for attempting it. "Besides, Her Royal Highness isn't here. She's gone to the dentist in Pretoria."

Brilliant.

Before 1996, when a decision was taken to make the Rain Queen more accessible – mostly in the interests of tourism – she was seldom, if ever, seen in public. Even when protocol was relaxed sufficiently to allow the queen to attend important functions, she could still never mingle with guests, no matter how exalted. If the function was in a university hall, for example, she would sit it out in an adjacent building with no more than one or two members of the royal circle to keep her company. Guests would be informed that the queen was present, but they'd never see her.

Still, I shouldn't hold it against Modjadji VI as she had some mighty sandals to fill. Her battleaxe of a predecessor was a formidable figure and everyone from staunchly racist former prime minister PW Botha to Nobel Prize winner FW de Klerk dropped by the kraal to pay their respects.

When Nelson Mandela expressed his desire for some quality time, she not only kept him waiting but apparently demanded a new Lexus and a four-wheel drive as part of the deal. When she eventually relented, he was permitted to address her through an intermediary and could only speak when spoken to. The relationship eventually thawed in the face of the famed Madiba charm, but it was conducted by her rules until the day she died.

With the Rain Queen mystique set to turbo wane, I started

off down the mountain in a light drizzle that seemed scheduled to mock my impudence.

Few regions of South Africa can rival this area when it
comes to tribal mysticism and my next destination was the
heartland of the Lemba tribe, who proudly regard themselves as the Black Jews of South Africa. Intrigued, I had set
up an interview with a tribal elder and was directed to the
small house a few kilometres out of town.

Arriving at her immaculate single-storey brick house, I
was warmly greeted by Dolly Ratsebe, a fifty-something
widow who was glad of some daytime company since both of
her children were now studying – accountancy and medi-
cine – at universities in Durban and Pretoria.

She greeted me with "Shalom", followed by hot cups of
tea and pound cake, then proceeded to convince me that we
were of the same stock. According to their oral tradition, the
70,000-strong Lemba migrated from Judea to southern
Africa between 2000 and 3000 years ago. Culturally, the similarities are evident. For a start, all Lemba males are circum-
cised. Unlike many other tribes, the Lemba refuse to
intermarry and refer to outsiders as *wasenshi* (the gentiles).
They do not eat pork, fish without scales or any creature prohibited by kosher law. They also never mix milk and meat in
accordance with Jewish custom. Furthermore, they will only
eat animals ritually slaughtered, and non-Lemba women
wishing to marry into the tribe undergo a strict conversion
process.

This was all information that Dolly clearly enjoyed sharing but felt compelled to interrupt with questions as to
whether or not I was married, the kind of living that could be
made through journalism, whether or not my partner was
planning to take up what she described as "the way of the

chosen people" and perhaps – most tellingly – how frequently I contacted my own mother during this trip to reassure her of my safety. It was as if she was constantly a syllable away from telling me to take a jacket in case.

Until recently the Lemba's claims of Semitic ancestry have been treated with a fair degree of scepticism, but recent DNA testing has strengthened their case. Analysis carried out in South Africa and Britain has found that Lemba males display an unusually high incidence of a particular Y chromosome, the Cohen Modal Haplotype (CMH), which is frequently found among Sephardi and Ashkenazi Jews, the two primary groups that emigrated from biblical Judea into the wider world. Although CMH is also found in other Middle Eastern populations, the incidence of this chromosome among Lemba men is 8.8 per cent – similar to that found among Jewish men in general.

Hanging out with Dolly was like taking tea with a long-lost aunt, and burdened by both regret and four slices of cake, I eventually hoisted myself from the armchair and took my leave. As she walked me to my car, Dolly asked how my Hebrew was. I tried to make light of the question by replying that it was on a par with my Lemba, but she was having none of it. Instead, she fixed me with a glance of unspoken disappointment.

The Lemba are not the only remarkable tribe in the region. Over the hill is a sacred lake whose waters are plied by a vengeful python god. The surrounding forest is an ancient chieftain burial ground guarded by a ferocious white lion.

The region is called Venda, which translates as Pleasant Land. It is the traditional home of the VhaVenda people, whose culture incorporates such a phalanx of spirits, gods and lesser sprites that it makes the ancient Egyptians look like dedicated monotheists. So deeply entrenched in water is their belief system that the VhaVenda will not eat any aquatic animal for fear that the rivers will run dry. Perhaps their most revered spiritual rite is the annual ceremony in which a child of the chief is chosen to place an offering on a rock in the sacred lake. A vine is tied to the child and if the offering fails to be accepted by the gods, malevolent water spirits known as *zwidutane* will cut the cord and the child will disappear into the opaque depths. If, however, the offering is accepted, the child walks on water. Sound familiar?

Evil aquatic nymphs aside, the lake is also known to be teeming with crocodiles the length of minibuses. According to the VhaVenda people, the forest that bounds this body of water is also home to the phoenix-like Ndadzi that soars on thunderous wings, carries rain in its beak and shoots lightning bolts from its eyes.

The ancient nature of the land, its inhabitants and their practices imbue the home of Modjadji, the Lemba and the VhaVenda with a spirituality that transcends religion. It simply feels sacred: a sense heightened by the hospitality, kindness and joyful nature of people who live in valleys of infinite charm under bountiful skies.

My lingering had thrown the itinerary into chaos and I had a daunting number of kilometres to cover before reaching my overnight accommodation at the Blyde River Canyon. Shortly after crossing a bridge over the swift and dark Olifants River, I caught my first sight of the muscular Drakensberg mountain range. So named by the early settlers for its resemblance to the ridges on a dragon's back, it stretches down most of the nation's eastern flank for 320 kilometres and marks the swooping border of the vast inland plateau that occupies the bulk of South Africa's land mass.

Millennia of erosion have etched bands of phosphorous yellow and terracotta into the flat-topped peaks so that they resemble massive slices of multilayered cake.

Moments after passing through the JG Strydom tunnel, I pulled over by a roadside market for a few horrendously cliched sun-setting-over-the-peaks shots. Here I was accosted by a woman brandishing a patently fake $20 greenback who asked if I would exchange it for the local currency. When I refused, she reached into the car, grabbed my can of cola and promptly drained it before my disbelieving eyes.

Through dusky light setting the valleys which plunged away from the roadside into picturesque relief, I made my way to a hotel complex perched on the edge of the world's third-largest canyon. I had stayed in a dormitory here during a school excursion and was mildly delighted to see that the place had hardly changed. It consisted of two dozen or so cottages made from rough-hewn stone topped by pyramids of slate tile. The resort also boasted a free-form pool, trampoline, minigolf course and a host of other charmingly nostalgic embellishments – here it was forever 1975.

Upon checking in, I was told that the resort prided itself on its dinner buffet and so once again I found myself in a restaurant where the staff significantly outnumbered the guests. And once again, the candle on my table was promptly lit to illuminate my solitude. For R70 (around AU$16) I was presented with a team of half-a-dozen impeccably uniformed chefs invading my tastebuds with ten starters, a handful of salads, a selection of stews, several curries and a dessert tray that was duly wobbled over the table when I could no longer rise from the chair under my own steam.

I slept the sleep of the supremely satisfied and mildly bloated.

* *

I'd been told that, on a clear day, dawn over the canyon was a sight one would treasure henceforth. I awoke to a pea-souper which offered all the visibility of draping a white sheet over one's head. When it cleared, the sun had risen high enough to burn away the fog and I drove the kilometre from my room to the lookout point.

Following a sign along a rocky pathway overhung with foliage, I made my way towards the lookout, pausing only for a minor coronary as a troupe of baboons screeched then scattered as I approached. Please believe me when I tell you that a fully grown male shares the dimensions and attitude of a psychotic Rottweiler.

I couldn't believe that I had been to a place of such magnificence before but could hardly remember it. Twenty-six kilometres long and higher than Sydney's Centrepoint Tower with the Harbour Bridge jammed onto its pinnacle, the canyon messes with your eyes, brain and ears as you struggle to comprehend the sheer scale and vacuum-packed silence of the panorama. The focal point of the canyon is a trio of conical peaks known as the Three Rondawels, which resemble enormous newly sharpened pencils. These are wrapped in a thick swathe of navy in the form of the Treur River which created the whole shebang through millions of years of erosion and empties into a glistening dam. It is a view so spectacular that you have to remind yourself to breathe.

The only other vista which had prompted such an awe-struck reaction in me was the Grand Canyon, and although Blyde River Canyon was admittedly more intimate in terms of dimension, I wasn't viewing it from behind a wire fence jammed elbow to elbow with oooohing Nikon-toters.

So vast, humbling and beautiful was the scene before me that I wished I had someone to exchange gobsmacked exclamations or reverential silences with. Viewed through a pair of binoculars thoughtfully chained to a post, the sheer quartzite cliff faces lost the velvet smoothness imparted by distance. Fissures the length and breadth of football fields had been hacked into the sedimentary rock formations like knife wounds, while a softer shale strata led into the wooded inclined slopes at their base. With the sun still rising, the arid north-facing rock walls morphed in colour from ground cinnamon to deep honey. Those that faced south, however, wore an evergreen coat whose tails trailed into dozens of valleys that crisscrossed the canyon.

Beneath a pair of martial eagles making what the musical theatre fraternity would term "lazy circles in the sky", I returned to the car and set out for my next destination: a geological curiosity known as the Bourke's Luck Potholes. These potholes are in fact a series of cascades, whirlpools and rapids, the result of the strong-flowing Treur River slamming into solid rock formations at its confluence with the Blyde. Through millions of years the water-borne sand and rocks caught in these strata indentations have scoured smooth-sided, perfectly cylindrical holes from the riverbed. It looks as if the area has been shaped with a butter knife, resulting in a Martian landscape of rich ochre and tumbling white water.

The experience was somewhat dampened by the final entry in the visitors' book. Peter and Petra – suspicious names to begin with, and hailing from the UK and Germany respectively – described their visit as "marginally interesting". Honestly, some people deserve to be bitch-slapped into next Tuesday.

The road between the potholes and the town of Graskop

could have starred in innumerable television commercials where a young couple in a convertible, flushed with the excitement of an imminent shagfest, tool down languidly curved stretches of tarmac.

Thick rafts of leopard trees emblazoned with sulphur-yellow flowers stood sentinel in dense patches, while the odd stream drew one's eye like the first broken capillary on a young alcoholic's face. A few kilometres later the road climbed to a spot known as the Devil's Office. Pine plantations sprung up around me as a cold fog banished the sunshine through which I had driven for most of the morning. At times the precipitous road bent sharply, leaving nothing but an edge and an infinite grey murk, the fog was foreboding enough without it momentarily clearing to reveal sheer drops and I could have done without the curtains of thick cloud that blew across the tarmac reducing visibility to such a degree that I wondered whether I had just set a record for contracting glaucoma.

Eventually the road plateaued, the seething maw receded and the swirling fog gave way to leaden, pregnant skies. Located conveniently close the Devil's Office was God's Window. One of the most famed lookouts in South Africa, it is framed by a deep cleavage of rocks that hang like tied-back curtains before a valley. On a clear day it must have spectacular. It wasn't and it wasn't.

The road to Graskop hugged the lip of the canyon then arced its way through the mustard plains after which Graskop is named and onto Pilgrim's Rest, a restored mining village that is not so much a town nowadays but a glorified tourist bus stop. It's essentially a single street flanked by corrugated-iron stores laden with scented candles, packets of fool's gold and the saving grace of locally produced fudge that's richer than Bill Gates with a winning lottery ticket.

The town was declared a national monument in 1972 but its contrived gentility and picturesque charm belies a history marinated in bloodshed, greed and depravation. Scottish miner Alex Patterson's 1873 discovery of alluvial gold in the creek which runs beside the town saw a wave of fortune-seekers descend on what was then a remote location bounded by mountains and choked with bush so thick that an hour's hacking saw explorers advance less than a metre.

So arduous was the terrain that one prospector reported taking forty-eight days to get from San Francisco to London to Cape Town then finally onto Durban – while his trip between Durban and Pilgrim's Rest lasted sixty-eight.

The travel seemed like a pleasure cruise once they arrived. Aside from the rampant theft of ore and frequent murder for claims, the alluvial gold was buried under three metres of topsoil and enormous boulders of quartzite. Scarcely a day went by when some fortune-seeker with poor reflexes wasn't rendered two-dimensional by one of these orbs rolling through the diggings.

I returned to my car after an amble around the town to find it glistening. Scam alert. As I was preparing to drive off, an impish face sporting a grin and a half appeared at the driver's window. "Hello baas," beamed the teenager. "I washed your car."

That was all he said, despite the clear implication that he was hopeful of more than a polite thank-you on my part. In most instances where I am requested to cough up for a service I didn't request I become such a miser that, to paraphrase Ferris Bueller, if you shoved a lump of coal up my arse, you'd have a diamond in a fortnight. Not this time. His strategy of performing the task without any guarantee of remuneration was as risky as it was admirable – all he could do was the best job possible and hope that his prospective client agreed. I did and handed him a crisp note, then added another.

I spent the night in Nelspruit, a prosperous yet characterless city where I was made to pay for brochures at a government tourist office staffed by personnel apparently recruited from Surly Indolents R Us. After checking into my hotel, I was shown to a distant granny flat that might have been designed for a particularly trying mother-in-law with a bad hip and a vicious tongue. The airconditioner was on the fritz, the cable was down and the evening carvery was replete with items bearing the same cadaverous shade and texture as the shoes worn by the risk-management analysts that had converged on the hotel for a conference.

The clinical accommodation and the tepid town only heightened my anticipation for exploring a province where Gandhi and Churchill shared battlefields, whose major city regards itself as "the last outpost of the British Empire" and from whose bosom arose a bastard of a warrior so fierce that entire tribes fled their ancestral homes at the mere mention of his name.

Chapter 8

A Tribe Called Quest

"There is lovely road that runs from Ixopo into the hills." So begins Alan Paton's novel, *Cry the Beloved Country*, which every South African schoolchild read at some point (and deluded ourselves that we were racially progressive as a result). Driving through KwaZulu-Natal, the province in which it was set, two things swiftly became clear: that Paton's statement could be applied to almost every stretch of tarmac in the place; and why it is known by the local Zulu tribe as the Kingdom of the People of Heaven. The dramatic cliff faces that marked the border of the highveld yielded to endless undulations of jade green embroidered with rippling streams. Small herds of black cattle grazed in the grassy valleys where smudges of mist lingered. Traces of fragrant woodsmoke from the whitewashed rondavels that dot the hillsides scented the air.

Yet these serene surroundings have seen more bloodshed per square kilometre than any other region in the country. In the first postapartheid election campaign, hundreds were hacked to death in conflicts between Zulus and Xhosas aligned to opposing political parties. Here, too, the bastard son of an inconsequential chieftain created the fiercest fighting force in African tribal history.

Revolutionising everything from weaponry to training and tactics, Shaka exacted a gruesome toll on rival clans, Voortrekkers and British forces (the latter of whom eventually turned on each other). Consequently, a network of battle sites runs through KwaZulu-Natal like cracks in a shattered windowpane.

The town of Dundee was touted as the ideal base from which to explore the battlefields, but even despite being surrounded by hills that once echoed with the sounds of musket fire and blade meeting flesh, it was worth a tarry. Set in the gumdrop hills of the Biggarsberg range, it was once termed Coalopolis because of the enormous collieries on its outskirts. However, it hardly feels like an industrial town but rather a diamond-shaped grid of oak-shaded streets lined with handsome homes, candy-apple-green churches and inviting parks in which vine-clad pergolas threw soft shadows onto still ponds. It was all relentlessly genteel.

Until this point in my journey small-town streets were named after either Voortrekker leaders or just called plain "Voortrekker", but these bore labels such as Union, Gladstone and Browning. This was an English-and-proud town, a fact crystallised when the pair of ladies manning the information centre didn't have to make the obviously draining mental switch from Afrikaans when dealing with my request for accommodation, as they had done everywhere else.

The next morning, as the sun gilded farmland that rose and fell like a sleeping child's chest, I made my way to a scene of slaughter more prolific and barbaric than any British army had ever suffered before.

Isandlawa is a dust-choked plain that extends for twenty

kilometres and at the centre of which stands a monolithic fist of rock. To the British soldiers camped in its shadow, it looked like the sphinx that sat on their collars as a reminder of their victory in the Egyptian campaign in the Napoleonic wars.

They were here thanks to a blatant land-grab on the part of the forces of Empire; the Zulus, however, were having none of it. On 17 January 1879 Zulu chief Ceteshwayo addressed a vast contingent of warriors at the enormous military kraal at Nodwengu instructing them to repel the whites "who have invaded Zululand and driven away our cattle".

By the day of the battle, the Zulus had reached a valley some six kilometres south of the pinnacle of rock where I now sat, but they decided against any attack as tribal lore dictated that the night's full moon was not an auspicious sign. A small party of scouts did, however, venture out of the valley and were spotted by a handful of British cavalry who gave chase. One can only imagine the stupefied terror these mounted Brits felt on reaching the lip of the bowl in which 20,000 warriors were crouched in utter silence. It was on for young and old as the Brits turned tail and the Zulus gave baying-for-blood pursuit.

Despite having had twenty-four years' military experience, the British commander made the fatal assumption that the regiment's stay at this location wouldn't be long enough to warrant digging trenches or forming a defensive laager of wagons. Charging in their ox-horns formation, the Zulus overran the British soldiers. As the ground shook to the sound of 40,000 stone-hard feet slamming into the dirt, the battleground was thrown into eerie darkness by an eclipse. Hostilities ceased for a few minutes in which all the combatants could make out were the gurgling screams of the dying.

Aside from protecting their homeland, the Zulu warriors found additional motivation in sex and drugs. Traditional lore stated that no man could take a wife until he had "dipped his spear in blood", and some scholars suggest that although the training regimen of Zulu warriors undoubtedly provided them with the stamina to run a half-marathon then mix it up on the battlefield, they were also assisted by powerful herbal *mutis* concocted to boost their aggression levels while inhibiting fatigue receptors.

Recalling the battle, Kumbeka Gwabe, a member of the uMcijo regiment, said, "I myself killed only one man. Dum! Dum! went his revolver as he was firing from left to right and I came beside him and stuck my assegai under his right arm, pushing it through his body until it came out between the ribs on his left side. As soon as he fell I pulled the assegai out and slit his stomach so I knew he would not shoot any more of my people."

By the time the battle was over two hours later, this process had been carried out 1357 times. "You could not move a foot either way," wrote a British officer who arrived at the battlefield later, "without treading on a body." Every British soldier would have been disembowelled in accordance with the Zulu tradition of releasing the enemy's spirit once he is slain, while the Zulus were felled with bullets designed to flatten on impact, cause massive tissue damage and splinter bone lengthways. Piles of white stones now stand sentinel over the mass graves that dot the battlefield.

One thousand Zulus died at Isandlawa. Their monument lies at the gate to the battlefield and consists of a four-metre-wide replica of the Isigqu necklace warriors would receive from the king in recognition of their feats in combat. Fashioned from copper and set against a granite slab, it is shaped like the traditional oxen horns battle forma-tion with one pincer advancing quicker than the other. No plaques or epitaphs are required.

Even in bright sunshine, a sombre and poignant air hangs heavily over the valley. You can somehow feel that thou-sands were butchered here, and the soil seems soaked in the memory of lives cut short.

The defeat at Isandlawa sent shockwaves of humiliation through the British military, which desperately sought to salvage some pride from events unfolding in Zululand. Its spin doctors received a godsend in the form of a battle that took place a few hours later, some ten miles east at a mission station called Rorke's Drift. Consisting of a chapel, home-stead and cattle enclosure, it was here that a handful of Brit-ish troops saw off a 4000-strong Zulu contingent over a twelve-hour attack. It was a display of gallantry that military historians still get misty-eyed about over 130 years later.

A record eleven Victoria Crosses were awarded but the uncommon valour displayed at Rorke's Drift was sullied by a general feeling among the higher-ranking British officers that these were not genuinely deserved but were being doled out to deflect attention away from the disaster at Isandlawa. Some of the upper brass charged with pinning these medals on the recipients couldn't even be bothered getting off their horses to do so.

The final stop of the day was Blood River. For anyone attending a South African government school in the 1970s and 80s, few historical events were more mythologised and glorified than the battle that took place here. With a name that rings of boy's own adventure, it was presented to us as a tale of revenge that was not only justified but rubber-stamped by God Himself.

Nine months before the battle a Voortrekker leader named Piet Retief had conducted what he thought was a successful land transaction with the Zulu chief Dingane. In exchange for sixty-three head of cattle plus eleven rifles, the Zulus would hand over the territory between the Thukela and Mzimvubu rivers.

When Retief returned to the kraal after the initial negotiations, he had brought the beef but not the bullets. Dingane then invited the party inside for a drink and – hello! – requested that they leave their guns outside. Their Voortrekker corpses were discovered shortly thereafter along with a land deed signed by Dingane. This document formed a crucial part of the story drummed into us at school but many historians never believed the deed existed and it apparently mysteriously vanished during the Anglo–Boer war.

A tall pistol-toting farmer by the name of Andries Pretorius, who accessorised his well-cut suits with a cutlass, was chosen to lead a punitive mission to avenge Retief's death. Shortly after setting out on 9 December 1838, Pretorius reportedly climbed onto a gun carriage before 468 heavily armed commandos whom he asked to join him in a vow before God. The basic gist went like this: if the Big Guy made sure they won, the day of victory would be commemorated in his honour. Recent research has questioned whether this vow actually took place, and the promised commemoration certainly wasn't observed in the years immediately following the battle. But not wanting to let the truth stand in the way of prime propaganda, the apartheid regime's education department consistently painted this vow as a powerful backdrop to the events that unfolded at the end of the rutted dirt road I followed past the endearingly named Fort Mistake.

With the rain settling into a persistent pelt and no way that I was going to leave without exploring the battlefield, I thrust my hands into my pockets, launched into the sulky walk that most of us have but rarely admit to, and slouched down a slippery mud trail towards the Afrikaner equivalent of the Wailing Wall in Jerusalem. Arranged in the D-shape that Pretorius pulled his wagons into when scouts spotted a Zulu column nearby are fifty-seven life-size replicas cast in steel and bronze.

Had the Zulu chief Dingane not offed his half-brother Shaka ten years before, the battle that changed the course of South African history would probably not have happened. A few unsuccessful skirmishes had taught Shaka that the chances of storming a laager of wagons were not only slim but inevitably came at the cost of massive casualties. Only on the grounds that is was Shaka's theory, Dingane chose to treat it with contempt, and in the early morning fog of 16 December Zulu warriors attacked the wagons in their standard horn formation. Three waves of attackers were in the words of one observer "literally mown down" by muskets and grapeseed.

The combination of solitude, inclemency and charcoal darkness punctuated only by the pair of lanterns that hung from poles at the front of each wagon charged the battlefield with a maudlin eeriness. Soaked through and standing by a dripping cannon that had faced the bulk of the Zulu onslaught, I recalled the words of Boer chaplain Sarel Cilliers who after the battle noted that "the word of the Lord was fulfilled", before adding "the Kaffirs lay on the ground like pumpkins on a rich soil that has borne a large crop".

Those who fled were ruthlessly hunted down. Over 400 Zulus found hiding in a nearby ravine were systematically executed and those who attempted to escape across the river were picked off by the Boer sharpshooters. Many of the 3000 warriors who died that day did so on the river's banks or midstream. "And that," as my history teacher Mr Hockey would say in a tone most often associated with the phrase 'and they all lived happily ever after', "was how the battle got the name Blood River."

On the opposite side of the river is another monument built by the South African government in 1999 to honour the Zulu nation and those who paid the ultimate price in battle.

Having squelched back to the car and smelling like a roll of corduroy that had been soaked then abandoned in a musty attic, I drove to the museum to get a different perspective on an event whose details I had learned by rote at school. Here is the sum total of what I discovered. The river was known by the Zulu as the eNcome – "praiseworthy" – due to its constant flow and evergreen banks. And I only know this because it was etched into a board by the locked entrance booth above which was a closed sign.

In the course of a single day I had stood where thousands of men had lost their lives in the name of God, greed and pride. Desolate places where bloodshed means tourism and tourism, hopefully, means understanding.

Chapter 9

High Tea if it Kills Us

Her name was Juana Maria de los Dolores De Leon. The last three words of which might have been a suitably exotic title for a town named after a Spanish beauty described by her countryfolk as *muy picante*. Unfortunately Juana Maria had the misfortune to be married to a former Cape Governor named Sir Harry Smith – who famously annexed a swathe of Xhosa land, informed the respective chiefs of this decision without bothering to dismount then concluded the meeting by giving them permission to come forward and kiss his feet. As a result of this union, the welcoming burgh that bears her name is known as Ladysmith.

Just before the turn of the twentieth century Ladysmith was thrust into headlines as the scene of a siege that gripped the Empire. Having fled British rule and established the independent Orange Free State and South African republics, the Afrikaners' worst fears were realised when English interest in incorporating their land reached suspicious heights following the discovery of gold in 1886. Three years of wrangling, veiled threats and intimidation followed.

On 11 October 1899, with British troops massed on the borders of the South African republic, a 5pm deadline for withdrawal issued by Paul Kruger expired along with hopes for a peaceful resolution to the conflict. Britain believed the bands of ill-equipped Boer militia would crumble by Christmas but, as Rudyard Kipling noted, they were to give Queen Victoria's best "no end of a lesson".

Determined to rid themselves of the Brits, the Boers decided to not merely defend their land but push the British soldiers back into the Cape. The wily Afrikaners got the better of their adversaries at Dundee and captured a well-stocked military supply train at nearby Elandslaagte to boot, then pursued the retreating Brits to Ladysmith and took scores of prisoners.

Most military historians agree that had Boer general Piet Joubert decided to take Ladysmith – so to speak – she would have yielded with all the resistance of a lonely nymphomaniac. With the Port of Durban following shortly thereafter. However, in an act of gallantry tantamount to a spectacular tactical blunder, he refused to allow his commandos to pursue the defenceless Brits. "When God gives his little finger," he famously – and in hindsight moronically – told compatriot General Louis Botha, "you don't take his whole hand."

The story of what happened next is evocatively told in the winding corridors of the Siege Museum which commemorates a bombardment that lasted from 1 November 1899 to 28 February 1900 when British forces relieved the town. Two hundred and twenty-one soldiers were killed, but it was dysentery and typhoid that were the real enemy.

Despite their circumstances, however, the people of Ladysmith remained defiant. The local newspaper continued to pump out a fresh edition every day and the banner headline on 23 December screamed: "LADYSMITH

BOMBSHELL. THE CONVENT IS NOW EMPTY. NUN LEFT."
So proud were the locals of their defiance that when the
town hall was damaged during the deluge, they didn't
bother fixing the hole in the clocktower until 1923 and
instead wore it like a proud battle scar.

Another of these battle scars occupies display number 21
in the museum. The envelope-sized piece of skin bearing a
small tattoo is all that remains of a soldier burned to death
during the nearby Battle of Spioenkop. It claimed the lives of
so many Liverpudlian troops that the town's football team
named the most parochial section of its Anfield stadium "the
Kop" in their honour. Several generations of museum staff
have reported that, during quiet periods, they have seen the
reflection of a forlorn, dishevelled soldier peering longingly
into the cabinet.

Where other towns in the region capitalise on their history through hard facts, solemn memorials and mordant
battle sites, Ladysmith adds to the hard data of its turbulent
past with a supernatural soupçon. The otherworldly encoun-
ters that have been matter-of-factly discussed by locals for
years are now a bold element in Ladysmith's tourism drive.

One of those behind the strategy is Fifi Meyer, who works
for the local council and was instrumental in establishing
the town's ghost tour. There are certain people you encounter on the road that you instantly warm to and Fifi was one of
them. In my experience, women with this name divide
neatly into two categories. The first are prissy princesses who
"relate" to *Sex and the City* and believe they regularly mingle
with the working classes because one does their pedicure
every week. The second are garrulous types who wear bold
prints, can hold their Scotch and if pressed can generally

complete limericks that begin, "There once was a girl from Nantucket". Fifi belonged squarely in the latter category.

Although the spectral circuit is a self-drive affair, Fifi couldn't resist getting me started with a personal tour of the town hall. Built in 1883, it consists of a Renaissance Revival facade atop which sits a clocktower. The midsection of the building is given over to a Tuscan portico with half-a-dozen council offices on each side. Beyond this lay a grand civic hall with a parquet floor, soaring walls painted in a dignified burgundy and under whose patterned plaster ceiling hearts were broken and romance blossomed at scores of dances.

"There was often an uninvited guest though," whispered Fifi. "Guests would frequently be heard muttering about the obviously intoxicated violin player who they thought was part of the orchestra. He would be glimpsed clowning around amid the guests and his favourite party trick was climbing the balcony wall, staggering, swooning and pretending to fall onto the dancers below. There were even instances when the orchestra leaders were reprimanded about his conduct, but they responded by saying that they had no violin player who even remotely matched his description."

Fifi's eyes flickered with intrigue at the conclusion of the tale. Sensing that I had chosen to merely wade into it as opposed to dive in headlong as she had, Fifi checked herself with the most endearing half-apology that has ever been thrown my way. "I really get intoxicated by the exuberance of my own verbosity," she smiled before equipping me with a map for the remainder of the tour.

La Verna Convent sat on a ridge overlooking the town and was now its primary hospital. It turned out that the area also functioned as Ladysmith's top make-out spot and the area was lined with a handful of vehicles whose shock absorbers emitted rhythmic sighs while the occupants within did likewise. Shrouded in a pearly mist, the hospital was all creaking doors and echoing corridors. It could have been the setting for one of those horror movies in which busty trainee nurses are transformed into catheter-wielding zombies by a demonic surgeon. The spirits that apparently roam this former nunnery are somewhat kinder. Numerous patients have emerged from fevers with a request to thank the pretty nun who straightened their bedding during the night. However, the only habits that have been in the hospital in decades have been confined to the detox unit.

The next morning I wandered into town in search of a cappuccino. With froth on my nose and sun on my back, I'm not ashamed to say that I developed somewhat of an infatuation with Ladysmith. Its slumbering streets were edged with whitewashed homes topped by pitched corrugated-iron roofs in mint green. Many of these were guesthouses peeping through French doors onto rose gardens and rugs of kikuyu.

People chatted with the easy familiarity of those who had pretty much the same conversation the day before. On the main street I browsed in shop windows made all the more intriguing by a universal reality of country retail: the charmingly incongruous display. With a modest population to service, many family-owned establishments are understandably wary of specialising too narrowly in terms of the stock they carry and instead opt to be all things to all people. Call me old-fashioned, but I like the fact that there are some shops where you can still pick up luggage, a bicycle and some cookware and have the staff address you by name without having to read it off your credit card.

Unlike Dundee, which lives somewhat in its past – albeit

graciously – Ladysmith has a quiet modernity which has been achieved without compromising its sense of small-town snugness.

It is also the home town of South Africa's most successful musical export. Led by the honeyed tones of Joseph Tshabalala, what started as a backyard a cappella group became Ladysmith Black Mambazo, the group that transfixed audiences around the world after they collaborated with Paul Simon on his *Graceland* album. What makes the group unique is that, unlike those globally successful artists who their countrymen think of as cheesier than a *quattro formaggio*, the locals can't get enough of them. In South Africa they have outsold the Beatles and Michael Jackson. When Nelson Mandela was awarded the Nobel Peace Prize in 1993, he took them along to belt out a few numbers at the ceremony.

A hall in the town's cultural museum is given over to the group and their remarkable story. Their style, known as *isicathamiya*, is not strictly a derivative of gospel but more a product of the harsh labour system of South Africa's mines. Working six days a week, the poorly paid miners would fill their desolate compounds with sounds of joy into the small hours of every Sunday morning. The singers referred to themselves as *cothoza mfana* (tiptoe guys) because of the softly-softly dance steps they choreographed so as not to attract the ire of the mine security guards. When the miners drifted back to their homelands, the sound went with them and local towns soon pitted their groups against one another in competition. These contests continue to take place in YMCA halls and church basements throughout what was once known as Zululand, and sometimes the traditional prize of a goat is still awarded.

With a posse consisting of his brothers, cousins and friends, Tshabalala entered the fray. But before a note could be sung, the group needed a name. The Ladysmith component is self-explanatory. Black refers to the type of oxen regarded as the strongest animal on the farm. Mambazo is the Zulu word for axe and stems from the group's proclivity to chop down the opposition. After a time they were so dominant that they were forbidden from entering competitions but achieved a large local following. A bootleg tape sent to a Los Angeles DJ eventually found its way to Paul Simon and six million albums later the group ranks alongside Miriam Makeba and Hugh Masekela as keepers of the sound of South Africa.

With a newly purchased copy of their Grammy-winning *Shaka Zulu* album blaring from my car speakers, I drove out of Ladysmith and into the misty valleys that rippled towards the distant coast. Hoping that my proximity to Durban meant that I'd finally escaped the saccharine clutches of Jacaranda FM, I scanned the radio dial. Perfection comes not in stretches but snatches and I experienced precisely four minutes and forty seconds of it. Best of all, it came with an Australian twang in the form of Powderfinger's "My Happiness".

It was the bespoke musical backdrop to a landscape which felt like a perfectly measured collage of sapphire-blue sky, vast sugar cane lakes and dark conifer forests that pressed into the road on both sides like a lecherous uncle on a blushing bridesmaid.

At times cairns of stones would appear at crossroads. The Zulu refer to them as *isivavini*. In traditional culture, when a man set off on an important journey he would stop at the first junction and search for a generously sized stone. Holding it to his forehead and closing his eyes, he would then make two wishes. The first was intended for those who had walked this road before him and conveyed the hope that their journey had been fruitful. The second featured the same sentiment but was reserved for those yet to travel this path. The stone would then be placed on the pile by the side of the track. Thoughts of personal good fortune played no part in the process as, according to this practice of Ubuntu, your needs are covered twice over by those who have gone before you and those who will follow.

The *isivavini* is just one manifestation of a tribal culture that is equal parts savage and enlightened. The country's other major tribal force, the Xhosa, who think of themselves as far more cerebral and form the bulk of the ANC's brains trust, often deride the Zulus as dim and aggressive bully boys who stab first and ask questions later. The descendents of Shaka, however, now refer to the power players in South African politics as the "Xhosa Nostra". Pretty smart if you ask me.

When it comes to friendliness, the Zulus don't exactly go out on a limb and greetings are returned but rarely offered. That said, their courage, sense of self-worth and pride in their heritage is palpable at a distance – and intimidating close up.

Nowhere was this more evident than on the freezing night of 20 February 1917 in the middle of the English Channel. The commandeered liner SS *Mendi* was carrying hundreds of black South African troops – the overwhelming majority of them Zulu – to Le Havre from where they would head to the front line at Flanders.

War-time regulations forbade the use of lights on ships and another vessel crashed into the bow of the *Mendi*. To a man, the troops raced to deck from below, formed ranks and awaited further instructions. Having been briefly addressed by a Zulu clergyman on a black and lilting deck, the men stripped. "Barefoot and naked, the way their ancestors went to battle, against the noise of the wind, crashing seas and creaking plates of the doomed vessel," wrote Roger Webster in *At the Fireside*, "they began stamping their feet in the death drill, celebrating their onrushing doom with the war songs of Shaka. It was a scene, the survivors declared, that would be burnt into their memories forever – those singing men slipping into their cold grave in the English Channel."

Boer war general, staunch Afrikaner and South African prime minister Louis Botha moved a motion of sympathy in parliament for the mourning relatives. No sooner had he finished than the entire whites-only assembly rose to their feet and bowed their heads in silence. It was the only time black heroism was honoured in this fashion.

I stopped for lunch in Pietermaritzburg. Ensconced in a ring of apple-green hills, it is named after the Voortrekker leader who founded the place in 1838 but presents itself as a captivating outdoor gallery of Victorian and Edwardian architecture so Disneyesque British that I was half expecting Dick Van Dyke to appear at any second followed by half-a-dozen animated sheep bleating, "It's a jolly 'oliday with Maaaaaary". All I needed to complete the picture was a street urchin, a flower seller with immaculate bone structure and a harrumphing bowler-hatted toff who used the word "awfully" when he meant "very".

The City Hall is the star attraction in Pietermaritzburg's stellar architectural gallery. According to Ripley's "Believe It or Not" it is the largest all-brick building in the Southern Hemisphere. Three storeys of Victorian wonder, it is emblazoned with ornate friezes, arch-framed balconies, stained-glass windows, lashings of Corinthian columnettes whose purpose has more to do with aesthetics than structure, and contrasting brickwork that lends the entire structure a subtle motif of horizontal stripes. Topped by a handful of cream domes that surround a clocktower containing a dozen bells, it would not look out of place as the centrepiece of some chic Parisian rue. However, it is all the more charming for the fact that it's located in this regional centre. It also boasts the second-largest organ in the Southern Hemisphere and we'll leave it at that.

With hamburger grease on my chin and a mustard trail in my wake, I spent a marvellous hour wandering along Pietermaritzburg's broad and dozing thoroughfares. Understated charm lurked at every turn. Beside a neat park exploding in pyrotechnic outbursts of purple and pink tibouchinas stood an octagonal bandstand bedecked in Chinoiserie with a roof designed to resemble a Mandarin hat. Fine examples of Collegiate Gothic architecture mingled with Magpie Tudor, Palladian and Classic Revival like genteel guests at an embassy cocktail party.

The sky had been occupied by bruised clouds which descended on Pietermaritzburg like a bully trying to psych out his victims by invading their personal space. I had been warned that the road into Durban was one of the most treacherous in the country and was keen to avoid adding to its perils with slick surfaces and poor visibility.

Too late. Fat splats hurled themselves onto my windscreen like kamikaze pilots from the battleship cumulo-nimbus. The carnage on South African roads is unfathomable to international visitors. For example, between 1 December 2002 and 9 January 2003, 1210 locals lost their lives in a mess of mangled metal. The road death toll for the same period in

Australia, where traffic volumes, weather and road conditions are comparable, was 66.

Road-safety organisations lay the blame squarely at the
government-issued boots of the nation's 8000 traffic police,
suggesting many are inexperienced, insufficiently trained
and easily bribed because they are poorly paid.

I can vouch for the last from personal experience as my
brother-in-law has escaped numerous speeding fines by carrying extra sandwiches for traffic officers. At times he has
had to also reach for his wallet, but a roast beef on rye has
done the trick on more than one occasion. Similar strategies
are also routinely employed by the owners of rust-chomped
taxis who always carry cash in anticipation of this work
expense.

These frequently unroadworthy vehicles are routinely
loaded with so many passengers that even the most
innocuous of dings can become a potentially fatal affair.
Only the day before I headed into Durban, traffic inspector
Deon Fredericks had pulled over a minibus near the town of
Laingsburg in the Karoo desert. En route to Cape Town, it
was licensed to carry twenty-one passengers. Forty-six piled
out. In addition to the van having no lights, bad brakes, a
faulty steering mechanism and tyres buffed smooth by years
of wear, the driver was four sheets to the wind.

The story had apparently been the source of ribald hilarity
in at least one national newspaper office and that morning's
edition had featured a cartoon of a minibus wrapped around
a lamppost. Limbs protruded from every window; contorted
faces complete with swollen eyes and scratches were pressed
against side windows. Surveying the scene were two traffic
officers, one of whom was excitedly yelling out the

punchline: "It's okay, I've found the missing two passengers in the glove box!"

Laugh? I thought I'd never start. This perilous state of affairs becomes all the more dangerous for motorists when you consider that the metal doors and roofs that protect signal-box controllers fetch a small yet sufficiently attractive sum with Durban's more unscrupulous metal dealers. Scores of the city's traffic lights are then disabled as a result of exposure ot the elements. So widespread is the problem that civic bosses have ordered pepper booby-trap mechanisms to be installed to curb not merely the theft but the dozens of gut-churning smashes at volatile intersections.

I was soon to discover that the reality of a minibus crash was far different from the comically confused version in the morning paper. With the rain still tumbling, I descended a steep mountain pass at a crawl and thought it odd that few vehicles were approaching. Distributed around the crumpled fragments of a minivan ahead of me was an array of ambulances and police cars. Nearby lay eight bodies covered in blue tarpaulins while a dozen battered survivors wailed in grief as paramedics battled to save a small boy. Shards of glass lay like frost on the tarmac and the air smelled of petrol. It was the first time I had seen blood on a road and I hope it's the last.

Soon afterwards I reached the squatter camps that mark the outskirts of Durban. Balanced gingerly against plunging hillsides strewn with litter and dead dogs, the tin shacks and cardboard dwellings appear to have been dropped from a considerable height. With no evidence of sewerage facilities and running water but plenty of overcrowding, they converge upon one another like a domino stack. I was left with the impression that a collapse near the bottom of the stack would send dozens of these structures tumbling towards the gurgling brown sludge at the base of the hills.

When I was growing up in apartheid South Africa, poverty meant not being able to afford a colour TV. We knew that black people did it tough, but the scale, spread and specifics of the poverty were unfathomable. Nothing would give me more pleasure than being able to report that the lot of South Africa's needy has improved since the transition to majority rule. The sad reality is the rich have grown even richer while the poor have not so much slipped below the breadline but are on their hands and knees foraging for crumbs.

As anywhere, the spin doctors are quick to spring into action with counterinformation. For example, the South African Advertising Research Foundation proudly proclaims that between 1994 and 2001, the percentage of the population that falls into the poorest-of-the-poor category fell from 20 to 5 per cent. Buried in the small print is the fact that this bottom rung earns less than $500 per year, while the next one up has an annual income of between $500 and $1200.

Admirable efforts have been made with 1.4 million homes being delivered to needy South Africans between 1994 and 2002. Electricity access rose from 58 to 80 per cent of households in the same period. However, at ground level these initiatives look like a couple of sponges trying to mop up a dam-wall collapse.

Economists, too, have been furiously waving the flag with the National Press Club naming the rand as the 2002 Newsmaker of the Year for gaining almost 40 per cent against the US dollar. Unfortunately it's 40 per cent of sweet fuck-all.

A small but conspicuous number of black movers and shakers have been catapulted into the highest strata of society and have made millions since apartheid ended. However, according to a survey by Statistics South Africa, many of their brethren were actually better off under the old government. Between 1995 and 2000, the average black household was slugged with a 19 per cent fall in income, while the average white one enjoyed a 15 per cent increase. In 2000 the average white household earned six times as much as the average black one. In 1995 the ratio was four to one.

The real-world results of these inequities are hunger – a study by the University of the Western Cape's School of Government found that 70 per cent of the 750,000 residents in the greater Nyanga area had insufficient food last year – crime and the other calling card of Third World destitution, child labour. According to the Department of Labour, 36 per cent of South African minors are engaged in labour that by its own definition is "exploitative, hazardous, or otherwise inappropriate for their age, detrimental to their schooling or social, physical or moral development".

Nowhere was the disparity between the fat cats and ferals more obvious than at the turn-off to Umhlanga, a resort town where I had spent a number of Christmas holidays as a child and which is a mere twenty minutes from downtown Durban. The moment I pulled up at the traffic lights my car was besieged by four filthy children begging for coins. Distended bellies inflated their threadbare shirts. Glassy eyes stared at me from sunken sockets, and beneath their snot-crusted nostrils lay streaks of the spray paint that offers a diverting intoxication when sniffed from a bag. The light changed as I was fumbling for a donation and as I drove away, the coins failed to land in the palm of the intended recipient and scattered on the road instead. I heard a squeal of brakes behind me and in the widescreen format of the rear-view mirror I saw the kids scrambling for silver amid flying fists, utterly oblivious to the vehicle that had almost ploughed into them from behind.

Within minutes I was surrounded by palatial holiday homes propped on a lush spur garlanded with mauve Star of India and surveying 180 degrees of placid Indian Ocean. These worlds of opulence and poverty were no more than a kilometre apart.

The handful of hotels I remembered from my childhood had become a ritzy conglomeration of tiered town houses, corporate headquarters inspired by the "who gives a fuck as long as it's shiny" school of architecture and a shopping mall so vast it could have qualified for its own postcode. The beachfront strip was, however, much as I recalled it. My family always stayed at the Cabanas, a twelve-storey faux-Mexican *casa grande* where I would routinely catch head lice in the swimming pool and spend the rest of the holiday reeking of carbolic acid shampoo. Which was just what I needed at that hormone-soaked juncture in my life when a holiday romance was a priority for the first time and my best efforts at wooing were hampered by a larynx that leapt between registers of its own accord.

My other most distinct memory of the Cabanas was the discovery that guests – even young ones – could order whatever their sugar-craving hearts desired and sign them to the room. It was only at the end of one three-week stay that my father was presented with a bill that included almost fifty chocolate sundaes, whereupon he had a conniption so fierce that I couldn't wrench my gaze from the vein that was throbbing in his neck. I could tell that he was mad because he used the phrase "with all due respect". Refusing to pay for items he was adamant he had not ordered, he demanded to see the bills. These were duly produced and when he caught sight of the signature at the bottom the temperature in the room dropped ten degrees. Thus began the great pocket money drought of 1980.

With nostalgia seeping from every pore and a suspicious itch in my scalp, I enquired about the price of a night at the Cabanas. The response made me instantly realise why Dad had chucked that tanty. For a fading four-star resort that had a TV blaring in the lobby, the room rate took the concept of exorbitancy into a perverse new realm.

Flanked by an embankment of waxy green shrubbery on one side and a blanket of champagne sand on the other, the concrete beach path hadn't changed a smidge. The air tasted like the rim of a margarita glass and the spray threw misty drapes over the breakers. I walked the length of the beach shin-deep in warm water with a mild sun on my face. It was fourteen types of marvellous.

On this Friday evening in low season, the handful of pubs a block back from the beach were occupied by locals flushed with hard spirits and the contented countenance of those rich or lucky enough to call Umhlanga home. I wandered into a bar with a crowded terrace overlooking a seascape iced with pink meringue clouds. Here I wiled away the evening as a middle-aged cover band ripped into "Hotel California" and "The Boys are Back in Town" while I did likewise with a laager or three.

Between songs, the balding troubadours made "this is one of our personal favourites and we hope it's one of yours" in-jokes. These were mainly for the benefit of a table of brassy blonde groupies in lycra, Wonderbras and the throes of hormone replacement therapy. Having spent most of their lives in the seaside idyll, they had skin like Louis Vuitton luggage.

This was a clear sign that it was time to call it a night. Ditto the fact that it had reached that juncture of the evening where a number of the single male drinkers began playing air guitar in their seats.

I was collected the next morning by Andy Heimann, an old family friend who had kindly offered me a lift into Durban. On the way he switched on the news. The top story revolved around a minister who was negotiating with a large German vehicle manufacturer regarding a defence contract and had accepted one of their flashy cars as a heavily discounted sweetener.

An ebullient, gregarious type, Andy had spent his two years' compulsory military training either running "get captured and we'll deny you exist" insurgency raids into Angola or guarding the apartheid era state presidents under constant threat of assassination. He rolled his eyes at what he described as "daily reports of government corruption".

"Of course it also happened under the white government," he said, "but few of us thought it would be so prevalent under the equality that so many of the current ministry suffered for during the Struggle. Maybe I was naive, but I expected more from the government after what its elected representatives went through in the past. Instead a lot of them have been tearing the ring out the chicken."

It was an expression I'd never heard before but which required no explaining.

"When the government changed over in 1994, there was so much reorganising going on that anticorruption mechanisms weren't high on the agenda in the new constitution. Certain black politicians who were suddenly in positions of power and influence made a lot of illicit money very quickly. The nobility of the struggle against apartheid led many of us

– of all colours – to underestimate human nature and assume that the new regime would somehow be immune to public officials on the take. But it happens everywhere else, so why not here?" he asked as we made our way onto the Durban foreshore.

If the city were a woman, she'd be wearing too little clothing and too much make-up. Despite the skullcap of dark roots, desperate attempts at flirtation and breasts bubbling from a mutton-as-lamb top, it would be clearly evident that in her day she was a stunner. Now she's more like Lola at the Copacabana with faded feathers in her hair and a dress cut down to for-God's-sake-put-it-away.

It is a sad shell of the playground city that so entranced me as a child. The wave-shaped Elangeni Hotel, once the zenith of sophistication, still presides over the Golden Mile – which is actually four – on Marine Parade. But it is now a Holiday Inn. The same fate has befallen the Maharani next door whose neon outdoor elevator had provided me with hours of gawping entertainment as it glided heavenward to a disco on the roof. The rickshaw drivers lined up out the front in intricately patterned capes of glass beads and towering headdresses comprising ostrich feathers, bulls horns and leopard skin have been replaced by security guards.

At one stage there were 1500 rickshaws ferrying visitors along Durban's subtropical boulevards and I remember squealing with glee as our driver leapt into the air between strides, sending my mother and I sliding about the zebra-skin covered seat. With its beaming rickshaw drivers (many standing over ten feet with their headdresses on), neon-trimmed roller-coasters, beachside slippery dips, reptile parks and dolphinariums, a childhood trip to Durban was like stepping into a fantastic story – except you were in the illustrations.

For adults it was a hedonistic playground where pith-helmeted doormen waited to welcome you to a day at the races or the Georgian grandeur of the Durban Club where women are still not allowed to become members and can only enter the premises in the company of a male.

A few handsome Art Deco apartment blocks in pale pastels still stand on the beachfront but they look like ageing actors who've mistakenly wandered into a casting for a grunge video. Despite names like Seaspray, Blue Waters, High Tide and, oddly enough, Las Vegas, most of the waterfront is taken up by red-brick boxes with rust-blistered gutters. The funfairs and putt-putt courses have long since gone and the mini town replica of the city we faithfully made pilgrimages to – although neither ever changed – is boarded up.

After trying briefly to talk me out of my intention to stroll around the precinct that had so enchanted me as a child, Andy dropped me off at a once-grand hotel with ocean views. The grassy promenade between the street and the beach was awash with fast-food wrappers, beer bottles and young alcoholics with old faces. The pristine sunken garden built by the unemployed during the Great Depression and given a Tuscan pep-up by Italian POWs during World War II was as magnificent as ever, but I couldn't be certain whether the most rudimentary maintenance had merely made it appear so against its surroundings.

Things improved marginally at beach level. Dreadlocked surfers with boards tucked under their arms lounged at ramshackle fast-food kiosks scanning the break. I had been warned that a stroll in this area would most likely result in me requiring a blood transfusion before nightfall, but in fact, it was almost pleasant. Homeys with their underwear showing cruised by on skateboards, pausing to bob along to the freestyling rappers busking. Families kicked around footballs near public barbecues and omigods – a collective noun I've just invented for teenage girls because it's their most predominant call – stole surreptitious glances at six-packed lifesavers.

Hauling flailers from this stretch of water presents the kind of challenge that would have your average Australian or Californian lifeguard hanging up their Speedos. Aside from the constant and abundant threat of sharks, those who decide to take a dip here frequently don't know how to swim. When the whites-only signs came down, tens of thousands of black South Africans descended on beaches they'd previously been forbidden from. Christmas and New Year's Day are particularly popular and archived press photos show bathers standing forty or fifty deep and shoulder to shoulder like peak-hour commuters in a train carriage.

"How many rescues do you think we performed on this stretch of beach on Christmas Day last year?" asked Eric Themba, a lifesaver in his late teens. Not wanting to dampen his justifiable pride I responded on the outlandish side with a figure in the low two hundreds. "Try a thousand," he beamed. "And we only lost thirteen."

The city's harbour precinct has been touted as the genesis of a process of urban revitalisation, but the once-magnificent maritime buildings festooned with arches, domes and fluid fretwork still share the dilapidated air of the Nigerian prostitutes who occupy them. This part of town is the province of cashed-up sailors who routinely drop anchor in the largest port in Africa, the hookers who welcome them and the pimps who prey on both.

The only evidence I could find of the promised renaissance was a shudder-inducing sign on some vacant land informing passers-by that this was soon to be the home of the Shaka Island Casino.

At the water's edge stood a modest collection of restaurants that Andy had instructed me to visit for a seafood orgy. Overlooking the shipping channels beside the cigar-shaped hill known as the Bluff, these eateries were all he had promised. Fresh oysters accompanied by the sight of a curious sea lion and salt water paved diamante by a high sun – Durbs still had some threads of the old magic in her fraying coat.

The ninth-largest harbour on the planet, Durban lacks one of the natural attributes most crucial for its purpose: deep water. As a result, a network of lanes were dredged into the sand. At low tide it is possible to walk ankle-deep to the edge of these precipices and dozens of fishermen over the years have been taken by sharks who leapt from the opaque darkness at their feet.

In the 1850s the virgin bushland around Durban gave way to sugar plantations and the harbour witnessed an influx of indentured labour from India. Back-breaking toil for a pittance held sweet FA in the way of allure for the local Zulus, and so land barons turned their attention to the Empire's most abundant source of labour: the slums of Delhi, Madras and Calcutta. For ten shillings a month, hundreds of thousands bade their families farewell, lost their names – henceforth being referred to as Coolie Number whatever – and boarded cramped vessels for a month-long journey into the unknown. Motivated by starvation, they accepted a deal whereby they were to be indentured to a particular planter for up to seven years. After this period, they were obliged to remain in Natal for a further five years as a 'free labourer', after which they were made an offer: gratis passage back to India or a small grant of Crown land.

By law they were meant to be provided with food, clothing, medical attention and an annual increase of a shilling a month after the first year of service. In practice the attitude towards these labourers was neatly expressed in an editorial in the *Natal Witness*: "He is introduced for the same reason as mules might be introduced from Montevideo, oxen from Madagascar or sugar machinery from Glasgow. The object for which he is brought is to supply labour and that alone. He is not one of us. He is in every respect an alien, he only comes to perform a certain amount of work and return to India."

The fragmentation of families was common, as was the deportation of ill children and wives. Few complaints ever made it to the authorities as the labourers were forbidden from leaving estates without an employer's permission and absconding warranted terrifying retribution. When the overworked coolie immigration agent did make it to plantations to check on the wellbeing of these units of labour, his inspections were always in the company of employers or foremen whose presence ensured smiles and silence.

Not surprisingly, many were worked to death. The customary cremation favoured in India was banned in Natal and some open ground beside a slaughterhouse in Durban was set aside for Indian corpses. The mourners, anxious not to get their scant wages docked, dug the shallowest of graves and the bodies were routinely exhumed by feral pigs who had acquired a carnivorous bent thanks to offal dumpings from the nearby butchery.

As the Indian labour community in Natal flourished and those who had served their period of indenture began to establish modest private enterprises, a new wave of travellers from the homeland began to arrive – at their own expense. Mostly Muslims from the state of Gujarat, they were of a higher caste than the majority of labourers, had extensive education and were sufficiently cashed up to make the local retail sector their own. Employing members of their family, they could trim business overheads and undercut their opposition to the point that increasing numbers of bargain-hunting whites became their clients. Their main customer base, however, was indentured or ex-indentured labourers and these high-caste merchants associated with them only to the degree that successful business practice demanded.

In the eyes of the whites, Indian was Indian, no matter what caste. That meant 9pm curfews, police brutality, and statutes which prevented traders from opening their stores on Sundays – the one day that indentured labourers could do their shopping.

These grievances formed the core of an ignored appeal this educated elite sent to the Colonial Secretary in London. When the local authorities were granted responsible government in 1893, Indian appeals to their homeland or England were effectively extinguished. If South African Indians were to combat discrimination, they had no choice but to put aside the social barriers that would have prevented them from associating in the old country and unite in a campaign for political and civil rights. Even though they didn't know it, the Indians were at this point pre-empting Bonnie Tyler by almost a century in holding out for a hero.

He arrived in Durban on Tuesday 23 May 1893, intending to spend no more than a profitable year in town then head home first class with a fat wallet. Mohandas Karamchand Gandhi was born in Porbandar on 2 October 1869, the son of a senior public official. He married at thirteen, became a father before his next birthday and left for London five years later to study law. Called to the bar in 1891, he returned to his family and opened a string of unsuccessful law practices in Bombay and Rajkot. Through his brother, Gandhi secured a contract with the firm of Dada Abdullah and Co. which had branches in Porbandar and Durban and was involved in a claim between two Indian businessmen for some £40,000 – serious potatoes in 1893. Gandhi's role was to instruct counsel, dispose of English correspondence and translate Gujarati documents throughout the duration of the case which was to be heard in Pretoria.

A bitter taste of what was to come presented itself on his third day in Durban when Gandhi went to the magistrate's court so he could become better acquainted with South African legal procedure. Equating his traditional turban with a hat – which was required to be removed in a court of law – the magistrate ordered him to lose it. Gandhi refused. It was an act which made two papers the next day, one article carrying the headline "AN UNWELCOME VISITOR".

A fortnight later he set out to Pretoria for the case. A first-class seat had been booked in his name on the train, but when it reached Pietermaritzburg a white passenger entered the compartment and promptly went off like a prawn sandwich. Livid at the idea of being made to share the journey with a person of colour, he returned with two rail officials who insisted the lawyer shift into cattle class.

His first-class ticket counted for diddly in their eyes and Ghandi's protestations saw him tossed from the train with his luggage.

For reasons that remain unclear to this day, the railway officials on duty deemed it necessary for Gandhi and his bags to spend the night in separate rooms. Bitterly cold and fearing the possible repercussions of asking for his overcoat, he endured a sleepless night during which he had ample time to consider his future. A return to India was one option, but cowardice was not in his nature. After being met in the morning by some local Indian merchants who shared their tales of bigotry with him, Gandhi did not have the epiphany that has been widely mythologised. There was no grand vow to spend the remainder of his life fighting prejudice and working for racial harmony. In fact, a year after the incident on the train, Ghandi was back in Durban preparing to head home to India. During a farewell bash thrown by his boss, he was shown a newspaper article dealing with a bill seeking to remove the rights of Indians to elect members to the Natal Legislative Assembly.

As the canapés were circulated, a local businessman asked if he would stay for an extra month to help the community mount a legal challenge. Gandhi agreed and although the bill was eventually passed unopposed, the Indian movers and shakers who had attended meetings presided over by the young lawyer knew they had someone special in their midst and begged him to stay on to fight for civil rights. Gandhi and his cohorts then set about forming a permanent lobbying organisation called the Natal Indian Congress.

After three years of eloquently agitating for the rights of Indians, Gandhi realised that this was not going to be a short African sojourn and he returned to India to collect his family. When news got back to Natal that this coolie had developed a severe case of the uppities and was telling anyone who would listen about the mistreatment of his countrymen, newspapers exaggerated his statements and anti-Indian demonstrations erupted in Durban's CBD.

In the years that followed Gandhi became increasingly

influenced by the life of simple, honest toil that Tolstoy extolled. Ruskin's *Unto This Last* had a similar effect, particularly the assertion that "the good of the individual is contained in the good of all, that all work is equal and that the life of labour of the tiller of the soil and handicraftsmen is the life worth living". For a man who had been born into relative wealth to a family in which professional success was as cherished as the ingrained prejudices of the caste system, this was a shift of seismic spiritual proportions.

Gandhi put his newly found ideals of truth, equality and fairness into practice by forming a self-sufficient hundred-acre community twenty-six kilometres from Durban. Known as the Phoenix Settlement, it contained a spring, a few orange and mango trees and cost £1000. It was here that he printed the weekly *Indian Opinion* newspaper, a moderate mouthpiece for the Natal Indian Congress.

Over the course of the twenty-one years he would spend in South Africa, Ghandi developed the political strategy of satyagraha – meaning "truth firmness" and often translated as passive resistance. It formed the cornerstone of the Struggle for half a century and was only abandoned when Nelson Mandela and his cohorts realised that the white man's heart was hardening over time.

Already being hailed as a mahatma (literally a great soul), Gandhi returned to India in 1914 and his son Manilal arrived in Durban to preside over Phoenix House. The settlement remained a sanctuary of peace until 1985 when squatters from a nearby shantytown rampaged through the grounds burning homes, looting their meagre contents and sending terrified residents fleeing for their lives.

Thanks to wads of cash from the Indian government, the local community and the city council, the squatters have now been relocated to vacant land nearby and work has begun to restore the gutted buildings as a national monument. Writing to Maganlal Gandhi about the name of his newly formed settlement in 1909, the Mahatma noted, "As the legend goes, [the Phoenix] comes back to life again and again from its own ashes, it never dies. The name serves the purpose quite well for we believe the aims of Phoenix will not vanish even when we are turned to dust."

At last count Durban's Indian community numbered around the million mark – 70 per cent of whom are Hindu, 20 per cent Muslim and the remainder Christian. When I was a child its heart and soul was to be found not by the breakers but at the sprawling Victoria Market. A seraglio of raised walkways leading to what felt like acres of stalls over three levels, the market had always been a highlight of our annual Durban daytrip.

You smelt it before you saw it. Wafts of garam masala, clove and cinnamon enveloped you like scented arms. The scores of spice traders who operated out of the market displayed their wares in enormous metal buckets from which rose infant-high peaks of fragrant powders in shades from cream to deep orange. In addition to the usual suspects such as rogan josh, vindaloo, korma and tikka, each would offer intriguingly named custom blends like "Honeymooners' Delight", "Mother-In-Law's Tongue" and "A-Bomb".

Dispersed between these were fabric emporiums where columns of sari silk in gold-flecked magenta, turquoise and acid green stood cheek by jowl with shop dummies sporting natty safari suits which could be custom-made within twenty-four hours. Samosas – deep-fried on the spot and served with a dollop of cucumber raita – were sold at a dozen locations throughout the market. Condiment specialists invited visitors to sample a spread of aromatic chutney on still-warm pappadams and linen traders offered "special prices for a beautiful lady" whenever my mum wandered by.

A part of me knew I had romanticised the experience but another chose to ignore that. I had been warned that the market was no longer what it had once been, but this proved to be euphemistic in the extreme. The pavements on the surrounding streets had been commandeered by vendors hawking malodorous Zulu herbal remedies – one of which purported to cure both AIDS and cancer – sad arrays of fruit in plastic bags, and packets of sweets. Inside, the market less than a half-a-dozen of the spice traders remained. The buckets of flavoursome powder were still on display, but judging by their lack of pungency – and the ready-mixed jars on the shelves – these were merely window-dressing hauled out every day rather than freshly mixed and replenished through demand. The textile kings had abdicated their thrones and the remainder of the stalls were selling mobile phone covers, crappy Chinese yapping dog toys and knock-off Beckham football jerseys.

Hoping there was still a fresh samosa to be had on the premises, I made the mistake of asking for directions to the food hall. As a journalist I had once spent a nausea-free day with a forensic doctor as he examined a murder victim to determine the cause of death. A bone saw, numerous scalpels and the phrase "Would you mind holding the cavity open?" were involved and I therefore consider myself fairly strong of stomach.

Or at least I did until I entered the food section of the Victoria Market. A fluorolit pavilion of warehouse proportions, it was packed with row upon row of butchers and fishmongers hacking into flesh with rusty cleavers. Carcasses hung from hooks at every turn, ventilation was nonexistent and the stench of rotting entrails filled my nostrils, prompting an evacuation drill further south.

A hurried and pale-faced departure later, I was in the posh end of town and the Durban I remember. The Berea is a sedate hilly burb where frangipani trees drizzled with palm-size buds of yellow, white, pink and mauve peep over low walls. Stately old-money homes with oak-lined gravel driveways glanced down the hill towards the harbour and in a garden or three a Union Jack snapped in the warm breeze.

The city had always seen itself as a bastion of British civility looking inland towards a landscape and natives of conquerable savagery. They may have won battles, but they lost the war. Now suburbs you can count on one hand take on the role the entire city once did as decay and degradation steal metres each day. That said, I was glad to be ending my stay in a part of town fiercely determined to maintain its quiet dignity while privately moaning about what had become of itself. What could be more English?

Chapter 10

Walking the Dragon

To the Zulus, they looked like the blades of the gods and were called uKuhlamba, meaning "barrier of spears". To the white settlers whose hearts undoubtedly sank at first sight, they resembled the scarred scaled ridges on a dragon's back.

The Drakensberg range runs down the right side of the country like a 1100-kilometre vein before swinging south-west into the Eastern Cape where it transforms into capillary mountain chains. Three hours northwest of Durban, the Berg, as it affectionately known, is at its most spectacular.

Bordering the nation of Lesotho in the shape an arrow-head, the Drakensberg soar in excess of 3000 metres with the highest peak out-altituding the Matterhorn. A crescent of national parks surround the Berg at its base and the region was declared a World Heritage site in November 2000 on account of its staggering biodiversity and numerous works of San rock art dating back 5000 years.

For those who don't have the luxury of weeks to explore the Berg, the Royal National Park is the mountainous equivalent of a tasting plate. Turning off the highway towards the northern section of the range, the road bisected pancake plains of russet farmland before passing through the amiable town of Winterton with its smattering of oak-lined streets, cellar doors and cosy B&Bs. The landscape eventually began to assume an incline. Grassy ridges serrated the topography as lazy cattle grazed beside catatonic rivulets. These sandstone and shale tumescences are known as the Little Berg and as the name suggests are merely support acts to the main gig.

The headliner at this rock festival is undoubtedly the Amphitheatre. A elliptical wall of solid basalt half a kilometre high and stretching five, it is framed by the flat-topped Sentinel (3165 m), the jagged Beacon Buttress (3124 m), while the Eastern Buttress (3121 m) looks on indifferently from the left. It is a sky-consuming vista exuding a mystical beauty that renders superlatives impotent. The entrance to the Royal National Park lies at its base.

In the visitors' centre was a framed photograph of Queen Elizabeth and South African prime minister Jan Smuts taken here in the 1950s. She is wearing her standard polite smile while he has a "so what were you saying about Ben Nevis?" gloat writ large across his dial.

It was a Monday afternoon, few visitors were about and a ramble was in order. The map I had purchased offered myriad options and I settled on the Fairy Glen trail on the grounds that it was the closest to where I was standing and perfectly described a close friend. Colour me gobsmacked, but this was like stepping into a fairytale forest.

On one side of the path a steep embankment of double-storey ferns swept toward the crest of a spur. On the other, a percolating brook glinted in the freckles of sunlight that pierced the canopy. Scarlet butterflies drifted by as distant birdsong harmonised with the river's soundtrack. After crossing the stream on a wooden pole bridge, the path traversed a hillside ablaze in red-hot pokers, lichen-dipped boulders and mauve bell agapanthus.

The closer you get to the Amphitheatre the less uniform the landscape becomes. Furrowed and cracked, it is a melange of pinnacles, saddles, cutbacks and ridges projecting outward at right angles from the escarpment. It is also draped with waterfalls that tumble from the precipice like streamers from an ocean liner about to set sail. From my vantage point, I could make out the Thukela Falls which drop 850 metres from summit to valley floor in five tumultuous cascades.

Another of the names by which the Drakensberg is known is "the cradle of rivers" and the mountainside was crisscrossed by rivulets that could be leapt in a single stride or clumsily sloshed through depending on how much attention you were paying to what lay on the ground in front of you. Not an easy feat when surrounded by the majestic backdrop used for the film *Zulu Dawn*, a rug of weeping lovegrass and irises that appeared to have been tossed over the spur as if it were a couch in need of some pizzazz, and a family of curious bush buck.

The track eventually turned into a camp ground consisting of a hectare of lawn, spotless ablution blocks with thatched roofs and a small general store. Shirtless men with beers in one hand and tongs in the other presided over barbecues, campers dozed under trees with newspapers on their chests, and children rode their bikes around a series of pathways on the periphery of the grass. Meandering through the camp site, I scanned the conversations for accents and found only locals.

That night I called my mate Andy – who had recommended the Royal – and asked whether many international tourists visit the Berg. "Don't be a *doos*," he said, the last word being an Afrikaans one whose literal translation is "box" but is more often reserved for those with a tendency to plumb the depths of moronic behaviour. "They see a few lions, take the cable car up Table Mountain, buy some diamonds and go home. They aren't too interested in the Drakensberg." He didn't seem overly disappointed by this, a sense that was confirmed when he added, "So don't you go making them."

From the camp site the path tracked a glassy stream five metres across and strewn with smooth boulders. Conifers dipped their branches into the rush like nervous swimmers testing the temperature of a pool. Thick rafts of yellow-tipped gladioli and cream gardenias sprung from the banks.

At the risk of coming over a bit Thoreau, there are few things to beat a drink from a mountain stream on a hot day, and nothing to top dropping your daks for a swim. Although the temperature took a few minutes of adaptation, I was soon happily floating on my back with the Amphitheatre upside down behind me.

Consulting the trail map when I got back to the car, I was surprised to discover I had covered eight pristine kilometres. I had booked a room that night at a local institution called the Cavern which is nestled between a pair of ridges a short drive from the Amphitheatre. The place is a series of tiers upon which perch wide-fronted thatched terrace houses. Below these lie tennis courts, a swimming pool and a further series of terraces ablaze with leonotis, strelitzias and purple daisies which found their way into the vases on every table at dinner. The Cavern has its own bowling green, a dance is held every Saturday night and tea is included in the room tariff but served strictly at 11am and 4pm when a gong is sounded.

With the 1960s on the horizon, guests christened it the "resort of many happy returns", but at the Cavern it was still and would forever be 1958. And when I was refused entry to the sparsely populated dining room on the grounds that I was not wearing a collar, the Cavern grew on me even further.

The next morning I awoke early and stepped out onto the balcony into air so crisp that it felt freshly laundered.

Wearing nothing but boxer shorts and the stupefied grin of contentment that only surfacing to a summer's day in the country can bring, I wasn't quite expecting company. However, the occupant of the room next door had also decided to venture onto his balcony and thought it rude not to introduce himself.

"Francois Du Plessis," he said in the confident tone of a man answering an early-round question in a quiz show, before thrusting a hand and a ready smile in my direction. A civil – exceedingly so, in fact – engineer, he was attending a national conference at the hotel and assumed that I must have been a colleague from a regional office. Making a mental note to re-evaluate the underwear which had so effortlessly lead him to this conclusion, I started chatting and it soon became clear why Francois was so anxious to network.

He had been unemployed for three years and believed that as a white Afrikaans male in the job market, his opportunities had been not merely hamstrung but amputated by the government's affirmative-action employment policies. "By law, every level of every company now has to have a certain number of what are called Previously Disadvantaged Persons or PDPs," he said. "If, for example, my company bids for a road-building project, we have to prove that we are black empowered before being considered. By that I mean 75 per cent of the board of directors must be black, women or preferably both and they must genuinely run the firm. A lot of companies tried to pretend that the guy who was cleaning the toilets yesterday got an overnight promotion to GM and the government stung them big time. If you are tendering for a government contract in South Africa today and are not a proven black-empowered company, your quote has to be 20 per cent lower (than those who meet the criteria) to even be considered. Even if you get the job, 15 per cent of the work must be subcontracted to PDPs or the government will slug you with extra tax to the same amount."

Francois acknowledged that while this policy had forced companies to boost their black staff numbers to qualify for tax concessions and government contracts, he was convinced it was a double-edged sword. "The generation of whites that voted for change is being punished," he said. "When the concept of merit is thrown out of the window and a person gets a job on the basis of his skin colour being darker than mine, that's reverse discrimination. I understand that wealth and all levels of jobs should be open to everyone, but I'm not convinced that throwing someone without the skills, experience and training into the deep end is the solution. Often through no fault of their own, they will drag down the company's performance and international investors will turn away. I mean, would you sink your dollars into a firm that didn't employ the best possible people in the marketplace?

"You hear all these stories about the white brain-drain because of the crime or the big money on offer overseas, but in many cases they have just become redundant here. I can tell you one thing," he added, the faintest trace of anger entering his voice, "if I was a black lesbian in a wheelchair, I wouldn't have been unemployed for three years."

Some unconscious element in my reaction must have betrayed my scepticism and Francois darted into his room to return with the Sunday paper. "Do me a favour," he grinned, "tomorrow morning, pick ten jobs from the employment section, call them up, say you're a white male who is qualified for the position and ask if it would be worth sending in your résumé."

Up for the challenge, I did as instructed and followed the script with positions ranging from media and manufacturing to IT and sales. In all but one of the cases I was told that the job was for a PDP but they would keep my résumé on file should a more appropriate role become available. The majority of the people I spoke to during these conversations – and who, judging by their accents, spanned a number of races – were far more sympathetic than I thought they would be. But as I'm certain Francois would tell you, sympathy don't pay the mortgage.

The conversation I had with Francios was repeated time and again with other white South Africans. On the one hand most of those I spoke to recognised the need for the majority of the population to be able to access the highest levels of management. On the other, they privately recoiled at the notion of effectively barring many of South Africa's best and brightest from entering the workforce because they were too pale.

Like Francois, many took the economic rationalism approach, arguing that companies forced to employ quotas would dilute the quality of their workforce. This in turn would impact on the firm's performance, which would send potential backers scuttling towards Asia (I don't know why Asia was continually singled out, but it was).

Others were more circumspect, saying that at some point the country had to start paying the cost of apartheid and if it took a generation for the average South African worker to boost his or her skill level and experience, then so be it. The nation would eventually be all the stronger for it.

Bloemfontein, which lies close to the heart of the country was everything I expected and less. The judicial capital of South Africa, it brought to mind Spike Milligan's likening of Woy Woy on the New South Wales central coast to "the world's only above-ground cemetery". Like many state capitals, it had failed to capture the city vibrancy that it was prepared to sacrifice its country charm for.

Even when I was growing up under the apartheid regime, the Orange Free State was viewed by many South Africans as a redneck backwater. It's an argument supported by the fact that the Free State is still home to communities such as Orania, a town of staunch Afrikaners who believe that the only way to preserve their heritage and identity is to establish an autonomous ministate so far away from the Rainbow Nation that everything is still black and white. The town was purchased from the Department of Water Affairs and in order to fulfil their vision, these descendants of the Voortrekkers did something that none of their forebears could ever bring themselves to: they got rid of their black and coloured servants. Yet Mandela has visited Orania and was treated like an honoured guest.

This is one example of how the Free State has always been and probably will continue to be a soft target for stereotypes when in fact its history is far more complex. It was here that the architects and administrators of apartheid, the National Party, was established in 1914. It was here, too, that apartheid's primary foe, the African National Congress, set up shop two years earlier.

The centre of the city is given over to a historic precinct that is stately yet compact. In essence a roomy square, it consists of a trio of imposing two-storey buildings all fronted by ionic columns. One of these is the Afrikaans Literature Institute, which I was heartened to see was still a bustling academic centre despite commemorating a language that many feel was apartheid's mother tongue. This of course makes as much sense as vilifying German because it was the language of Nazism. In this instance civil service pettiness seems to have been put aside and government funds allocated to preserve Afrikaans. Yes, twelve years of compulsory Afrikaans study was foisted upon all South African students under the apartheid era, but it was the medium of conscience-jarring, soul-poking writers I would never have had the privilege to sample otherwise.

Twilight was approaching and I joined the throngs making their way towards the rugby ground where the reason for my visit — a Super 12 clash between the ACT Brumbies and the local Cats — would be taking place. Despite the fact that it seemed to have had a charisma bypass, Bloemfontein felt like a town that was doing all right, content within itself and clocking up milestones like being the capital of the first state to elect a black woman premier, Dr Ivy Mastepe-Casaburri.

My mate Francois would have said she was a shoo-in for the job, but for a region that had produced many of apartheid's staunchest advocates this was no small irony. Unlike Johannesburg, Durban and even Pretoria, Bloemfontein felt safe. They were no armed guards watching over every ATM and no wailing sirens every few minutes. In fact, the only crimes I witnessed were those against fashion and let me assure you that you haven't lived until you've seen a man wearing a short-sleeved mustard safari suit jacket with a long-sleeved burgundy shirt beneath it. There was only one accessory that could have done justice to this ensemble and the wearer nailed it: a comb-over.

My sense of personal wellbeing vanished shortly after entering the stadium. After migrating to Australia I became a rabid supporter of my new national team in whatever sport was being played, and if truth be told, there's nothing I like better than when the Aussies take it to the Jaapies.

Steep-tiered and designed to intimidate visitors with the appearance that it is closing in on you from all sides, this stadium was the venue where generations of Afrikaner Springboks – farm-toughened and powered by an unshakeable belief in their racial superiority – slayed Lions, Wallabies and All Blacks. This paddock was one of a select few on which a rugby nation came to believe it was the world's best. It was a notion which only grew stronger during the sports boycott of the apartheid years when teams of rebel has-beens were crushed by young, skilled men in green and gold and culminated in the 1995 World Cup victory. For a few glorious hours after Nelson Mandela – wearing the rugby jersey of blue-eyed Afrikaans skipper Francios Pienaar – handed the William Webb Ellis trophy to the beaming captain, the nation was united in a collective delirium the likes of which it had never seen nor will again.

Like junkies chasing that first rush, South African rugby fans have never quite replicated that dominance. Since these halcyon days, the elite coaching staff of South African rugby have rolled over like rent boys at Mardi Gras in an elusive chase for victory. They have even taken to importing Australian coaching talent such as Tim Lane who would be guiding the Cats around the paddock in the game I had steadfastly maintained I was going wear my Wallabies jumper to. I swiftly discovered that good-natured rivalry had long been replaced by hardened bitterness as team after South African team across a variety of sports choked on the threshold of victory over Antipodean rivals.

By the time I had covered the ten metres between the booth and the turnstiles I had already been called Bruce four times and told that I was "going to get the crap beaten out of me in that shirt" by a concerned security guard.

The match was scheduled for a 7pm kick-off, but being a Friday most of the spectators had knocked off early and were enjoying numerous frosties in the beer garden adjacent to the stadium. Seething with antagonism and the contents of half-a-dozen longnecks calling their small intestines home, the punters who were still sober enough to make out where my loyalties lay fixed me with narrow-eyed death stares. Others merely alerted their pals to my presence by giving me the bird with one hand and nudging their pals amid a sideways "look at this fuckwit" with the other. The solitary smile I received that evening came from Owen Finegan as the Brumbies' bus rolled by.

Having been sent reeling by a series of shoulder charges, I found my seat. Which happened to be next to an Afrikaans family who clearly viewed me with the type of virulent disdain usually reserved for war criminals and Bon Jovi impressionists.

The taunts dissipated as the home team edged in front by half-time. Lulled into a false sense of security, I brazenly got to my feet at the referee's whistle and was promptly pelted with a well-directed mandarin to the bridge of my nose. Upon which most everyone seated in the adjacent sections burst into heartfelt applause.

Temporarily blinded by an explosion of citric acid, I groped my way to the men's room. Having doused my burning retinas, I foolishly decided to pee. No sooner had I taken my position at the trough when I felt a meaty hand in the small of my back deliver a powerful push. Yes, in a horrifying revisitation of schoolyard humiliation, I was launched feet first into the urinal.

Shortly after the second half commenced, a Brumbies winger bolted across the line for a try that was not converted, thus giving the visitors a six-point lead. The tension in the stadium built as penalties were awarded and missed, the ref dropped some clangers in the face of obvious foul play and time ticked away towards a victory for the Australian team. All the while the glares and taunts I drew became more threatening.

A glimmer of redemption was mercifully delivered in the last minute of injury time when the Cats fullback glided over in the corner for a five-pointer. With the siren wailing and the home team still a point behind, he slotted the conversion from a miraculous angle. Joyous pandemonium broke out and as the beaming Afrikaner family beside me packed up their esky, their seven-year-old son who hadn't made a sound all night craned his golden-fringed head to look me dead in the eye and beamed, "Vok jou".

Chapter 11

Highs and Lows

The region surrounding Bloemfontein is known as the *platteland*, which imaginatively translates as "the flat land". It is a prosperous agricultural belt and consists of hectare after hectare of cattle-strewn paddocks and wheat fields. Mildly agreeable to begin with, the scenery very quickly begins to feel like it's on an audiovisual loop and tedium rides shotgun shortly afterwards.

The odd troupe of monkeys and stoats standing up on their hind legs in the yellow grass by the roadside made fleeting appearances – as did raptor specks gliding against a backdrop of liquid sky – but mostly it seemed like just interminable stretches of same old, same old.

My destination was a church in the restful village of Adelaide near the town of Somerset East. It began life as a military outpost during the Frontier Wars and then became a sheep-farming hamlet of unpretentious charm – a quality it has regained today – until British forces rode into town during the Anglo-Boer War. The troops commandeered the local Dutch Reformed Church, turned it into barracks and left things in such a state of disrepair that the locals had to embark on a funding drive to restore their place of worship.

Offers of labour and time were abundant, but the townsfolk simply could not afford the expensive materials needed to complete their task.

Three months after the donation drive was abandoned through lack of results, it seemed the congregants' prayers were literally answered when two wagons rolled into town stacked with cut timber, a hand-carved pulpit of intricate allure and a matching chair. Believing that the master builder in the sky had seen fit to bestow this miracle upon them, locals quickly set about fulfilling their part of the bargain and restored the church immaculately.

The packaging on their gift revealed the items had been imported from England and locals viewed them as a spiritual lesson that all races had goodness in their hearts. They believed that their former enemies' consciences had got the better of them and the timber had been sent as an apology. The time had come to live and let live.

A few years later, however, a letter arrived addressed to the town mayor. It was from his equivalent in South Australia and read: "Dear Sir, It is with some trepidation that we enquire as to whether a consignment of oak wood, which we ordered from England about two years ago for our new church, has not, perhaps, by mistake been delivered to your town in South Africa instead of ours." The locals admitted to nothing and the church they restored remains one of the prettiest in the nation.

After cutting through a succession of dry, dull and dusty towns, the road began to traverse a series of jagged charcoal peaks. Lined up in tight formation behind one another like overweight relatives at a bar mitzvah buffet, they signalled the start of the Kat River valley. A compact cluster of citrus orchards set between a succession of gentle ridges, this it was one of those rare places where agriculture has complemented Mother Nature rather than being a boil on her pristine bottom. Wooden roadside kiosks offered kilogram-bags of plump mandarins for R10 ($2). Fruit hung in the trees in such profusion that they looked like spatters of luminous amber flicked from a paintbrush onto a bottle-green backdrop.

By the time I reached my destination of Grahamstown it was late in the afternoon and the air was beginning to chill. I had never been to the town before but it was there I would most likely have studied had my family remained in South Africa.

After a brief conversation with a hotel receptionist about evening distractions in town, I was directed to a pub called the Rat and Parrot. By the time I arrived it was thrumming with the kind of crowd that only university towns can muster. Women in the unfortunate combination of G-strings and hipsters pretended not be interested in floppy-haired lads nursing beers and Foucault. Rugby boys were already losing their ability to pronounce consonants as jug after jug of Castle Lager was consumed, and Ashanti was blaring from the speakers.

Using that ever-reliable technique of buying students' company with alcohol, I began chatting to a group of English majors nearby. Boisterous, amiable and opinionated in the way that only undergraduates who have happily fallen on an unexpected source of booze can be, we spent a couple of mildly inebriated hours discussing everything from sport to politics to racial integration. When I asked why there were so few – or more precisely, zero – black students in the bar, one of the girls replied, "They have the bars they prefer to go to and we have ours. Obviously no one is banned from going anywhere but human nature is such that like tends to stick with like. Jews hang out together. WASPs gravitate towards one another. It's just a matter of choice."

Some hushed discussions then followed during which I wondered whether I had overstepped the mark with the race question. In a telling blow to my coolness count, they were actually debating whether or not I was a narc. Having decided that I probably did not make a living from law enforcement, an architecture student named Tim asked if I had sampled any zol on my trip. It was one of those words that I recalled from when I lived in South Africa but whose meaning I momentarily struggled for.

My glimmer of confusion presented Tim with what seemed like a linguistic opportunity he had been awaiting for some time. "You know," he beamed, "grass, dope, ganja, green, the sacred herb, skunk."

His mates dissolved into giggles as Lexicon Boy went through his pace and I replied in the negative. "Well," he said, producing a joint from his pocket, "it's time to fix that."

Minutes later we were in a cobblestoned laneway out the back of the bar, passing the Duchy from the left-hand side. Several other groups clustered around glowing cherries were also imbibing. What else would you expect from a university town located in a region where *Cannabis sativa* grows like a wild weed?

Long before white occupation, the Xhosa tribe had cultivated a thriving dope business and exchanged the crop with Zulus for beads and iron. Today it is a primary component of South Africa's rural economy.

Despite exhaustive eradication programs aimed at reducing supply beyond the budgets of consumers, the price has remained stable for decades and in some cases has even dipped. In fact, it is frequently cheaper to get stoned on dope in South Africa than it is to get drunk on beer or buzzed on espresso.

It is mostly produced by poor black farmers who supplement their subsistence existence with an easy-to-grow cash crop that flourishes several times a year alongside South African staples such as corn and cabbage. By the time the foliage has gone from farmer to wholesaler to retailer to street dealer it has been divided into what are known as "bankies" – the plastic bags banks use for storing R100 worth of coins – selling for around R50 ($10) each. Those in the trade are there to get by and it is not a hugely profitable business. In fact, the estimated gross profit of one dagga house selling hundreds of bankies a day in a well-to-do area of Durban is little more than R15,000 ($3000) a month.

The real money is overseas. South Africa has knocked Jamaica off top spot as the single largest supplier of cannabis to the United Kingdom and is importing vast quantities of club drugs from Blighty in return. So widespread is South Africa's THC reputation that enterprising travel companies are now running tour groups through the Eastern Cape and Natal so that overseas travellers can sample Durban Poison and Maritzburg Gold at ground zero.

That evening we were enjoying the former, referred to by those in the herbal know as DP. The smoke had the sweet tang of caramel and the pungency of football socks forgotten behind the couch. Within seconds of a petite puff, my head began to implode in slow motion and I felt myself withdrawing at light speed to a galaxy far far away. My companions, however, coherently maintained a conversation about whether human beings inherently knew right from wrong or if we needed a moral system imposed upon us to prevent anarchy. At times, one of their voices would penetrate the fog between my ears to ask my opinion. To which I could offer no more than a glazed smile and a shoulder shrug followed by the kind of convulsing squealy giggle that eventuates when feather meets armpit.

I waited for waves of wellbeing to wash over me but instead currents of nausea ripped through my abdomen. Then paranoia joined the party. I formulated a cogent hypothesis that I was about to become victim of a well-rehearsed gang that fleeced visitors of their belongings and pride, leaving their quarry naked on the main street as they swapped postmodern bon mots.

I mumbled something about an early start in the morning, thanked the group for their hospitality and wandered off in the opposite direction from my hotel. The broad oak-lined street featured half-a-dozen pubs clearly designed to attract different faculties: there was a sports bar for the engineers, an avant-garde (read: sign upside down, lots of neon and Kraftwerk remixes) for the fine arts mob and a candlelit coffee bar where a doleful guitarist was bleating about some misery or other for a clutch of twenty-year-olds in anti-globalisation T-shirts.

I ended up at a late-night diner decorated in a 50s rock and roll motif where I had the best banana milkshake, toasted cheese sandwich and choc-fudge sundae of my life.

I woke up the next morning surprisingly clear-headed but accompanied by the flaky remnants of a block of chocolate that judging by the packaging had once been the size of a roof tile. It was a bright warm morning and Grahamstown was mine to explore. Its streets were wide enough to allow for two rows of parking in the middle, separated by a concrete flowerbed awash in yellow and purple pansies. Students with second-hand jeans but top-of-the-line laptops dawdled their way towards the grand archway at the entrance to Rhodes University; townsfolk browsed shop windows to see if anything had changed from yesterday, and shopkeepers swept footpaths in the sunshine. The high street couldn't be a more different scene for eleven days in July when the Grahamstown Festival transforms the town. Second only to the Edinburgh Arts Festival in scale, it is twenty-nine years old and in 2002 it showcased around 200 plays, cabarets, art exhibitions, films, concerts, dance performances and lectures. There are also two separate jazz festivals – no one would tell me what caused the ruction – a separate fringe, a literature fair and a thousand craft stalls. From the sound of it, things get awfully bohemian around festival time with some locals apparently offering floor space to weary pilgrims while others embark on a gouge-fest at the dozens of B&Bs.

The town was established in 1812 by Colonel John Graham as a military outpost on what was the eastern frontier of the Cape. The surrounding region was essentially one enormous battlefield where nine frontier wars were waged over a century. Each had its share of treachery, slaughter, vengeance and provocation, but it says something for the resilience and military ingenuity of the Xhosa that they resisted the mightiest army on earth for almost one hundred years while the proud Zulu fell in a mere handful.

Like most frontier towns, Grahamstown's early residents could be neatly divided into two distinct groups: the pious and the bonkers. Grateful for their survival on the edge of civilisation, almost every religious denomination with a congregation in the town set about constructing their own house of worship. It soon became a case of keeping up with the Jehovah's and today almost forty spires rise from the compact town centre. It's like someone put Prague in the tumble-dryer.

The brooding Methodist Commemoration Church with its Gothic revival facade topped by a quintet of spires and ten stained-glass windows is magnificent. Not least for the winged figure of Peace, commemorating the Anglo-Boer War dead, sitting atop a plinth out the front with a plaque written by no less than Rudyard Kipling. It is not a particularly moving piece of prose and reading it I couldn't shake Groucho Marx's response to the question, "Do you like Kipling?"

"I'm not sure," he said, "I've never Kippled."

Grahamstown's most prominent landmark is rather unsurprisingly another church. The Cathedral of St Michael and St George is a jaw-droppingly gorgeous edifice in early English Gothic. Its spire is the tallest in South Africa and peers into backyards like a nosy neighbour on the hunt for scandal. Before the word had all meaning flogged out of it by the extreme-sports crowds – "that wave was awesome!" "your bungee jump was awesome!", "my socks are awesome!" – it would have been tailor-made for the space.

Having faithfully visited a handful of the buildings built by the devoted, it was time to explore the doings of some of Grahamstown's other main players: the eccentrics.

After the Fifth Frontier war, 4000 Britons were granted land and passage to the area to consolidate the empire's power base. As military activity continued to push eastwards, Grahamstown blossomed into South Africa's second largest city after Cape Town. Aspirations to grandeur accompanied its growth. Imposing public buildings, such as the colonnaded sandstone Town Hall with streamlined clocktower, sandstone law courts and stately libraries took their place among the ornate churches and stretches of Victorian shopfronts.

The civility, climate and picture-book charm drew genteel oddballs by the dozen, but HG Galpin made the rest look like mere dabblers. His home – a cream two-storey Victorian town house with a turreted clocktower – has been preserved as the Observatory Museum. The architect, surveyor, civil engineer and chronometer-, watch- and clockmaker bought the pile in 1859 and over the next twenty years added a basement, three storeys to the back of the structure and a rooftop observatory.

Picture Henry Higgins's home in *My Fair Lady*, up the bizarre Victorian gadget factor by around 30 per cent and you'll have some idea of the restored Galpin residence. Beside his bed was what appeared to be a mahogany shoe box but my guide Walter Pamca deftly opened a latch in the middle to reveal a porcelain commode. The man of the house's faded burgundy smoking jacket and fez were arranged on a Chippendale by the window while the polished floorboards were strewn with lion, zebra and, oddly enough, tiger pelts. Heavy velvet curtains decorated with lace framed the windows; photographs (at least one of Queen Victoria in every room) crowded the walls; and the library was dominated by a celestial globe, a terrestrial globe and an exotic insect collection in a mahogany cabinet. On the wall swings the five-metre, 136-kilogram pendulum from the rooftop clock.

On the second floor is a meridian room, on whose walls are traced the arc of the sun. It was here that Galpin and his son Walter – one of seven boys who all wore dresses until they were eight – determined the orb's position at noon to maintain the accuracy of the rooftop clock. After all, what kind of watchmaker couldn't keep accurate time?

The inner workings of the rooftop clock occupy the Science Room next door and are a scaled-down replica of those at the Royal Courts of Justice in London. They are hand-wound four times a week.

Up a tight spiral of thirty-six steps is the house's pièce de résistance. A camera obscura is an ingenious contraption which uses an angled mirror and convex lens to project images of the exterior surroundings onto a central table in the darkened chamber. It can be tilted and rotated through 180 and 360 degrees respectively so that the activities on pretty much every street in Grahamstown's CBD could be observed in private by Galpin.

As intriguing a novelty as the camera obscura was and continues to be – there are only five in the world and this one is it for the southern hemisphere – Galpin's finest moment was to be in the ground-floor drawing room in 1867. It was a mild autumn day when Dr William Atherstone, who rented a small surgery space in the Galpins' house, lobbed in and excitedly asked for a moment in private.

Atherstone, who was also instrumental in establishing the world's first mental hospital nearby in 1875, had been dabbling in geology for two decades and, much like the current students of Grahamstown, was always searching out his next stone. From his pocket, he retrieved a pebble and letter which he presented to Galpin. The missive was from the acting civil commissioner in the town of Colesberg who reported that the stone had been found on a local farm and asked if it was perhaps of some value. Galpin tested it for hardness and concluded that 21.25 carats of pure diamond had been sent through the mail. A specific gravity test was then performed at the home of the local Catholic bishop, the Right Reverend James David Richards. It confirmed Galpin's assessment, whereupon the bishop grabbed the diamond, strode over to a nearby window and scratched his initials into the glass. The inscribed pane forms the centrepiece of the exhibition on the ground floor of the Observatory Museum, while the gem which carved it proved to be the first of thousands which altered the course of the nation's history.

The myriad charms of Grahamstown were only heightened by the air of malevolence and decrepitude that blew hot and fetid through my next destination.

Port Elizabeth is known in South Africa as The Windy City, a title I long thought of as not quite doing justice to the laid-back beach town I had been to on holiday as a child. Until I got there as an adult and discovered that the constant breeze was in fact that city's only refreshing attribute. I entered PE through a malodorous stew of silos, factories and saltworks that had turned the sandy lagoons on the city's outskirts to a purple-green never seen in nature.

The air smelled of chemicals and the industrial tangle of streets was flanked by decaying sidewalks from which chunks of concrete were missing. These were presided over by faded Vaseline billboards with smiling black families below which the words "your skin, your pride" appeared. On the side of the road were lines of rusting taxis in which gun-toting drivers slouched asleep in the passenger seat awaiting the peak-hour rush.

The once quaint buildings were stained by the fumes of the thousands of vehicles which crawled by on the way to somewhere more picturesque. Sun-blistered paint, garbage and bitter eyes seemed to be the prevailing motif in this part of town. Cresting a ridge, however, it seemed I had turned into transmogrificationville. Avenues of skinny, triple-storey terrace houses in fuchsia, mustard and burgundy streamed away in both directions. Set against the broad sweep of steel-blue harbour and interspersed with the odd sandstone steeple, it could have been a San Franciscan hideaway.

As I was to discover, PE is somewhat of a schizophrenic city with pockets of startling beauty in a coat of crime, grime and slime.

On the advice of the students I'd met in Grahamstown, I booked a room at the gracious Edward Hotel, which happened to be celebrating its centenary. It was three storeys of pale yellow Edwardian elegance located at the top of a hill which commanded a fine view of the harbour and had a park the size of a city block on its doorstep.

The place had recently been taken over by a national chain. This fact was made apparent through various pieces of marketing that could only have come about as the result of the semi-intoxicated ramblings of a focus group. The first of these was the slogan on the hotel's brochure. Bearing in mind that it was a hundred years old, magnificently stuccoed and dominated by a glass-domed atrium below which cane ceiling fans revolved graciously over flagstone floors, you'd think that they could come up with something more tempting than "probably the best value in the country". All over the land you could hear potential customers crying, "Fuck Bora-Bora, we're going to the Edward where there's a good chance the rates are reasonable".

My exasperation may seem a little hysterical but in an era of contrived old-world elegance this was a rare real deal. The plan had been to dump my bags and begin exploring the city, but on the pretext of organising my notes, I spent three blissful hours in the palm court while waiters in red velvet waistcoats ferried a succession of tea, crumpets and Singapore slings down a mahogany staircase and into my gluttonous maw.

I dillydallied the afternoon away exploring the place. The bar was panelled in dark wood, plushly carpeted and decorated with a dozen aging pendulum clocks which didn't so much tick as groan like a group of old men simultaneously vacating their chairs. The Edward was of such elegant decrepitude that it had to have at least one resident ghost. The manager duly informed me that the previous owner and his wife who were murdered on the premises in 1972 by a sommelier – "Who's breathing now, punk?"– have made their presence felt from time to time in the form of footsteps in empty corridors and objects that leap from tables seemingly of their own accord.

I had tarried in the Edward too long and the tourist office was closed. In fading light I wheezed up and almost tumbled down the hilly streets of the central district. Despite its sprinkling of parks, shabby Georgian cottages and church after quaint church, I couldn't shake the feeling that the region was trying to put on a brave face amid increasingly frequent crime. Even the smattering of second-hand book stores had the kind of security systems you only see at jewellers in other countries.

As I trawled the shelves at one for a local history, the proprietor bemoaned the decline of the area and warned me not to leave any of the nearby bars with an attractive woman who might approach me. Many a tourist had apparently fallen for the sting in which he gets back to her place and is confronted by a gun-wielding accomplice who then accompanies him to an ATM, forces him to withdraw the maximum amount, then holds him hostage for as long as it takes to empty the account.

Once the city's bohemian heartbeat, this area was now more "ho" than "bo". A succession of prostitutes began to filter out of the down-at-heel apartment blocks that bordered the district. Some smiled suggestively as I approached, pimps watching on from parked cars. Others looked at me with dead eyes and asked if I "wanted to party". One offered me oral sex in exchange for a hamburger.

I got back to the hotel to find a noticeboard welcoming participants to a "Prevention of Crime Against Tourists" conference. The pall that PE had cast over me darkened further when the top story on the news that night revolved around a father of three who had been murdered in front of his wife and children while driving past a nearby beach. He was not the target. Nor was his wife. Or even their car. The attackers wanted his mobile phone and when the man tried to get in between them and his children, they shot him four times from point-blank range. Despite the standard warning given by the newsreader, I was dismayed and sickened by the sight of a man ten years my junior slumped through a car window with his blood spattered along the driver's side door.

Seeking an experience which would remind me of the idiosyncratic vibrancy of this nation where I first drew breath, I asked the concierge to recommend one of the six African jazz bars I could see from my hotel window.

"Listen to me nicely please, sir," he said, his voice dropping low and earnest. "Please don't go to any of them. Terrible things have happened to some of our guests there."

I needed no further convincing and took up his recommendation of the Boardwalk, which was essentially a casino and shopping mall arranged on two levels around an over-sized pond. "It's the safest place in town," he said.

The journey required me to vacate the high ground occupied by the Edward and navigate the jumble of overpasses and freeways that blight the city's foreshore like looping concrete scars. Worse still, the marvellous Victorian facade of PE's original docklands and beach strips had been destroyed in the 1960s to make way for these monuments to woeful city planning.

As I was nearing the Boardwalk, screaming sirens and a unnerving orange glow filled the night air. Nearby, a hotel made of logs had gone up in flames. The night smelt acrid, fire trucks sped by in rapid succession and cinders blew across the road. With the image of the murder victim still fresh in my head, the smoke, the inferno and the wailing emergency vehicles added to the impression I had wandered into an urban version of purgatory.

Things began a little more promisingly the next morning, as I tottered down impossibly steep streets – enlivened by intermittent sprays of bougainvillea from behind high walls – towards the city. The hub of the CBD is Market Square, a hectare of paved promenade surrounded by a series of impressive public buildings.

However, it was like putting a fine gilt frame around a pornographic centre-spread. The square smelled of diesel and looked like a demolition derby. It was scattered with overflowing garbage trucks, and loonies screaming Bible verse paraded about the place chastising the vagrants who collected in a brandy-scented pile at the base of the Queen Victoria statue in front of the public library.

Aware that I might be misjudging PE, I decided to head to the city's surf strip. If Durban's beach front was an ageing beauty trying to pass off her mutton as prime lamb, Port Elizabeth was the bloated aftermath of a B-list gigolo beset by erectile dysfunction.

It was a motley jumble of patently neglected attractions such as snake parks and aquariums I couldn't face the prospect of visiting through fear of seeing the animals forced to live out their days there. A wicked wind whipped sand from the beach against my cheeks as I was buffeted along the promenade. The swimming baths where I had stood up on a concrete water slide, slipped over and suffered my first concussion still stood near a pier which must have once had a tinge of Mills & Boon melancholy about it but now appeared clinically depressed. Still, hundreds of happy holidaymakers with suntans and beach towels slung over their shoulders dawdled towards the surf.

Port Elizabeth's coast reminded me of no-frills ice cream – it wasn't unpleasant as such, there was just next to zero chance of me going back for a second helping.

Chapter 12

Pardon Me Boy, is That the Outeniqua Choo Tjoe?

An hour west of Port Elizabeth I turned off the highway towards the home of the perfect wave. Local and international waxheads make pilgrimages to Jeffreys Bay for the freakishly reliable sets of glassy breakers that build offshore then roll towards the cream sand beach offering rides of unparalleled smoothness and duration.

A smattering of guesthouses, weatherboard cottages and boutique hotels pepper a low bushy hillock overlooking a placid lagoon. On the other side of the rise, the beach runs away into the distance where the boundaries between sand, sky and ocean blur. JBay, as it is otherwise known, is everything a surfy village should be. Laid-back, unpretentious and with the commercial enterprises, whose lifeblood is the Super Tubes break, set back a block from the beach.

Surfboards airbrushed with tropical sunsets and buxom bikini babes are displayed in shop windows alongside shots of locals doing time in the green room. Every second store seems to be draped in Billabong and Rip Curl promotional material.

In addition to the ubiquitous surf stores, I noticed the usual procession of agreeably hippyish retail outlets opened by those who flee the city for a sea change. Hand-made pottery in an Aegean colour scheme was precariously stacked in one store while the healing centre next door featured an entire wall given over to an incense display of hundreds of varieties including the intriguingly named Black Love. The proprietors of both were no doubt those soft-spoken types who smell faintly of ylang-ylang, drop the term "ki" at least once every ten minutes and refer to "their former life" as a stockbroker, arms dealer or lawyer, which financed this one.

Also prominent were a handful of bars with broad decks overlooking the sea. Their doors were plastered with flyers offering discount drinks to anyone who showed up in a bikini. Unadorned and honest, they were the kind of place where a request for a Cosmopolitan would not see you loudly ridiculed but politely directed down the road to a newsagent.

It was around seven-thirty in the morning when I rolled into town and Jbay was still rubbing the sleep from its eyes. The only shop that was open was a bakery. With a steaming coffee in one hand and a buttery croissant in the other, I meandered down to the beach for breakfast.

Here I was greeted by salt-tanged air, a crushed-glass sea and the splendid isolation that comes with being up early in a town where the majority of inhabitants go hard every night. I could have been in Byron Bay, Curl Curl or Lennox Head, and for the first time since leaving Australia I felt a pang of homesickness.

Eventually lone surfers and trios in faded boardies drifted onto the sand, took a moment to assess the break, splashed some water on their faces as if anointing themselves and paddled out. Most had dropped their belongings on the beach in piles, barely bothering to conceal the car keys, wallets and mobile phones that protruded from beneath sun-bleached towels. Port Elizabeth, where people were routinely butchered for any one of these items, felt like another planet.

After an hour, most of the surfers emerged as the tide began to recede. Those for whom this daily communion was a private affair were mainly men and women in their thirties, although a couple of decades of sun damage made accurately gauging their ages something of a challenge. Those in trios or foursomes were primarily men of the extensively pierced and tattooed variety for whom this activity offered a competitive outlet. The bigger groups were grommets and grommettes who wriggled out of their rashies and threw their school uniforms over still-wet bathers before tucking boards under their arms to dash off in the direction of a distant bell. With the waves cleared of surfers, a five-strong pod of bottle-nosed dolphins decided to ride the swell. With the waves backlit, they formed a crisply silhouetted quintet surfing in perfect parallel.

By the time I got back to the main street, shops were open and populated by perpetually peeling locals whose skin bore the strap marks that come with swimming every day in the same bathing suit. I could only imagine the daily torment that life held for the lone Goth – there's always one – at Jeffreys Bay High.

I found a coffee shop where a freckled backpacker in a backless dress didn't respond to my request for a short black as if I'd just scraped the bottom of the politically incorrect barrel but presented me with a dark and pungent brew.

One of the questions I am most often asked when people

find out I am a migrant is whether I would ever return to South Africa. JBay invalidated my well-rehearsed answer – "Yes, but not to live". It was the quintessence of coastal idyll. Reluctant to leave, I revived the sulky walk that characterised much of my childhood on my way to the car.

The nearby resort towns of Saint Francis and Cape Saint Francis almost eclipsed JBay for beauty with three kilometres of sparkling beachfront and thatched whitewashed holiday homes perched along dozens of canals dredged from a lagoon on the Kromme River. The marina was occupied by a fleet of yachts that would require the GDP of a Third World nation in annual upkeep, and the local tourist brochures displayed an inordinate fondness for the words "exclusive", "discerning" and "US currency accepted". As undeniably picturesque as it was, Cape Saint Francis struck me as the type of ritzy locale into which bloated magnates would roll with their mistresses du jour. Ask a barman for a Cosmopolitan here and he'd most likely sneer that the drink was "soooo twentieth century".

I tracked west to the Garden Route, a heavily touristed coastal plain whose stunning pulchritude has been only marginally dimmed by decades of ill-conceived development. The coastal scrub which cocooned Jeffreys Bay gave way to dark cool forests. I had reached the Tsitsikama, a beguiling world unto itself bordered by inhospitable blue peaks from whose feet ancient rainforests run to a craggy shale coastline battered by the tempestuous Indian Ocean. The ancient Khoisan people called the area Sietsikama (The Place of Clear Water). It was a particularly apt name as the rainforest traverses seven rivers. On their steep course to the sea, these have produced idiosyncratic erosion patterns resulting in dozens of skinny waterfalls that crash into icy pools and plummeting ravines whose rock faces interlock like teeth on a zip. The Tsitsikama is also home to rivers rendered mahogany by tannins in the surrounding foliage.

Keen to get among it, I pulled into the first signposted car park and within minutes was surrounded by ferns the size of traffic lights. The Tsitsikama works its alchemy on two scales: massive and minute.

Reaching heights in excess of fifty metres and frequently measuring a metre in circumference, the outeniqua yellowwood trees are just one of numerous gargantuan species that ascend from the forest floor. These lofty characters are matched in height by the scores of stinkwood (named after the odour the cut wood emits), kalander and assegai trees that form the upper reaches of the forest.

Frequently dripping with old man's beard lichens, their scale only becomes apparent up close. After reaching the end of an elevated walkway trail to the imaginatively named Big Tree, I was confronted by an object taller than a five-storey office block. Its girth equated to eight humans huddled in a group.

On a macro level, the Tsitsikama is even more mesmeric. Agog at the dimensions of my surroundings, I took a seat on a bench thoughtfully fashioned from a collapsed stinkwood trunk and swiftly became entranced in the details I had missed. The floor was a blanket of undulating seven week's fern randomly illuminated by the droplets of sunlight that pierced the canopy. Booties of lime-green moss clung to the roots of thousand-year-old trees beneath tangles of witchhazel, milkwood and forest elder. Wild pomegranates and tiny buttery-yellow flowers sprung from overhanging boughs, and traces of native gardenia scented the breeze.

A flicker of movement shattered my meditative calm.

Aside from bush buck, bush pigs, porcupine, honey badgers and caracals, leopards still pad their way through the soft undergrowth and would have no trouble sneaking up on a daydreaming tourist. Instead, two metres in front of me was the strangest, most beautiful bird I had ever seen. Of the 220 species found in the Tsitsikama, 35 are endemic and this was one of them. The Knysna Lourie is an opalescent olive green and has a head shaped like a mohawk haircut, the tip of which looks as if it has been dipped in coconut cream.

Human voices soon began to rip through the forest as tourists toting video cameras and children made their way along the boardwalk. Grateful for my ninety minutes of isolation in the forest, I returned to the car. Turning back for a last glimpse, the forests appeared big enough to accommodate the groups now piling out of coaches in the car park. They seemed to be subsumed by the green depths and eventually became shadows trekking along the trail.

Having been unencumbered by the presence of large groups of tourists throughout my journey, it was a rude shock to see the service station beside the graceful arch of the Storms River Bridge clogged with buses, tantrum-chucking toddlers and spouses wearing that unmistakable "I told you we should have gone to Club Med" glare. I couldn't have agreed with them more.

By the time I reached the Tsitsikama National Coastal Park down the road, I begrudgingly acknowledged that as many people as possible should get to experience such natural majesty. The gateway to its eighty-kilometre canvas of seascapes is the park's visitor centre. A modest collection of log cabins set against sloped foothills. It was populated by bronzed holiday-makers still damp from a dip, retirees on deckchairs dozing by the water's edge and groups of excited hikers setting off on one of the dozens of trails that radiate into the bush.

I naturally opted for the least taxing on offer: a concrete pathway that hugged the shore until reaching a suspension bridge over the mouth of the Storms River. Were I condemned man, I would have foregone my last meal for the opportunity to complete this walk.

The path descended to a beach where a lone swimmer was floating on her back in water whose crystalline purity is more often associated with a full-time pool boy and enormous amounts of chlorine. Perhaps twenty metres from her bobbed a Cape clawless otter, equally at home in salt and fresh water.

As the path climbed into the forest again, the embankments to the left of it became a collage of boulders and ferns sparked with filigree flowers of hot-coals red, purple and apricot. Each turn brought with it a postcard of steel-blue sea and salt-misted crags framed by an artfully placed bough. All set to a soundtrack provided by breakers on rock.

Being a rather gangly type, I tend to clip along at a moderate pace and thought nothing of overtaking a middle-aged posse of European tourists. However, by the time I reached the suspension bridge spanning the river mouth, I had only managed to zip by a third of the group.

Halfway across, on some unspoken signal, they simultaneously burst into an oompa song they had all apparently been taught as children. Call me old-fashioned, but crowds of chanting Teutons can still make your average Semite a little edgy. However, with overtaking on a suspension bridge about as realistic a notion as making acid wash elegant, I had no choice but to smile and just keep on walking. Two verses and three choruses later we reached solid ground. All the while I, too, was singing quietly. "Germans to the left of me, Germans to the right. Here I am, stuck in the middle a Jew."

My overnight destination of Plettenberg Bay was an hour away on one of those cliff-hugging roads out of a film where a glamorous couple in a roadster collapse into cap-toothed giggles as the buxom blonde passenger's Hermes headscarf blows off her peroxided head and into the blue depths. Christened Bahia Formosa (Beautiful Bay) by Portuguese explorers, it is a slab of ocean-lapped temptation sheltered by the natural breakwater of the Robberg, Outeniqua and Tsitsikama mountain ranges. Overlooked by the lush Peak Formosa it's the undisputed playground of South Africa's rich and famous.

Once a well-kept secret, Plett, as it is known, became an alternative destination for Johannesburgers who found Cape Town too crowded and Capetonians who felt the same way. The attraction is understandable. Here, a pair of spurs, bisected by a lagoon, overlook two camel crescents of beach lapped at by an aquamarine surf. Between the beaches lies a rocky outcrop upon which sits the world's most hideous hotel.

My family had holidayed at the Beacon Island when I was eleven and it was still much as I experienced it. Incongruous, ludicrously expensive and devoid of warmth. The speckle of houses I remembered on the ridges were now suburbs.

Even two decades ago, Plett had a Millionaires' Row. Today it's more like Billionairesville. From behind hibiscuses on the hillside, homes bear testament to almost three decades of the architectural whimsy that only the obscenely wealthy can indulge in. Casa de Bad Taste butted up against faux Tuscan, while white-cube minimalism only accentuated the ugliness of the myriad glass and chrome octagons perched here and there like futuristic garbage bins.

On the other side of the hill, however, the locals lived in pastel weatherboard cottages, neat bungalows with blossoming unfenced gardens and surfboards on the lawn. Dads just home from work walked hand in hand with excited kids towards the beach; a woman tossed a Frisbee to a Labrador-cross on a sandy oval, and in the molten light of a late afternoon, I became swiftly, irretrievably and unstintingly enamoured of the place.

I checked into a hotel on the main street which offered "disabled facilities in public areas" and sure enough they were. My infatuation remained undented as I found myself peering into the window of a real-estate agent. It was at this point that depression set in. For the mortgage I was paying on an innercity semi in Sydney, I could pick up an ocean-view double-storey home in Plett and have enough dosh left over to get the hell out of town every December when the tourists arrive.

The downer was, however, fleeting. As it would be when you find a open-decked restaurant set high against a knoll where the waiter's opening line is, "Welcome to happy hour". A seafood and daiquiri frenzy for one ensued as I watched the sun melt into the horizon in pinks softer than a butterfly kiss.

I had planned to laze on the beach for most of the next day before heading to the same restaurant for a second round of indulgence, but I awoke to murky skies that didn't so much threaten rain but imply it. It was the kind of day that screamed theme park, so I made a beeline for Monkey Land. These types of establishments are notoriously soft targets and I was – rather shamefully in hindsight – taking no small measure of glee from the prospect of dispensing copious amounts of withering scorn on the place. I imagined the Primate Palace where one could buy sugary concoctions identified by torturous puns such as Orangeutang and Limeur, while for the grown-ups there would be a creamy cocktail named International Vervet. Instead, I found the world's only free-range sanctuary for primates rescued from caged existences as pets, circus animals and laboratory experiment subjects.

Monkey Land is set over twelve hectares of indigenous forest that has been fenced only at the borders and nestles under a net canopy strung high above the trees. It is home to 15 species and over 200 individuals.

I joined a tour group led by a Steve Irwin type dressed in khaki and radiating infectious enthusiasm. The first creatures we encountered were a pair of Madagascan lemurs. Black and white in the panda fashion, they were exquisitely long-limbed and wore a perpetual expression of faint concern. They are the only animals in the world with two tongues, which of course makes it rather difficult to understand what they are saying.

A rustle in the canopy above us saw a pair of gibbons descending like dive-bombers to a raised platform the size of a breakfast tray which was piled with fruit. Although the park is a contrived ecosystem, the rangers do what they can to minimise human contact. Hand-feeding is verboten and the speedy orange tamarinds who loitered around the cafe to scavenge biscuits from unwary visitors were frequently sent shrieking into the bush as a staff member with a spray gun aimed a jet of water in their direction.

Gibbons are the undisputed aerial masters of the primate world. Not only can they swing between trees at around thirty kilometres an hour, they can also clear gaps of thirty metres with ease. And unlike humans, they have one lifelong partnership.

As we followed a trail through the forest and across the longest single-span rope bridge in the southern hemisphere, I got the distinct feeling that we were being cased by hidden eyes. A piercing shriek from the rear of our group followed as a woman's sunglasses were snatched off the top of her head by a capuchin monkey apparently overcome by the need to accessorise. They are so named because the cowl-shaped colouring around their heads resembles the hoods worn by the Capuchin friars.

According to our guide, these sneaky bastards are the Mensa members of the animal kingdom. Adopting the tone of one of those insufferable parents who feel compelled to tell you of their child's every academic, sporting or questionably adorable achievement, he rolled out a list of attributes that I'm embarrassed to say I did not believe until I confirmed them through various websites.

For a start, the capuchins are those little buggers frequently seen beside organ-grinders. Why? Because they can be trained to dance, clap and solicit donations quicker than practically any other species on the planet. With the exception, perhaps, of backpackers.

Capuchins apparently make a fine fist of assisting the disabled and can be trained to turn on lights and memorise up to ten phone numbers. They can also be taught to administer injections and have mastered the art of basic communication with humans through a card system. On one occasion when a paraplegic visitor came to Monkey Land, a capuchin handed him a card that read, "Don't worry, Superman, your secret's safe with me". Actually, he gave him a red piece of cardboard signifying a recognition of illness.

In the wild, capuchins are equally canny. For example, they rub the bark of the hard pear tree on their skin as it contains cyanide – a mosquito repellent. They also have a thing for scorpion sashimi and instead of being stung in the pursuit of lunch use weapons such as sticks or stones to break their bones.

I enjoyed my Monkey Land experience more than I thought I would and made a point of dropping a note into the suggestion box urging them to rethink the name – I believe the words "it intimates a third-rate carnival" were used.

Turned out, however, Monkey Land was merely a bracing appetiser to the day's main course. Heading west towards the town of Knysna, I drove through forests once home to multitudes of elephants. As incongruous as the combination of rainforest and pachyderm may seem, by retreating deep into the thick clusters of yellow-woods and stinkwoods the area's elephants prolonged their survival far more effectively than their plains-dwelling counterparts.

Even up until the 1980s rumours persisted that a few ageing cows still wandered the fern-covered floor. But as their habitats diminished along with the prospect of procreation, these proud stragglers died lonely deaths. In the lobby of the Knysna Elephant Park is a grainy photograph of the last wild elephant in the local forest. She looks proud yet mournful. Today a quartet saved from a cull in a northern game park have been introduced into the habitat and the rainforest once again shakes to the occasional rumble of a behemoth hitting its stride.

As commendable as such initiatives are, it's like treating

cancer with a band aid. The manner in which South Africa has treated these animals is a disgrace and the elephant park's museum made for a sickening enlightenment. In 1913, when authorities may have been excused on the grounds of naivety for seeing elephants as an inextinguishable resource in South Africa, the United States imported 200 tonnes of ivory just for piano keys. That's 5000 dead elephants. According to a display at the museum, the slaughter continued unabated until at least 1998. In July of that year, American conservationist Craig Van Note wrote of South Africa that " as a CITES [an organisation that binds nations to wildlife conservation by treaty] member which projects the image of a conservation-minded model for Africa, it is in reality one of the biggest wildlife outlaws in the world".

His vitriol comes from evidence suggesting the nation's military encouraged Jonas Savimbi, the leader of Angola's rebel UNITA army, to fund his civil war effort by slaughtering 100,000 elephants. The ivory was then allegedly carried back into South Africa on the military planes and trucks which had transported weapons into Angola. Vast stockpiles of Angolan ivory are still rumoured to be held in South African military storage depots.

Van Note's assertion is supported by an eyewitness account from a South African colonel who recounted, "Elephants were mown down by the tearing rattle of AK47 rifles and machine guns. They shot everything: bulls, cows and calves."

The park's star attractions are four teenage orphans who roam the hundred hectares of open space that features grasslands and a forested section. They sleep under cover in individual pens and visitors can choose to interact with them in one of two ways. You can either spend half an hour or so feeding them vegetables before the next group of half-a-dozen arrives to take their turn. Or, as I did, go on an elephant safari, which entails a walk with them through the forests at sunrise or sunset.

The slogan emblazoned across the park's pamphlet is "Be Touched By An Elephant" and I had a phalanx of single entendres to trot out when it came to describing my visit. The unexpected truth of the matter is that the pitch encapsulated the essence of my experience.

Granted, these were mere three-metre juveniles who only tipped the scales at a couple of tonnes, but up close they radiated a humbling gentleness. Their skin felt like old luggage and was covered in coarse hair; the tips of their trunks worked like opposable digits to almost tenderly grasp food from my palm, and their benign eyes were framed by lashes as long as my hand. They evoked a sense of awe-filled wonder I hadn't felt since childhood and didn't believe I was still capable of.

So as not to defile the experience with any further hyperbole, I'll turn to the words of Henry Beston who in 1928's *The Outermost House* described elephants thus: "They move finished and complete, gifted with extension of the senses we have lost or never attained, living by voices we shall never hear".

Twenty-two kilometres west is the town of Knysna where I had planned to stay for a single night but was seduced into remaining for two. It was payday and jovial lines trailed from ATMs while nearby groups of kids busked, using plastic washing tubs as drums. Between the de rigueur curio shops selling zebra-print everything were galleries displaying abstract seascapes by local artists, oak-panelled bookstores and a fine public library made from hand-carved sandstone.

Pubs and cafes spilled onto the pavement with cane tables shaded by umbrellas and, in one ingenious case, deckchairs with milk crates as tables.

Also in evidence were the day-to-day shops that facilitate small-town life: a discount mattress outlet, a video store, a post office and so on. It was this final element that gave the place not so much a resort feel but one of real life, albeit a charmed one.

By 6pm the pubs were filled with locals enjoying the first of many, weekenders from Cape Town and backpackers living high on the Euro's back. Pushbikes, which seemed to be the transport of choice for many residents, were littered outside. Lured by the golden light pouring out of its windows and the sounds of a precociously talented acid jazz ensemble, I squeezed into a crowded bar which emptied into a courtyard where clusters of bobbing groovers warmed their hands on fires in tin drums.

Although the crowd had its fair share of hemp accoutrements in the textile and toke varieties, it was distinctly designer hippie. In South Africa these often well-to-do new-age types are marvellously known as Trustafarians. Yet along with their distressed cargos and ironic soft-drink T-shirts, they also wore welcoming smiles. Many were curious about Australia in terms of lifestyle, culture and how the general public felt about the Howard government's refusal to formally apologise to the stolen generation. Some levelled allegations of racism at my homeland whose attitude to Aborigines they said was on a par with apartheid, and my inclination to agree saw the conversations meander from sport to politics to recommendations for the rest of my journey.

Politely declining an invitation to the next bar, I struck

out in search of food and ended up in a dimly lit cafe strewn with tea lights where a chanteuse was running through a Joni Mitchell/Tracy Chapman repertoire. Knysna is home to a large gay population who absconded from the larger South African cities in search of a quiet life and now run many of the town's most attractive establishments, outside which the pride flag snaps, crackles and pops.

This one was presided over a by a square-jawed maitre d' of indeterminate vintage named Jacques, whose aplomb at working the room was interrupted only by the odd visit to the microphone to out-Ronan Ronan Keating. My waitron – as they are known in this gender-phobic nation – was from Cairns and when she alerted Jacques to the fact that another Australian was in the house, he promptly told her to take the next half-hour off and sent a bottle of wine over to the table. Charmaine had come to Knysna for a two-week stay. Three years on, she wasn't going anywhere. "I adore this area," she said. "It draws writers, potters, artists and loonies. The region is home to hundreds of forest fairies – people who disappear into the bush and don't come out for years. Plus, the South African equivalent to [Sydney's Gay and Lesbian] Mardi Gras is held here. It's called the Pink Lourie."

"What do the local make of it?" I asked.

"We are the locals," she replied. "Unless you mean the Poppies." This, I was told, was a term used to describe a certain type of Afrikaans woman in her twenties or thirties who lived in the area. Her defining features were, according to Charmaine: "Auburn hair that should have her colourist banned from going near a human head again, red lipstick worn with orange lipliner, eighteen-carat-gold nails and fondness for brandy and soda with a specified number of ice-cubes – fail to provide that exact figure and the drink is sent back to the bar."

Unbeknownst to us, Jacques had been hovering and swooped in on Charmaine's shtick with, "My dear, you cannot believe the hair colour. There's just no way those drapes match the rug."

After many Dom Pedros – a local concoction made from vanilla ice cream, whiskey, Drambuie or both — I made it back to the hotel somewhere in the am and set my alarm for what felt like the ungodly hour of seven as I had a train to catch.

Belching smoke at the station by the lagoon around which Knysna sits was the Outeniqua Choo Tjoe. Its name is derived from two sources. The Outeniqua element – Khoisan for "they who bear honey" – relates to the mountain range which forms the backdrop to the sixty-seven-kilometre journey to the town of George. The Choo Tjoe refers to the sound made by the hulking black 1924 steam locomotive which hauls a dozen suburban side-door carriages along what must surely be one of the most spectacular stretches of track in the world.

Groaning and creaking out of the station, the Choe Tjoe trudged along the perimeter of the olive wind-whipped lagoon at the centre of which floated dozens of oyster beds. As it picked up speed and the carriage became scented by coal smoke and brine, the track leaned hard into a conifered embankment that ran at an angle of seventy degrees to an achingly gorgeous settlement of white wooden houses topped by green tin roofs.

Surrounded by the pale fragrant shrubbery known as fynbos and sporadic fern outbursts, the track crested the incline and dropped into a basil-coloured mosaic of paddocks separated by ageing timber pole fences, wooded hillocks and slow shallow streams. It then crossed a succession of rippled saltwater lakes before running parallel to a beach for a few kilometres. Next, it climbed to cling against cliff faces so close to the ocean that mists of spray drifted through the carriage windows from waves crashing into the boulders below. Through Sedgefield, Wilderness and the riverside camping grounds of Fairy Knowe we chuffed, across arched bridges, tidal beds and fields where chestnut mares grazed. It couldn't have been more romantic had Lauren Bacall stepped silhouetted out of the smoke at George Station wearing nothing more than unconscionable amounts of chinchilla and a welcome-home smile.

Part of the Choo Tjoe deal was a shuttle bus back to Knysna on an uninspiring stretch of highway. Our driver was a retired Afrikaans teacher by the name of Corne. Not what you'd call the talkative type – something one might imagine would be an obstacle for a career in tourism – he responded to my enquiries about the area with a string of "I'm not sure's", "that's a good question's" and "I'd be interested in knowing the answer to that myself". He was, however, certain of one thing. When I asked what he thought about a story in that morning's paper which reported that a local farmer had transported the wreck of the late, disgraced South African cricketer Hansie Cronje's aircraft from the foreboding Outeniqua mountains to a shed on his property where he was charging an ogling fee, Corne shot me a withering look and spat the word "bullshit" in my direction. The elderly Welsh woman in the seat behind me gasped. I had clearly struck a nerve as raw as steak tartare. In many quarters the charismatic and devout Springbok is still viewed as a man who had the rare courage to admit to his mistakes and as a result became the whipping boy for the international cricket community. "If Shane Warne and Mark Waugh had been honest about those pitch reports," Corne said, before leaping headlong into a non sequitur that pushed the very definition into slightly intimidating new ground, "Hansie might still be alive today. But that's journalists," he hissed in what he believed was a subtle dig.

It was lunchtime when we arrived back in Knysna, so I headed to a pub by the heads where the lagoon empties into the open sea. The gap between the two rocky outcrops is no more than eighty metres with a frothing fury between them. Compressed into this narrow avenue, the tide surges and recedes into the estuary with such unpredictable fury that it was only thirteen years after the area was settled that the first ship attempted to navigate the passage. Cruise boats now ferry bilious tourists back and forth but I was thoroughly content to watch the spectacle from a table by the water's edge with two dozen local oysters and a chilled bottle of beer sweating droplets in the afternoon sun.

It was where I spent most of the afternoon in a state of mildly intoxicated bliss which manifested itself in a pounding headache by the evening. As much as the idea of another night of high camp with Charmaine and Jacques appealed to me, I had an early start the next morning and four hundred kilometres to cover before reaching a city where unfathomable beauty and brutality are separated by a mountain shaped like a table.

Chapter 13

Oceans Apart

Before reaching Cape Town – where I was due to meet Jennie and suggest we spend the rest of our lives together – I detoured off the main highway for lunch in Swellendam, which bills itself as the third oldest city in the country. One out of two ain't bad but it's no city. Instead, it is a town of utter loveliness amid plush fields watched over by the mauve Langerberg mountains. It was a Sunday morning and the main street was lined with the cars of the faithful who were singing up a reverential storm in the local Dutch Reformed Church. Dating from 1911, it's a snow-white cocktail of neo-Gothic, Neo-Renaissance and Neo-Baroque that is near perfect. Not least for the fact that it harmoniously incorporates elements of the Cape Dutch style of architecture.

Regarded as a national treasure, it is essentially the evolution of a seventeenth-century Dutch template which was adapted to meet the demands of a new geography. Whitewashed, thatched, single-storeyed and taking either the shape of an inverted "T" or recumbent "H", the most obvious and striking features of these buildings are their fluid gables set above a symmetrical facade punctuated by shuttered picture windows.

Between 1690 and 1850 these gables took a wide array of forms influenced by everything from the home-owner's pretensions to the neoclassical revival sweeping Europe. And so they appear, liberally sprinkled around Cape Town, the mountainous vineyard districts on the city's fringes and outlying districts such as Swellendam.

Guesthouses, upmarket gift stores and tearooms in this style stand shoulder to shoulder on the main street of Swellendam like pale soldiers on parade, and in the cool morning air the place looked freshly scrubbed in preparation for the weekend rush of day-trippers from Cape Town. Stiflingly picturesque, it is one of those towns in which you grew up feeling only one of two ways: either you can't bear to leave or you can hardly wait to get out.

Those who opted for the latter most often turned right at the highway and crested the precipitous Sir Lowry's Pass to Cape Town, where some lived like tanned royalty but most died before their time.

The sandy Cape Flats are a sea of corrugated-iron shacks, dilapidated concrete council flats and burnt-out cars that either function as single-occupant brothels or family dwellings. These badlands stretch relentlessly in every direction off the main road which heads into Cape Town from the east.

If you happen to be of the reincarnation persuasion, being born into a life on the Cape Flats would imply a serious fuck-up last time around. On the bright side, though, you won't have to hang around long. A 2003 report into living standards in Khayelitsha, one of Cape Town's biggest townships, found that 70 per cent of households had insufficient food the previous year, three-quarters of residents live below the poverty line and in over a third of all homes the main breadwinner had lost their job in 2002.

As they do around the world, poverty and squalor go hand in hand as refugees – one-third of South Africa's population are estimated to be illegal aliens – crowd into areas such as the Cape Flats, straining already meagre sanitation infrastructure. If it exists at all. As a result, the now-curable diseases that decimated the slums of Jack the Ripper's London run rampant. As do the rats.

As lung cancer victim Agmat Fischer, forty-one, lay dying in his corrugated-iron room on Sugarloaf Street in the Manenberg township, rodents reported to be the size of full-grown cats nibbled at his toes and feet. Too weak to shout for help, he was discovered by a relative who rushed him to hospital. He died the next day. A paraplegic named Billy Fisher who also lived in Sugarloaf Street was attacked by rats which gnawed their way into his room and didn't stop until his shins were gone. He, too, died the day after the assault.

Rats, polio and TB aside, the most prolific killer in these shanty cities is AIDS. For the poor, sex is probably the only form of free entertainment available, a few glorious minutes of escapism, and more than a third of South African nineteen-year-olds have fallen pregnant at least once.

That's just the consensual figures. The Minister of Safety and Security – who apparently admits to this title – reported that 181 crimes against children are logged daily in South Africa. Rape tops the list. That's 66,065 a year, for which the average conviction rate is less than 10 per cent. (So under-resourced are the child protection units that, for example, in the Northern Cape town of Springbok, there are no facilities for cases to be heard so the process has to take place in Cape Town. But wait, not only is there a dearth of facilities, there is also an acute shortage of police vehicles, resulting in the accuser and the accused often having to travel over 400 kilometres in the same vehicle.)

So horrific is the toll taken by AIDS that one million South Africans live in households headed by children under eighteen – with some as young as eight.

If the present rate of infection continues, by 2009 the average black resident in Cape Town will clock off at forty, a drop of fifteen years from the current life expectancy. Coloured people will see a decade shaved off their average lifespan. In the country's prisons AIDS has turned practically any incarceration into a death sentence. Not only are 90 per cent of deaths in custody attributed to the disease, but prison gangs are now using the virus as a weapon of coercion. Known as a "slow puncture" those who refuse to pay protection money are raped by a series of HIV-positive men, with the assault being named after the rate at which death presents itself.

The government's response has ranged from the ludicrous to the inhumane with President Thabo Mbeki stalling on the roll-out of antiretrovirals because he was not convinced of the link between HIV and AIDS.

Citing the not inconsequential challenges faced in trying to promote condom use in traditional tribal cultures and the utterly ridiculous notion that medication alone is not the answer – a claim critics counter with "it's a bloody good start" – the government's approach to AIDS has infuriated South Africans from every social strata. "Once upon a time, not so long ago, we had an apartheid regime in South Africa that killed people," wrote AIDS activist and satirist Pieter-Dirk Uys in his autobiography *Elections and Erections*.

"Now we have a democratic government that just lets them die."

The South African government's AIDS prevention campaign has been only marginally more effective than its response to citizens who have contracted the disease. For example, to combat unsafe sex practices it commissioned … a musical. Which died in the arse after a handful of performances and took R14 million out of the health budget.

In another case, a well-meaning but spectacularly misguided local safe sex organisation decided to distribute 44 million free condoms with instructions on how to use them plus a blurb on the importance of safe sex. Which they *stapled* to the prophylactic packaging.

In his show *For Facts Sake*, Uys recommends that the schoolgirls in his audience carry a condom at all times in case of the deplorably high chance that they will become a rape victim. "At least hopefully you'll be able to say: 'If you're going to rape me, use a condom'. If he says, 'I don't use condoms', then lie. Say: 'I have AIDS, you'd better use a condom'."

Solid advice in a nation where the lack of any coherent and pervasive AIDS education campaign still sees many rural black men believing that they can cure themselves by having sex with a virgin.

A marginally less life-threatening township diversion is drugs. The isolation that came with apartheid practically insulated South Africa from the heroin, cocaine and ecstasy booms; it was only after the fall of the white regime that significant amounts of these drugs began to appear. Until then – and for many still – the drug of choice was mandrax or "buttons" as it is known by users. No other country has an industry based around this combination of methaqualone (the primary ingredient in Quaaludes) and diaphen-hydramine (an antihistamine found in cold medication) or diazepam (otherwise known as Prince Valium).

A potent sedative when popped, it is more frequently smoked like crack, thus enhancing both the high and the chances of addiction. Often vaporised in a bong-like con-traption known as a white pipe and teamed with marijuana that has been dried with paraffin or other solvents, the initial rush is so powerful that many users "earth" immediately after use and drop unconscious to the ground.

The raw chemicals required to produce a kilogram of man-drax can be purchased for around $200 and cooked in a five-litre bucket on any suburban kitchen stove. In addition to the main ingredients, hydrochloric acid purchased from swimming-pool supply stores is thrown into the mix to draw off excess oil. Unlike the wide variety of markings – Calvin Klein logos, white doves of peace and Mitsubishi branding – that appear on ecstasy tablets, buttons are most commonly marked with a swastika. It is no small irony that these sym-bols of white supremacy are sprayed around township schools to indicate the presence of an on-site dealer.

Cheap to produce and highly addictive, mandrax has long been shadowed by a conspiracy theory which suggests the apartheid government flooded townships with it, thereby sabotaging the chances of black unity and mass uprisings. Such speculation would have forever remained in the realms of crop circles and grassy knollsters had it not been for the anguishing Truth and Reconciliation Commission which aired apartheid's dirty laundry in the wake of the transition to majority rule.

One of those interviewed was Dr Wouter Basson, head of Operation Coast, the white government's secret chemical and biological weapons program aimed at combating the pro-democracy movement. Aside from attempting to culti-vate HIV for use in biological warfare and untraceable con-tact poison that was applied to a victim's clothing and mimicked natural causes of death, Operation Coast manu-factured quantities of street drugs that made Pablo Escobar look like a narcotics minnow.

The official line is that the drugs were to be used as a crowd-control mechanism to be spread by tear gas. However, mandrax was incinerated in the vapour-dispersion process, thus rendering it useless. No plausible explanation was offered as to the scale of production – we're talking tonnes – or why it was necessary to press the chemicals into tablet form with a logo designed to mimic that of the original pharmaceutical source.

No one is suggesting that the mandrax issue was solely created and fostered by the government, but there are many who will swear blind they gave it a kick along.

Regardless of who was manufacturing the buttons, they couldn't be profitably disseminated without a distribution network willing to put their own material wealth ahead of the wellbeing of the communities in which they operated. Enter the gang-bangers who rule townships from Johan-nesburg to Port Elizabeth to Cape Town. Facsimiles of American-style gangsterism down to dress codes, slang graffiti, tattoos, hand signs and symbolism, the merciless numbers gangs (which originated in prisons and take their names from their cell blocks) rule the Cape Flats. Each defends its turf with extreme force while monopolising illegal business activities and extracting protection money.

When the inevitable confrontations occur, they are

bloody and ferocious, and stray bullets frequently claim the lives of children. With police outnumbered, under-resourced and so badly paid that the kickbacks from gangs make paying school fees for their children a more viable option, vigilantism is rife.

Yet, somehow, from these miserable slums has arisen a culture that crackles with wry wit, innate musicality and the wisdom to recognise that because life here is so often charac-terised by loss and pain, celebration should be consumed in lusty gulps.

The coloured community's best-known festival is called – I shit you not – The Coon Carnival, a name which has sur-vived the recent tide of political correctness and which the community has steadfastly refused to abandon. Thousands of participants in gaudy, glittering costumes parade through the main streets of Cape Town strumming banjos, shuffling and leaping along to Afrikaans songs as they make their way to a local stadium for a day of festivities. In the South Africa where I grew up, this was the closest we'd get to interacting with the coloured community, though individuals still scrubbed our floors and made our beds.

The Cape Flats eventually morphed into rust-licked facto-ries, junkyards and silos, which in turn gave way to work-ing-class suburbs of neat brick homes where children rode their bikes in the streets. The light had all but been swal-lowed by the evening sky when I reached my hotel in the suburb of Seapoint. It was an area of which I had fond memo-ries. My grandmother lived in a residential hotel called the Kei Apple Grove off the main street, and it seemed practically everyone else's did too. Then this road was lined with tea-rooms, kosher delis and boutiques selling twin sets. The area was so heavily populated by ageing Semites that pretty much every Jewish joke we told began with "These two old ladies/men meet on the main road of Seapoint ..."

At night, however, when the oldies were tucked away with bedsocks on their feet and milk of magnesia in their tummies, Seapoint was the domain of the young, the hip and the dangerously suntanned who'd been sunning themselves at nearby Clifton Beach for weeks.

We waited in line outside discos while groups of girls dressed like Kim Wilde were ushered through hinged metallic doors which swung open to reveal gyrating bodies in a swirl of coloured light and artificial fog. Duran Duran blasted out of bars with pavement tables from which Kouros-drenched boys cruised girls in cut-off gloves who pretended not to notice the attention. Beside these were restaurants with candlelit corner tables that hosted dinners which were the hopeful prelude to third base. Further along the strip were burger joints, video game arcades – Galaga anyone? — and milkshake bars with names like the Purple Cow.

But we weren't in Kansas anymore. The few stores that remained were fronted by iron bars of such profusion that the retail precinct wore a penal institution motif. Seedy neon-trimmed brothels with names like Madonna's and Pleasure Palace stood on practically every corner. In their windows were dated posters of girls with big hair and breasts to match. These were apparently intended to provide an enticing glimpse of the calibre of female company which waited inside, but it seemed unlikely that Elle Macpherson had turned her back on a lingerie empire to make jiggy-jig with Portuguese merchant seamen on shore leave.

I stopped at a set of traffic lights near the hotel and was instantaneously greeted by a mahogany face at the window. Despite the fact that I was driving your bog-standard 1.8

Toyota Corolla rental, I immediately assumed that I was about to be carjacked. Not an entirely unreasonable premise given that only that day a seventeen-year-old Pretoria boy had taken his sister and brother hostage demanding guns, ammunition, two-way radios, R6 million in R200 notes ransom and his favoured getaway vehicle: a 1.6-litre Hyundai Excel. My point is the criminal mind works in strange ways and I was about to leap from the car begging for my life when my would-be assailant motioned for me to wind down the window. I did as I was told, only to be offered a choice of cocaine, ecstasy, marijuana or a buy-in-bulk-and-save combination of all three. Declining with a "no thank you but I appreciate the offer", I sped away in the direction of my hotel and turned into the driveway having seen the ugliest facets of arguably the most naturally beautiful city on the face of the planet.

I woke up the next morning ready to be seduced and glanced out my window at a 1000-metre-high aphrodisiac. It is impossible to overstate the presence of Table Mountain in Cape Town. Almost ten kilometres long and over three wide, it can be seen from as far as 200 kilometres out to sea and is the only landscape element on the planet to have a constellation named in its honour. It's called the Mons Mensa (Latin for Table Mountain) and is a next-door neighbour to the Southern Cross. The mountain is garlanded by more plant species than are found in England, Wales, Scotland and Ireland combined. It is wholly inanimate but possesses an undeniable soul. Viewed from the north, its sandstone ramparts coalesce into an amphitheatre whose dimensions are topped only by the magnificence of a vista that renders superlatives impotent. Six times older than the Himalayas,

Table Mountain presides over the city at its feet like a wise and kindly quartzite benefactor.

The first European to come over all Edmund Hillary upon seeing it was a Portuguese navigator and admiral by the name of Antonio De Saldhana. In March 1503 he packed some sandwiches and clambered up a perilously inclined skinny fault in the northern face known as Platteklip Gorge – the first word being Afrikaans for "flat stone" and we're not talking horizontal. Judging by the name he gave the mountain – Taboa do Cabo (Table of the Cape) which sounds more like one of those upmarket delis where the staff feel compelled to correct your pronunciation of tapenade – Antonio wasn't much for descriptions. That task was better left to another of his countrymen, explorer Livio Sanuto who explored the summit in 1588 and wrote that it "hath formed here a great plain, pleasant in situation which with the fragrant herbs, variety of flowers and flourishing verdure of all things, seems a terrestrial paradise".

Table Mountain is framed on one side by the conical Devil's Peak, so named because Lucifer apparently once lost a pipe-smoking contest up there to a local farmer. It continues to blow the stream of alabaster cloud that tumbles from its flat-topped neighbour and is known as the tablecloth. This phenomenon is actually caused by southeast winds that bring moisture-filled air from the sea into contact with the mountain, where it rises, cools and condenses into downy cloud quilts.

To the right of Table Mountain is the 699-metre Lions Head peak. One of its flanks boasts a marginally leonine rock protuberance and faces the Atlantic, while the other dips and levels out over a kilometre to Signal Hill, otherwise known as the Lions Rump. The combined effect is that of a recumbent feline, the tip of whose tail emerges several kilometres out to sea as Robben Island. Viewed from the string of eastern beaches and glittering bays, the mountain is a craggy behemoth butted up against a succession of nine peaks which wade ankle-deep in the blue ocean at their feet and are somewhat confusingly called the Twelve Apostles.

Johannesburgers like us always considered Cape Town as somewhat less cosmopolitan than our golden metropolis. But in truth, for me anyway, it was the voice of deep and abiding jealousy. I envied my cousins who spoke of volunteering for surf-livesaving patrols and coast-guard activities. I coveted the fact that they had a "home" beach. But I would have swapped it all for the mountain at their back door. Like meditation made manifest, it simultaneously stills and energises me.

A certain young lady who inspired precisely the same response in me was shortly to fly in from Sydney and I figured that the Mountain would provide no end of help in securing an affirmative response to a question I would pop once we hit the summit. Unlike the intrepid Portuguese adventurers and the numerous hikers who venture up one of the 350 trails to the summit, my plan called for a semblance of dashing charm and a speech bubbling with heartfelt declarations. Difficult enough to conjure without being marinated in your own sweat and wheezing between every syllable. Clearly this wasn't going to be a case of "you had me at 'stop complaining about those blisters there's only five kilometres to go'". So with a ring in my pocket and a lump in my throat, I steered Jennie towards the queue for the cable cars that ferry thousands of visitors a year to the summit.

Having asked Jennie's dad for his daughter's hand a few days earlier, I now thought of my own father and how he would never meet the woman who would, I hoped, take his name. He had, however, been beside me the last time I made this mountaintop pilgrimage. I have only two memories of the experience. The first was that the cars were cramped metal cages that resembled enclosed Ferris wheel seats. The second was that I picked out a relative's house way below on the shores of Camps Bay because of the distinctive shape of their swimming pool. I was told by my parents I was talking nonsense, which swiftly became "You're ruining it for everybody" as I continued to point out what I could clearly see and they couldn't.

The old cars had been replaced by high-speed models that rotated during the three-minute journey from the base station. Around twenty-five people can fit in each and the universal vowels of gobsmacked wonder plus the whir of camera lenses filled the cabin as we ascended. Being the premier tourist attraction in South Africa's premier tourist city, I had feared the mountaintop would be too crowded to find a secluded spot to do my spiel. Fortunately, there are three kilometres of walking tracks on the summit and within a few minutes we were sitting on a secluded precipice above a sweep of azure ocean pounding a succession of columned peaks. I found out later that my paramour was thinking, "If I had the balls, I'd ask him to marry me right now".

Somehow the lines I had rehearsed a million times on the road came out in the correct order. Perched on one knee with a sheer drop at my back, I placed the ring onto her finger and was greeted with the response, "Oh my God, you're doing it!" Which after a brief interlude of vexed clarification, I was told meant "Yes".

In a glazed daze we wandered the summit hand in hand

before repairing to a beachfront bar in Camps Bay for champagne.

Aside from being a creamy expanse of beach bounded by smooth boulders on either side, wide strips of lawn and chunky palm trees, Camps Bay is also the suburb in which three generations of my mother's family lived. It is one of the few places in South Africa to which I felt a genuine connection.

This strip of surf was the stage on which my Aunt Fay would strut with a hibiscus behind her ear and a midmorning martini in her hand. A kosher Mame who was something of a bombshell in her youth, she volunteered for the nursing corps in World War II on the grounds that she looked great in white. Family folklore has it that another aunt was walking on the beach one morning with a friend when in the distance a woman approached in an ensemble for which "makeshift" is too kind a description. "Look at that," said my Aunt Monica, "it looks like she's taken a sheet, sewed up the sides then cut two holes for the arms and one for the head." Lo and behold, Fay materialised from the mist with the greeting, "Darling! Don't you just adore my new caftan? I took a sheet, sewed up the sides then cut two holes for the arms and one for the head."

When darkness fell, we went to a nearby restaurant for dinner and began calling home to share the news as it was now early morning on the eastern seaboard of Australia. Although we tried to be discreet throughout the conversation with my prospective parents-in-law, fellow diners overheard the tale of the mountain proposal and sent over a bottle of champagne by way of congratulation. Although it was an individual gesture of kindness, it left us with an

affection towards Cape Town and its residents that will
endure henceforth.

Seapoint was a far more attractive prospect by day than it was
by night and the next morning we wandered along the
ocean-front promenade. The path is several kilometres long
and bounded by a stone wall over which frothy explosions of
sea spray leap. A string of coloured lights runs between the
lampposts on the path, which is bordered by patches of grass
large enough to accommodate dog walkers, several games of
six-a-side soccer and the odd wino howling at the moon.

The paths were packed with groups of shirtless lunchtime
joggers, mothers cantering along behind prams and even –
bless – a few retirees who gladdened my heart by bellowing,
"So this is a race track now?" to anyone who had the temerity
to pass them.

The shimmer of the Seapoint Public Swimming pool, a
sleek Art Deco collection of change rooms and admission
booths, was exactly as I remembered it. But the high diving
board on whose precipice I had cowered before hanging off
the edge by my arms and bellyflopping into the water was
inevitably more modest.

Alerted by the beep of a horn and a shrill cry of "Cape
Town", we boarded one of the crowded taxi minivans that
make up for the city's abject lack of public transport and
leapt out a few minutes later at the Victoria & Albert Waterfront.

Locals rave about the place and although it revitalised the
once scungy harbour district, replacing venereal sailors with
well-heeled tourists, it is, at the end of the day, a shopping
mall. Or more accurately a collection of them straight out of
that struts-and-plexi school of retail architecture whose

practitioners should be condemned to assembling IKEA furniture in hellish perpetuity. Save for the mountain peering down on the scene, we could have been in Sydney's Darling Harbour or San Francisco's Fisherman's Wharf and would not have known the difference.

Cape Town is a fairly compact city to navigate on foot, so we struck out towards the CBD past fishing boats unloading crates of rock lobster and tuna. Outside the impressive city aquarium stood a line of Muslim students in white fez-style hats, long navy trousers and matching shirts. They must have been six or seven and all looked immaculate despite the heat of the day and the volume of their clothing. A few of the scampish scoundrels at the back of the line even made sure they were out of the range of teacher's ears and shot a "Howzit pretty lady!" towards Jennie.

Unlike Johannesburg where businesses have fled the CBD in the face of horrendous crime and ambivalent policing, Cape Town's authorities took proactive action when they saw things heading the same way. The result is a city centre that teems with visitors, smartly dressed office workers of all races, roadside traders of one, and low-key security.

The foreshore sits on 240 hectares of reclaimed land and at a busy intersection near the main railway station is a statue of Jan Van Riebeck who dropped his ship's anchor in that very spot and stepped ashore to do what no white had ever done before: stay.

By the middle of the seventeenth century the Khoikhoi herders of the Cape peninsula had become quite used to the European vessels that stopped over as they plied the lucrative spice route to the East Indies. Almost two hundred years beforehand a Portuguese explorer named Bartolomeu Dias had strode ashore at Mossel Bay halfway between Port

Elizabeth and Cape Town. His party and the Khoikhoi eyed one another nervously and when the sailors made for a fresh-water stream, one of the tribesmen hurled a stone in their direction, only to be impaled by a bolt from a crossbow. And so at the first meeting between Europeans and Africans, the die was cast for their subsequent dealings.

Dias was exploring what was known as the Sea of Darkness — reputed to be boiled by a sun that turned all men to Negroes. His mission was to provide a solution to the conundrum that had hamstrung Europe's merchants for half a century: finding a sea route to India that would cut out the Arab middlemen who controlled the overland tracks. Dias reached Algoa Bay, but in a rickety ship and high seas, he was bound by his king to respect the majority decision of the senior crew and turn back. A decade later a compatriot named Vasco da Gama not only rounded what Dias had christened Cabo da Boa Esperança (The Cape of Good Hope) but continued up the east coast of Africa to modern-day Mombassa. He then sailed on to Goa, returning with cargo of cinnamon and pepper a year after leaving Lisbon.

Fast-forward a century and the sea route to Asia was being used by Dutch, English, French and Scandinavian merchant ships who occasionally landed on the Cape Peninsula to take in fresh water and barter sheep and cattle from the Khoikhoi pastoralists in return for iron and copper goods. A fair few of these vessels came a cropper around what also became known as the Cape of Storms. In 1647 the *Haarlem* – which belonged to the Dutch East India Company, the Microsoft of its day – ran aground in Table Bay. Rather than abandon the ship and its cargo, the master of the accompanying fleet ordered a contingent to remain until the following year's fleet swung by to collect them.

A sand fort was built and twelve months later the sailors were picked up as promised with their tenure proving that the land was habitable. One of those on the fleet making its way back from the east was Jan Van Riebeck, who was returning to his employers under a cloud of disgrace after being found guilty of private trading.

Anxious to restore his standing with the Dutch East India Company, he would have agreed to practically any assignment. They had a doozy in store.

The profitability of the spice trade was being undermined by the fact that the crew members had the annoying habit of popping their clogs en route. At least one sailor in six died between Europe and the Far East. The culprit was scurvy, a vitamin-C deficiency whose symptoms were an attractive package of swollen gums, loose teeth, lack of energy and bouts of spontaneous bleeding. As scurvy could be prevented by eating fresh fruit and vegetables, the company directors proposed an outpost at the Cape which could grow enough food to sustain both itself and the disease-ridden seamen that popped by.

Thus on 5 April 1652 Van Riebeck sighted Table Mountain and within a week began building the Fort of Good Hope, which still stands on the original site. He was under strict instructions not to lay claim to the land but merely utilise it. He was also was expressly forbidden from keeping anything but the peace with the Khoikhoi or any other powers that wanted to establish an outpost. From the outset the company demanded the settlement show a profit, and what better way to do that than by outsourcing. Five years after the fort was established, the Dutch East India Company slashed nine salaries from its bottom line and granted each of their former employees 11.5 hectares of land. They were exempt from tax for twelve years, given free licence to trade with the Khoikhoi on the provision that they did not undercut the company, and were encouraged to grow crops not already produced in the firm's garden.

With land, monetary incentives and free equipment; all they needed now was labour to produce on a profitable scale. However, the company had outlawed enslaving the Khoikhoi whom the settlement still depended on as trade partners, especially in livestock. Their prayers of subjugation were answered in 1658 when the *Amersfoort* pulled into port with a cargo of 170 slaves, the survivors of 250 taken off a Portuguese ship off the Angolan coast. The farmers were allowed to purchase a few human beings on credit while the rest were put to work by the company.

When Van Riebeck left the Cape in 1662, the original population of 90 had swelled to 463, around a quarter of which were slaves. In the years that followed, ever-increasing numbers of men were despatched by the company to the Cape where they were given tracts of land traditionally belonging to the Khoikhoi.

The indigenous population naturally resisted and in turn suffered retaliation that grew in brutality as the company and free settlers learned how to farm cattle — a commodity that for many years only the Khoikhoi could supply. Two periods of brief warfare and a batch of smallpox later, the Khoikhoi had been subjugated into servitude. It was during their first uprising in 1657 that what many consider the seminal act of apartheid was carried out. In response to raids on farmers' cattle stocks, Van Riebeck ordered the construction of an almond hedge to separate the settlement from the Khoikhoi. Parts of it still stand in Cape Town today.

As the Khoikhoi vanished, slaves continued to pour into

the settlement, but from a different source to the initial ship-
ment. Another maritime company – the Dutch West India
Company – had acquired sole trading rights (human cargo
included) for the West African coast and serviced the growing American colonies. The Dutch East India Company
turned to its concerns in the Orient and began importing
slaves from Java, Bali, Macassar, Timor, Burma, India and
what is today Malaysia. The trade was so extensive that ships'
officers returning from the east frequently picked up a few
slaves at cost and sold them for a tidy profit in the colony.

Life – if you could call it that – for slaves at the Cape colony
was so miserable, degrading and painful that many surely
wished they had perished along with those who routinely
died in transit. Families were broken up for sale; Van Riebeck
made it a condition that any household with slaves had to
have a whip or lash on hand for disciplinary purposes; and
such was the white fear of an uprising that more than two
slaves belonging to different owners were forbidden from
conversing at any time. Those who ran away and were recap-
tured were flogged, branded on the cheek or back with a
red-hot iron and condemned to a lifetime in chains. A second bash at freedom resulted in the ears, nose tip or in some
case the right hand being lopped off. This practice was later
abolished not for humanitarian reasons but out of concern
for the innocent people in polite society who had the misfortune to gaze upon such disfigurement.

By the time the nervy British occupied the Cape in 1807
(after an attempt in 1795 when everyone lost interest halfway through) it was mainly to prevent the territory falling
into French hands still dripping with the blood of the nobility. The new power banned slave trading and immediately
earned the ire of a group of outlying farmers who'd been

quarrelling with the Dutch authorities for years and had expanded their properties ever eastwards to do as they saw fit as far from the eyes of authority as possible.

Faced with diminishing amounts of land, the unforseen expense of now having to pay employees, and an oversupply of wheat and wine (neither of which travelled well, causing prices to slump), these battling, uneducated farmers were faced with two choices: remain in the Cape settlement and work as labourers (considered the scantest of notches above slavery) or acquire the nucleus of a herd, a couple of wagons and find a suitable area for watered grazing.

These fiercely individualistic farmers, known as the Trekboers, lacked the capital to buy the amounts of land required for raising sheep and cattle, so they travelled instead to the outer fringes of the colony and took over Khoikhoi pastures. These Trekboers were the forebears of those who would eventually flee British rule and establish independent republics to the north.

Those Capetonians unwilling to endure a harsh and isolated life on the edges of civilisation but who could not survive as farmers mustered their artisan skills. The businesses they created catered to the swelling number of visitors passing through a city that had become known as the Tavern of the Seas. As the nexus of two trade routes – agricultural produce from the interior was sold to ships which had brought in freight to be flogged to the rural community – Cape Town prospered. With a wealthy merchant class came aspirations to culture, and amid the brothels, pubs and early casinos, libraries, concert halls and ornamental gardens began to flourish. Along with the streams of visiting sailors, the city's civic foundations had been well and truly laid.

As early as 1764, Greenmarket Square was a vibrant

element of the Cape Town cityscape and 240 years on it's still kicking.

I heard Greenmarket Square before I saw it as the lulling throb of hand-slapped drums echoed through the narrow surrounding streets. And it's not just your *nts-nts-nts* shite either but a synthesis of beat and melody. Above these tip-toed harmonies produced by five painfully shy black girls who couldn't have been more than six or seven. Standing ramrod straight in their neatly pressed school uniforms they let rip with a multilayered rendition of "Nkosi Sikele Africa" so pure and heartfelt that it prompted me to do something I had never previously considered: folding a donation to a busker. I had to wedge said origami under the sparse array of coins in the cap at their feet or it would have blown away in the breeze that had just whipped in from Table Mountain. This brisk southeaster is known as the Cape Doctor as it sweeps away the city's pollution and was purely to blame for the particle that lodged in my eye the moment the choir hit their second chorus. See that's the thing about South Africa: she'll sicken you one minute, seduce you the next and steal your heart the moment your guard is down.

The cobblestoned market courtyard is bounded by hand-some deco office buildings and the Georgian Town House that is now a hotel. The wood and stone busts of regal tribes-men you see at every roadside market in the country were here too, along with compact discs, aromatherapy soaps, knock-off Gucci sunglasses and innumerable variations of the Table Mountain motif on everything from coasters to tea towels.

The stalls were separated by a central passageway where vendors sold cold drinks from metal tubs filled with dry ice, grilled ears of corn over iron barrels or enticed passers-by with *sosaties*, one of many recipes that Malay slaves brought from their homeland and adapted to local ingredients in their masters' kitchens. This particular example consisted of lamb chunks grilled kebab-style on a stick then anointed with a spicy apricot dipping sauce.

Jennie and I wandered through the market – which is mercifully a haggle-free zone – then took a seat in the window of a pizzeria that looked out over the square. It was a spin doctor's wet dream: tourists and locals of all races mingled happily beneath a cloud-wisped sky, the air redolent with percussion and barbecue. This was the South Africa that locals wished it could be – a happy bubble and squeak of cultures in which the past was never forgotten but did not infect the future. However, in quiet corners of this vibrant collage, the reality of deprivation and violence seeped through onto the canvas. Haggard street children barely into double figures but with war-veteran eyes hassled anyone with shoes for spare change, simultaneously casing them as a potential snatch-and-dash victim. White beggars, a contradiction in terms in the South Africa where I grew up, squatted on the pavement behind pieces of cardboard on which was scrawled their tale of woe.

Some locals looked over the rims of their latte glasses, through the faces of Third World squalor that ineffectually beseeched their First World sensibilities, and mumbled, "Isn't it terrible?" Others had their pizza leftovers packaged in takeaway containers which they handed to the hungry fringe-dwellers. It should also be pointed out that a significant few white South Africans also choose to forsake their prima veras for volunteer work in townships where the ricochet of stray bullets no longer warrants a head spin. As with so many other endeavours in the South Africa of the new millennium, stereotyping is a perilous business.

Our next stop was Saint George's Cathedral, a slender and elegant nod to neo-Gothicism designed by Herbert Baker and fashioned from Table Mountain sandstone. It couldn't have appeared more different from the Regina Mundi Church in Soweto but they had striking commonalities. Both were at one time the domain of Archbishop Desmond Tutu, both were symbols of defiance and both offered refuge to protestors fleeing the rubber bullets of police enforcing the apartheid regime.

Saint George's was the starting point for a rally of 30,000 multiracial protestors who made their way to the old City Hall on 13 September 1989. It was during this event that Tutu first dropped a phrase that for some is the catchcry of a new land, while for others rings disappointingly hollow: the Rainbow Nation.

Semantics aside, the pressure brought to bear at demonstrations like this played no small part in bringing about the death throes of apartheid. Less than twelve months later and only hours after walking free from twenty-seven years of incarceration, Nelson Mandela stood on the balcony of the very same City Hall to address delirious crowds.

Watching from Sydney I felt a joy that went beyond mere recognition of a grave injustice made right. It was only the clarity of hindsight that helped me identify the strange and overwhelming new emotion surging through me: I was proud to come from South Africa.

Although the pomp and pageantry of Mandela's inauguration took place in Pretoria, it was in Cape Town that he ended his long walk to freedom. The complicated business of governing majority rule was taking place around the corner in a Victorian amalgam of red brick and white granite fronted by a portico of Corinthian columns. The House of Parliament was a bastion of legally enshrined racism until the newly installed president Frederik Willem de Klerk realised that the inconsequential concessions made by the apartheid regime in the late 1980s didn't amount to squat. The writing was on the wall and it read "One white, one bullet".

On 2 February 1990 de Klerk announced that from that day on the ANC, PAC and South African Communist Party were no longer banned. Thirty-three domestic organisations such as the United Democratic Front and Congress of South African Trade Unions had all restrictions imposed upon them lifted; political prisoners incarcerated for nonviolent actions were freed, and capital punishment was abolished.

Although he took part in his fair share of duplicitous and underhanded actions, de Klerk's courage is often overshadowed by the lack of vengeance displayed by the man he released from the Victor Verster Prison nine days later. From his earliest days in power, Mandela pointed out that he was no messiah sent to rapidly deliver the South African masses from inequity. He was at pains to use the word "generations" in discussing his time frame for undoing the injustices of apartheid and distributing the nation's wealth more equally. When this message was emanating from a beaming Madiba, it seemed the people were happy enough to deal with their current hardships secure in the knowledge that change was going to come. The generation of ANC hierarchy which took the place of the retiring stalwarts such as Mandela and Walter Sisulu have not enamoured themselves of their constituents to the same degree. Granted, martyrs who spread the gospel of what they would do when righteousness saw them delivered into power have a far easier job than those charged with delivering those promises, but some of the sitting members have been behaving like out-and-out politicians.

For a start, President Mbeki became frustrated at the tedious business of dealing with commercial aircraft flight schedules and plundered the state coffers for R300 million for a private jet. That's a year's worth of AIDS medication for half a million of his countrymen and women. At the time of our visit, the country's premier anticorruption squad – the fabulously named Scorpions – had been sniffing around his deputy Jacob Zuma for months and the ANC's chief whip had admitted to receiving a cut-price prestige four-wheel-drive from a company who just happened to have been awarded a contract to supply the army with hardware.

Jennie and I followed Government Lane from Parliament through the botanical gardens exploding in crimson bougainvillea against a succession of pristine Cape Dutch buildings. Behind these lay the imposing edifices of such institutions as the National Gallery, Jewish Museum and Holocaust Centre, the Great Synagogue and the South African Museum.

At the top of the path lies another of Cape Town's grand dames: the Nellie. A rambling colonial hotel in the palest of pinks, the Mount Nelson is set amid rolling lawns and rose gardens behind an ornate archway flanked by pith-helmeted staff apparently under order to greet guests and visitors with a crisp salute.

The high teas here are a tourist attraction in themselves, as much for the location in which they are served as anything else. On the day of our visit the hotel's drawing room was lit by a pair of chandeliers and decorated in a manner that would suggest massive discounting in the Laura Ashley factory. The carpet was peach, the walls mustard, the armchairs were covered in Sanderson print hydrangea, and almost every horizontal surface was occupied by a flower arrangement in which you could secrete a toddler should the need arise. Pairs of overstuffed sofas with matching occupants faced one another around the edges of the room. However, the centrepiece was a mahogany table the size of a wading pool piled high with tortes, crumpets, scones, croissants and silver bowls aquiver with raspberry jam and cream.

A stately gent played Cole Porter tunes on a baby grand in a corner, the soundtrack augmented by the tinkle of silver-plated teaspoons being stirred in china teacups and half-hearted protestations of the "I couldn't possibly have another but since we've paid for it" variety. There was only one word for it: smashing.

Suitably refreshed and buzzing with a chocolate-mud high, we rolled out of the Nellie, tracked left past the eyebrow-raisingly named Labia Theatre – which in a happy symbiosis just happened to be hosting *The Vagina Monologues* – and back towards the city down Long Street.

Once a seedy cavalcade of brothels, bodegas and other dubious enterprises beginning with "b", the Victorian buildings – complete with wraparound iron-filigreed balconies – are now host to restaurants, African music stores, fashion design studios-cum-stores and marvellous second-hand bookshops. The cumulative effect, however, is greater than the sum of its louche parts and we decided to return that night for dinner at a restaurant known more for its live music than its food: Mama Africa.

Although many tour operators were offering evenings in traditional township drinking dens, the musicians who traditionally gave these raucous bars their sonic African edge had been lured to businesses like Mama Africa to play for audiences who gleefully handed over cover charges that would be laughed at in Soweto.

Yet without these township shebeens – a word many South Africans would bet the stashed currency in Switzerland has a local origin but was actually introduced by Irish members of the Cape Town police force and is Gaelic for "little shop" – South African jazz would probably never have flourished. As black migrants flooded to the cities in the wake of mineral discoveries and the establishment of manufacturing industries, these illegal drinking dens became centres of urban social life. Often run by shebeen queens – women who became relatively wealthy and wielded significant influence over their communities, police force included – the township bars were embroiled in fierce competition. Aside from offering patrons a wide range of drinks such as traditional maize and sorghum beer, noxious chemical brews like Kill Me Quick and commercial European liquors, they also tapped into the fact that musical performance was the traditional accompaniment to drinking in tribal societies.

At first the patrons themselves performed, but eventually miners and contract workers who strolled about playing African, Afro-Western and Afrikaans folk songs on guitars, concertinas and violins were yanked off the street and plonked on tiny stages.

The increasingly urbanised black patrons eventually grew bored of the traditional sounds and demanded ones which would reflect city life. By the 1920s musicians had responded by assimilating elements from every performance tradition they encountered into a single urban African style. It was called *marabi*, a word which signified not only the music but also the lifestyle of its listeners.

Thoroughly working class and overtly sexual – the word *marabi* also meant a category of people with low social status and a reputation for immorality – it coaxed African polyphonic principles into the western harmonic system. In other words, it was smokin'.

Marabi was, however, merely the precursor to a style of music influenced by the American jazz that flooded areas like Sophiatown and Cape Town's similarly multiracial District 6 (of which nothing remains but a museum and a musical).

The appeal of this type of music is apparent when you consider that blacks in the United States were also forced to make the difficult transition from a rural to an urban existence. In doing so they adapted the African rhythms that filled the slave ships into blues and then jazz. You don't need to be a rocket scientist to also figure out that music was one of the only arenas in which underprivileged black Americans were able to earn a form of respect.

Township bands like the Boston Stars, Manhattan Brothers and Jazz Maniacs, resplendent in lurid broad-shouldered zoot suits, tore joints apart and many were hired by the military during World War II to entertain the troops. For the conscripted white boys in the audience who thought Bing Crosby was pushing the envelope, this must have been nothing short of a revelation.

Rural black newcomers to cities took a while to get into the sophisticated facsimiles of Satin Doll and many were seduced by *tsaba-tsaba*, a brash blend of New York jive and traditional tribal beats that dared listeners to keep their feet still. One of these tunes by August Musururgwa called "Skokiaan" was renamed "Happy Africa" and topped the US charts in 1954. Penny whistles were soon layered over the *tsaba-tsaba* foundations by musicians agog at the conjuring of Benny Goodman and Artie Shaw. The result was *kwela* music – brash, ballsy, raw and frenetic.

Its rough edges were slowly smoothed with saxophones relegating the penny whistles to cameo appearances. *Kwela* jazz had arrived and, by the time the Group Areas and Separate Amenities Acts closed down many of its best-known venues, it had developed into a subtle, idiosyncratic and sophisticated entity whose foremost proponents such as Miriam Makeba, Hugh Masekela and Abdullah Ibrahim fled their homelands for sanctuary overseas.

Kwela jazz with a generous side-serve of percussion was on the menu at Mama Africa the night we visited. This was not your finger-snapping variety of music – it was all about foot-stomping and booty-shaking. Patrons left their tables to crowd around the ten-strong band, which syncopated fiercely while a trumpet and sax rose above the beat like the opening clarinet in *Rhapsody in Blue* then exploded like a mushrooming firework.

The sound trickled into Long Street as patrons edged through the doors to sway, grind or close their eyes with a half-smile and savour what was being created before them. We danced, drank and danced some more until the sweat-soaked band played one more encore then called it a night.

The older I get the worse I boogie, the more inclined I am to use words like boogie and the less I am sure of. However, I know for a fact that if South African music doesn't move you, it's time to start checking for a pulse.

Chapter 14

No Man is an Island

Having sped through the Cape Flats a few days later, we were meandering through what locals call the Wine Route, a term which could be applied, phonetically anyway, to a number of my single friends. While the bottled product of the region doesn't quite match up to that of Australia, France or California, the locale in which it is harvested makes the Hunter Valley, Napa and most of Burgundy look like the agricultural equivalent of a crack den.

Under a canopy of diluted sapphire, squat wide-fronted Cape Dutch homesteads sat in the midst of vineyards that looked as if they had been braided onto the buttresses of merlot mountains.

The first cellar door at which we stopped was located on the enormous Spier Estate. An ensemble of whitewashed restaurants and conference facilities complemented picnic areas along the fringes of a gurgling river with the vines on the opposite bank. Aside from hosting a summer arts festival whose commendable motto is "without new works there are no classics" and introducing a profit-sharing scheme with employees that has led to new housing developments for those most in need, Spier has also donated a portion of its voluminous land holdings to a cheetah sanctuary. There, Jennie and I posed for photos with the skinniest of the big cats. After being led into a wire enclosure, we sat on a couple of logs in front of which lay a dozing feline. As we ran our hands over its coarse coat and bony frame, the cheetah rolled onto her back like a kitten and playfully swatted at our hands. It was like playing with a tabby on steroids.

Of all the cats in Africa, cheetahs are the most threatened. For a start, they have no natural killing instinct – mothers have to literally show their cubs every aspect of hunting – and therefore lose out in the prey stakes to lions, leopards, hyena, vultures and wild dogs. As if to compensate for this fundamental shortcoming, they have a range of natural attributes that is unparalleled in the animal world. For example, under each of their eyes is a black strip of fur which cuts down glare, and the tips of their tails are as individual as fingerprints, allowing them to hunt in concert in long grass. Finally, a cheetah can also go from 0 to 120 kilometres per hour quicker than your average hatchback.

The greatest concentration of wild cheetahs is found in the arid and isolated farmland of southern Namibia and the Kalahari Desert (hence the nickname Kalahari Ferrari). Like most predators they will go for the easiest kill – the weakest victim – which frequently turns out to be calves under eight weeks old. Farmers in the area faced with stock losses began to lump cheetahs among other pests to be eradicated. According to a survey in the Cheetah Conservation Fund's June 2002 newsletter, in the decade up to 1991, only 10 per cent of 241 regional farmers interviewed said they had not slaughtered a cheetah on their property. The fund's education campaign saw that number jump to 24 per cent for the decade up to 2001. In addition to touring schools with the cheetahs, the foundation has also given away 170 Anatolian shepherd puppies to farmers. Bred in Turkey to protect herds from wolves and bears, this is a prop forward of a hound that ain't gonna take no shit from no pussycat and has proved a far more effective deterrent to stock loses than bullets have ever been.

From Spier we travelled to Franschoek, a village founded by the French Hugenots who fled to the Netherlands and travelled on to the Cape after 1685 when Louis XIV revoked the edict of Nantes which tolerated Protestantism. Before you could say pogrom, they had arrived in this bountiful valley with their faith unshaken and wine-making nous from the homeland. Enclosed by the saw-toothed Drakenstein mountains which take the form of cupped hands, Franschoek (literally the 'French Corner') is essentially a gentrified main street of Gallic symbols such a vignerons, fromageries and patisseries. While strolling towards the monument at the end of the road we were approached by a smartly dressed local schoolboy collecting for a gym, sports tour or charity drive of some sort. The reason I am so unclear is that I became immediately transfixed by the fundraising activity. For every R50 collected, a teacher of the students' choosing would spend half an hour perched in a tree outside the school hall. I handed over R100 on the condition that he nominated the cantankerous prick who got his jollies by repeating obscure questions to quivering students he knew didn't know the answer. Every school has one.

Franschoek is Cape Town's foodie mecca with eight of the nation's top 100 restaurants. We lunched on nouvelle nosh in a pretty restaurant named La Petite Ferme which overlooked the valley from a wooded ridge.

Despite growing up in a household that had its own

modest cellar and wine on the table at most meals, I'm
ashamed to admit that I never acquired a taste for the stuff.
Consequently, the allure of the numerous cellar doors that
lay at the end of oak-lined gravel driveways was purely aesthetic. That said, coachloads of ever-so-slightly-slurring
tourists were piling in and out of them carrying vacuum-
packed bottles. Although the quality of wine produced in the
early days of the colony ranked somewhere between burgundy dish water and bitter vinegar, things soon picked up
considerably and by the time Napoleon Bonaparte was doing
time on St Helena he would only drink wine from the Groot
Constantia estate.

Sorely tempted to stay overnight, we instead opted to
head back to Cape Town for cocktails at a certain seaside bar
where I would tell a joke that began, "A Texan, a South African and a Sydneysider were standing on the deck of a cruise
ship …"

On the way we passed through some of the most
sought-after real estate on the planet. Taking a circuitous
route back to our hotel, we traversed the leafy enclave of
Constantia. One of Cape Town's old-money havens, it is an
elegant composite of Cape Dutch gables behind don't-
even-think-about-it walls. Acorns and oaks overhang the
streets and the occasional clip-clop of hooves filter onto the
road from an unseen gulch. It is all frightfully civilised in an
Enid Blyton sort of a way.

Skirting the wind-whipped froth of Hout Bay, we crested
Chapman's Peak on a road hacked out of cliff faces that
couldn't be any sheerer were they made of organza. In the
distance below, bounded by a crescent of hyper-white sand
and an electric blue swell, nestled Llandudno – which looked
more like a Greek fishing village than a metropolitan suburb.

Darting this way and that like a schizophrenic serpent, the road eventually dipped a few metres above sea level at the seaweed-draped bay of Oudekraal. The angle of the slope eventually eased into foothills lined with homes of the multitiered, extensively balconied variety. We were back in Camps Bay.

The odd beachfront cafe I remembered as a child had mushroomed into a row of trendy wine bars, restaurants and cocktail lounges frequented by what the tourist brochures termed "the beautiful people". This turned out to be a euphemism for too-tanned models wearing fake Dior sunglasses and implants, affected waiters who were no doubt "really writers/actors/directors" and all manner of male poseurs for whom how much they could bench press was a valid topic of conversation.

We drove on to La Med, the bar in which I had envisioned myself at the start of my journey. Set on a rock promontory beside a bowls club my grandfather had helped found, it looked out over all of Camps Bay and its attendant Apostles. And that was just when you turned your head to the left. Directly in front of the outdoor terrace was an oval where paragliders who'd leapt from Lions Head would touch down to golf applause, and beyond that 180 degrees of shimmering open sea.

It was the eve of the World Cup cricket final and Australia were a cert to take out the trophy. With the hosts shooting themselves in the foot through bungled run-rate mathematics, Jennie suggested it might not be prudent to gather a group of locals for a joke about emigration. With the death stares I'd received at the rugby match in Bloemfontein still casting a malevolent shadow, I did the only thing I could: sulk and stare out to sea as my fiancée quietly asked herself

what kind of man she'd agreed to spend the rest of her life with.

As with most children, my mood brightened after a beer and a bowl of ice cream. On the drive towards Seapoint we passed through Bantry Bay, a cliffside retreat so exclusive and pricey that most of the houses have private funiculars beside the garage. After all, darling, do you know what steps can do to a pair of Blahniks?

Having spent most of the day imbibing, we skipped dinner in favour of a sunset amble by the sea. Eleven kilometres offshore lay the island where we would spend our final day in this enchanted city.

The Dutch word for seal is *robbe* and the seventeenth-century sailors who were the first Europeans to explore the 3.2-kilometre-long, 1.6-kilometre-wide island named it after the abundance of these creatures frolicking on the bone-white slivers of beach.

As early as the 1660s the Dutch authorities were using Robben Island as a prison where Khoikhoi who were suspected of theft were dumped after being branded, thrashed and chained. From its earliest incarnation, it was also a place to hide those with scandalous notions of racial equality.

The British needed little convincing of the island's penal value and everyone from the odd farmer who refused to grant freedom to slaves who had served their time, to tribal warlords were imprisoned here. Along with thousands who had committed the heinous offence of contracting leprosy.

At only seven kilometres wide, the stretch of water between the island and nearest landfall at Blouberg Strand seems to invite escape attempts. Until you consider that it's an icy coffin where if the hammerheads, great whites or hypothermia don't get you, the tenacious currents fresh

from the Antarctic will. According to some sources, the only successful bid for freedom from the island was made in 1658 by a banished Khoikhoi leader named Achumatu – bless you! – who only pulled off the feat because he stole a boat. Others point to the sorry story of Carel and Jacob Kruger, a pair of eighteenth-century vagabonds who reached shore in a boat fashioned from animal hide. After absconding into the interior, Carel was stomped into rigor mortis by an elephant, while his brother endured in the bush for two decades before being granted a pardon. God only knows how they found him to deliver the news, but on his way to Cape Town to formally receive his freedom, the poor bastard became lion food.

When World War II rolled around, the strategically valuable port of Cape Town was considered a possible target for a German attack. Robben Island was promptly outfitted with a battery of antiaircraft guns, 3000 military personnel and an infrastructure of accommodation, places of worship and recreational facilities. So real was the threat that city residents were instructed to black out their windows and cover car headlights with cardboard into which thin slits had been sliced. Air-raid sirens would scream across the Atlantic Seaboard several times a week for emergency drills. My mother vividly recalls diving under desks with her classmates at Mrs Lotz's kindergarten and biting down on the eraser they were required to wear at all times on a string around their necks. Presumably this would absorb the shock of a building falling on their heads.

Over half a century on, the island that would have protected the city from attacks which never materialised is now a tourist attraction so lucrative that only the Table Mountain cableway rakes in more cash.

A sleek concrete and glass terminal-cum-museum known as the Nelson Mandela Gateway is the departure point for the three-and-a-half hour round trip to Robben Island. Lumbering through the harbour populated by behemoths stacked with containers, compact fishing trawlers and the odd bobbing seal, the captain cranked the engine as we passed the breakwater of interlocking concrete fingers. Even with a calm sea and twin hulls, it was a matter of mere minutes before I was on the back deck focusing on the horizon as my stomach was flipped like a patty on a grill.

As we neared, the blurred mass whose highest point sits only thirty metres above the Atlantic began to acquire some detail. The white spire of a church was traced against a leaden sky, followed by a modest lighthouse and a string of low buildings with faded red metal roofs lining a jetty. Beyond these stood the rusting watchtowers.

When the retching prisoners arrived here, they were lined up along the stone wall by the jetty and herded through an archway bearing the motto of the prison service: "We Serve With Pride". Yep, and Arbeid Mach Frei.

A gunmetal-grey bus was waiting for us and we piled in for a spin around the island. It was dotted with more structures than I had expected: a football club, tennis courts, a domed Muslim shrine built on the grave on an esteemed cleric, the quaint Church of the Good Shepherd chapel erected in 1895 and designed by no less than Sir Herbert Baker.

When we pulled up at a stone cottage surrounded by razor wire, our tour guide swiftly lost her perky demeanour and adopted a quietly reverential tone. Zinzi, a vivacious twenty-something student who had up until that point delighted in playfully exposing the ignorance of the visitors, then asked who had heard of Nelson Mandela. Every hand on the bus was raised. She then asked who had heard of Robert Sobukwe. Only me and a pair of African-Americans responded in the affirmative. And in my case, it was only through the fortuitous coincidence that I had been researching this book.

Turns out the cottage had been home for six years to a remarkable man, who in my opinion is certainly in Mandela's league when it comes to selfless sacrifice for the betterment of all South Africans. Sobukwe was the founding president of the Pan Africanist Congress, a group which split from the ANC over the issue of co-operation with non-Africans in the liberation struggle. While Mandela and his cohorts believed any future democracy rested on the idea of obliterating racial divisions, Sobukwe favoured a policy whereby Africans would regain their sense of self-worth even if it meant turning their backs on other racial groups fighting for the same cause.

Although the ideologies differed – with Sobukwe's vision being broader than South Africa and entailing what he described as the United States of Africa – the ANC and PAC employed many similar strategies, such as anti-pass campaigns. Although the PAC never mustered the same following as the ANC, its message resonated in enough black South Africans to bring Sobukwe to the attention of the authorities.

On 21 March 1960 he presented himself, along with a small crowd, at the Orlando police station for arrest on the grounds that he was not carrying his pass. Between 3000 and 5000 people had heeded the PAC call and done the same at Sharpeville police station. And we know what happened next.

A leader of obvious influence and charisma, Sobukwe was jailed for three years for the pass offence. After which he was sentenced to six years of "preventative detention" on Robben Island thanks to a law specifically drafted to minimise his influence. From 1963 to 1969 Sobukwe was forbidden from communicating with anyone on the island. However, as the prisoners shuffled past him on the way to a lime quarry nearby, Sobukwe made a daily speech of rare power, poise and poignancy. When a free man, he was known for addressing his speeches to "sons and daughters of the soil". In prison he would grab a fistful of sand as his shackled audience marched by and let it drop to the ground as a visual reminder that they were sons of the soil, that Africa belonged to them and they belonged to Africa. Although Sobukwe was released in 1969, he was to spend the final nine years of his life under house arrest and severe restrictions.

Robben Island proved an effective mechanism for silencing those with dangerous voices and when Nelson Mandela and seven colleagues were found guilty on four charges of sabotage on 11 June 1964, life imprisonment on Robben Island was a fait accompli.

After years of non-violent resistance to the apartheid machine only engendered increasingly vicious responses, the ANC had established a militant arm called Umkhonto we Sizwe. Its aim was to destabilise the nation through the bombing of Bantu administration offices, post offices and other government buildings, as well as electrical and railway infrastructure. In the eighteen months from December 1961, 200 such attacks took place. The authorities responded with a predictable raft of draconian knee-jerks. One of these was the Ninety Day Act in which police were permitted to detain suspects on suspicion of political activities and hold them – without access to a lawyer – for three months of questioning.

This period could also be extended indefinitely, or as the justice minister of the time put it "to this side of eternity".

The last time Mandela spoke in public before being jailed for twenty-seven years was from the dock. He gave an impassioned statement that would sustain the armed struggle that he was being jailed for participating in. It concluded with the words: "During my lifetime I have dedicated myself to this struggle of the African people. I have fought against white domination and I have fought against black domination. I have cherished the ideal of a democratic and free society in which all persons live together in harmony and with equal opportunities. It is an ideal which I hope to live for and to achieve. But if needs be, for which I am prepared to die."

Mandela arrived on Robben Island to find a mix of political activists and hardened criminals. No distinction was made when it came to how they were treated and hard labour in the prison's limestone quarry occupied a significant amount of the prisoners' time. A blinding white face of stone, the quarry was continually buffeted by sharp winds off the water, resulting in a near constant haze of dust that would blow into the prisoners' eyes and lungs. Zinzi reported that Nelson Mandela's eyes are so sensitive as a result of years of quarry work that he cannot be photographed with a flash and his ducts are damaged to the point where he is physically unable to shed tears.

A seven square metre cave hacked into the rock functioned as the prisoners toilet and meal space. Two buckets were deemed sufficient for the ablutions of thirty prisoners over an eight-hour shift in the quarry.

Robben Island is now also a wildlife sanctuary and as we drove towards the finale of the visit – a tour around a cell-block led by a former resident – springbok, bantabok, steenbok and eland bounded between the eucalyptus and aloe vera trees introduced to the island in 1891.

Waiting in front of B section, a sombre grey bunker fronted by a pair of hefty metal doors, was Sipho, an ANC activist who spent five years on Robben Island. He ushered us into a wide corridor lit by fluorescent bars and pointed to a wooden door inscribed with the word *kantoor* (office). "It was where we were given our ID cards," he said. "From that second till the time you left, your name became a number."

If the authorities viewed the prisoners as numbers, the imprisoned ANC hierarchy saw them as students. Operating under the motto "Each one teach one", prisoners were instructed in everything from basic literacy and numeracy to biology, history and political courses with titles such as "Deepening and Broadening the Theatre of Revolution".

The secrecy of this education program is a matter of some debate as Mandela and others actively encouraged the warders to further their own education. That said, it is difficult to imagine approval being given for the structured examinations, assessments and ceremonial recognition of academic performance that took place on the island.

Sipho guided us into a courtyard that separated B block, where the high-ranking political prisoners were interred to minimise their influence, from C block, home to minnows and murderers alike. It was here that the ANC brains trust would conduct amplified conversations that functioned as lectures to the inmates who listened intently on the other side of the wall. The prisoners whose job it was to deliver food also slipped scraps of paper with topics for discussion or test results back and forth.

Next were the solitary confinement cells. On the walls were laminated remembrances from the prisoners who once occupied them. One of the most chilling was from Napthali Manana who was incarcerated on the island from 1982 to 1991. "During the medical check-ups," he wrote, "authorities would talk about which organs would be taken from our bodies for transplants."

Each of the fifty cells – with the strange colour scheme of grey to head height and white to ceiling – had one of these grim memoirs affixed to the wall. Except cell number 5.

Measuring six square metres, the cubicle which only just accommodated a metal cot, bedside table and steel bucket that served as a night toilet was Nelson Mandela's home for eighteen years. Of his period on the island he wrote that "time moved glacially". I was awestruck that he had emerged from these depths of deprivation and indignity not brimming with vengeance but possessing the quiet grace of man who always believed that his faith in humanity would be fulfilled.

What's to say about a man who not only invited two of his former jailers to his inauguration as president, but insisted one retain his job overseeing the facility when it became a tourist attraction? I have two heroes in life: one is my father for reasons too numerous, modest and sentimental to mention. The other is Mandela – no explanation required.

The tour ended in a dormitory measuring twenty metres by fifteen which Sipho and sixty-four others had occupied for half a decade. Pointing out his bunk, he smiled for the first time and said, "I'm home now". Shaking his hand as we made our way back to the bus, I asked if it was difficult coming back here every day to tell his story.

"Sometimes," he replied. "But it's easier when there are children in the tour groups. Aside from my wife, that's what I missed most: their laughter, their hope and the future of my country which they represented."

With the boat pulling away towards Cape Town harbour, I took a last look at the island, hoping to glean even a hint of stark beauty. There was none.

Robben Island is surrounded by the carcasses of thirty ships whose hulls were torn to tatters by shark-teeth rocks beneath the surface. The perils of sailing in this region are illustrated by the fact that on the night of 17 June 1722 ten ships were lost in Table Bay. Twenty-eight years earlier, the *Dageraad* was buffeted into a reef by a malevolent north-wester off the island. Seventeen chests of gold sank into the icy brine with her, but only a trio were recovered. The *Dageraad* is one of many ships laden with riches that disappeared off the rock-ringed island, and hushed rumours of undiscovered fortunes beneath the waves still flit around Cape Town every now and then. Who would have thought that a treasure beyond measure had been sitting in cell number 5, B block?

Chapter 15

Dangling a Carat

With Jennie on a plane and the knowledge that I would be home in three weeks, I left Cape Town before dawn the next day. By the time it had broken, I had passed through the Cape Flats and Hugenot Tunnel into the Hex River Valley. A quilt of vineyards surrounding white homesteads from which chimney smoke rose, the scene was dipped in toffee by the rising sun. This region, cradled by the Cape's highest mountains, is the largest producer of table grapes in Africa. The surrounding area is where much of the Western Cape's fresh produce is harvested. Beyond the mountains, however, lies the Karoo, a semidesert that covers almost a third of South Africa and is barely inhabited. The word comes from the language of the early Khoikhoi who coaxed food, shelter and water from the boundless wilderness. It means "hard".

The transition between farmland and scrubby plains was no gentle fade. Rather, it was like someone had a flicked a switch from fertile to arid. I had been warned to expect a visual palette bereft of variation and character, but after the tourist-clogged maelstrom of Cape Town and the Garden Route, the Martian landscape, clean air and shimmering lace of tarmac offered a gift of stark solitude.

Far from being visually monotonous, driving through the Karoo was rather like looking through one of those Viewmaster toys we had as children. Only this time I was clicking through a series of stark and desolate landscapes unified by an austere beauty. Georgia O'Keeffe would have done her nana in the Karoo, but as aesthetically pure as it was, it was the sound that I liked best. Or should I say, the lack thereof. For urban types, silence is the rarest of commodities and the Karoo is a repository of the stuff.

Nine hours after leaving Cape Town on a northeastern tack, I arrived in "the gem of the Karoo". Wedged in a niche of the Sneeuberg range where the Sundays River loops lazily back on itself, Graaf-Reinet was the precise centrepoint of Gondwanaland before the continents began absconding hither and yon.

Today it is a sedate town of gracious Cape Dutch and Victorian homes whose tumultuous history is acknowledged through its 220 national monuments and memorials. In addition to those commemorating locals who sacrificed their lives in World War I, II and the Anglo-Boer conflict, stood plaques, plinths and parapets of practically everyone who broke wind in the district.

The next morning I awoke at the positively uncivilised time of 4.30am to catch a sunrise at the aptly named Valley of Desolation. Thanks to fortunate timing, I arrived in time to see the first golden wash spill over Driekoppe Mountain into a vast basin shaped by a hundred million years of volcanic and erosion forces. The spectacle was framed by pinnacles of piled dolerite that could have been the columns to some ancient temple whose high priests I aped in a reverent and ritualistic salute to the rising sun. Between me and the horizon, so distant it was convex, was a sheer drop to hectare upon hectare of ochre soil. The odd low hill sprang up here and there but was swallowed by the red sand giving them the appearance of welts on a sunburned back.

I'm anything but a religious man, but such was the sparse magnificence of the Valley of Desolation that I couldn't help but wonder whether some supernatural guiding hand had been at work alongside the erosion and magma. A lone black eagle riding the zephyrs in the valley signalled the time had come to leave – it wasn't going to get any better than this and I'd heard the sound of shutting doors in the carpark.

At peace yet craving coffee, I headed to a hamlet in the hills called Nieu Bethesda. It is located at the end of a dirt track which barrelled along grassy dykes and fissures before twisting through a valley floor where willow-laced rivers ran and a handful of impassive sheep grazed in an emerald paddock. The population of the town barely scratched four figures yet it buzzed with a low-frequency hum that sat somewhere between mystical and "on the count of three, freak out". Equal parts isolated and inspiring, the town has long been a magnet for artists, but the most bi-polar of the lot was Helen Martins, whose home is Nieu Bethesda's prime attraction.

Born in the town, Helen left an unhappy marriage to a local farmer, then floated between Johannesburg, Cape Town and Port Elizabeth before returning in the 1930s to care for her ailing parents. Her mother died soon afterwards and her cantankerous father, whose less-than-affectionate nickname was the Lion, moved into a small windowless room off the verandah where he refused to have anything to do with his daughter. When he died in 1941, Martins painted his dwelling black and called it the Lion's Den.

It was the start of what is far and away the eeriest

endeavour in South African art. Martins was ill in bed one night shortly after the Lion had roared for the final time when she became transfixed by the moonlight shining through her window. It symbolised how grey and dull her life had become and she resolved from that moment to flood her existence with colour. The desire to embellish her environment manifested itself in the installation of coloured glass panes in place of clear windows. These bathe her home in technicolour reds, greens and blues with each room having a different mood. Walls and ceilings were coated with elaborate patterns of crushed glass embedded in bands of bright paint. Natural light was viewed as a fuel to be diffused, and an alcove in one room was entirely given over to a wall made of amber jars through which a golden sheen radiated.

The place is known as the Owl House, as a result of the emblematic bird images that work as a motif throughout, and walking through it is like wandering through an animated LSD trip. Once Martins had finished treating her home as a canvas, she turned her attention to the garden. There she utilised cement, wire and glass to create the hundreds of sculptures and relief figures that crowd her yard like a surreal mosh pit. Her favourite animals – owls and camels – abound in an otherworldly fantasia also populated by distorted sphinxes, Buddhas, bejewelled mermaids, acrobats and shepherds en route to a nativity scene in stable of tiered glass bottles. She and Lewis Carroll would have got on famously. On a cold winter's morning in 1978, unable to take pleasure from her creations due to failing eyesight, Helen Martins swallowed enough caustic soda to kill herself.

Despite the self-inflicted demise of its owner, the Owl House was an uplifting celebration of a fiercely creative life.

Following hard upon the sunrise over the Valley of Desolation, I left Nieu Bethesda with a light heart.

Hours later I crossed the Orange River and the desert began to recede in the face of the *platteland*'s rich farmland. Turning left at Bloemfontein – where as you'll recall I spent a weekend one evening – the road bisected paddock after paddock of sunflowers, their heads bowed as if in solemn remembrance. These gave way to fenced-off empty scrubland where what lay beneath the soil was far more valuable than anything that could be grown in it. Hang on to your tennis bracelets, ladies, because we've just reached diamond country.

One lazy afternoon in 1876, young Erasmus and Louisa Jacobs were exploring a riverbank on their neighbour's farm near Hopetown when they found a shiny pebble. The children duly handed it over to the farm's owner, Schalk Van Niekerk. Not knowing quite what to make of the curiously glinting stone and being a spectacularly trusting type, he transferred it into the custody of a passing trader named John O'Reilly. When O'Reilly showed it to some wizened heads in Hopetown, they dismissed it as being of little value, one trying to console O'Reilly with the suggestion that it was topaz. The trader was unconvinced and passed the stone – so to speak – to the Acting Civil Commissioner of Colesberg. Its next stop was our friend Dr Atherstone in Grahamstown.

It was a discovery which transformed South Africa from an Empire backwater to a source of unimaginable wealth. More deposits were unearthed shortly afterwards and by 1870 over 10,000 diggers from southern Africa, Australia and the United States were working plots along the Orange River.

A year later a prospector with the marvellously appropriate name of Rawstone was doing his thang on a farm called

Vooruitzicht, which has the uncanny meaning of Prospect. Semantic fate came to pass when an African employee of Rawstone's excitedly showed his boss three stones he had found on a nearby hill. Known as the Colesberg Kopje, the rise proved to be the head of an ancient pipe of diamondiferous lava and fell within the property owned by brothers Diedrik and Nicholaas De Beer. Eleven years earlier they had paid £50 for the land. In just over a decade they turned a major – if shortsighted – profit by accepting 6000 guineas for the property. Their naivety was set in precious stone when the new owners retained the farmers' name as the trading title of the company which would eventually dominate the global diamond industry.

Within two years 50,000 diggers were working the hill while a predictable brouhaha had broken out over which government owned the land. As it had previously been such an arse-end-of-beyond region, no one had bothered to lay formal claim to the place. Now, however, the Orange Free State and the South African Republic both put up their hands, as did the Cape Colony, and Griqua tribe who had lived there for at least seventy years. A British court found in favour of the Griqua, whose chief Nicolaas Waterboer promptly turned to the crown for protection. In 1871 the region became a crown colony and was formally annexed to the Cape in 1880.

The labyrinth of tents that sprang up around the diggings morphed into the city Kimberley, and Colesberg Kopje became the biggest hole in the world. This chasm is the centrepiece of a village-cum-museum which provides a glimpse into a society comprised of paranoid miners prepared to kill to protect their claim, genteel British administrators, grifters, bar flies, diamond dealers, saloon keepers and prostitutes.

The Big Hole is approached along a boardwalk which is enclosed in mesh and juts out ten metres over the edge. Enclosed by steep gradients that drop to sheer faces only to plunge into a pool of luminous lime water, this man-made gouge has a circumference of 1.6 kilometres and is over 182 metres deep. Its true scale is only seen in contrast and semitrailers travelling the highway near the opposite rim looked like Tonka trucks. Aside from its vastness, the most striking aspect of the Hole is the way it absorbs sound making for a sense of desolate peace.

At the peak of operations, 30,000 men worked around the clock in the huge pit. When Anthony Trollope visited, he observed, "The stuff is raised on aerial tramways, wires are stretched taut from the wooden boxes slanting down to the claims at the bottom. As one bucket was taken down empty on one set of wires, another comes up on the other set full of blue. It looks to be so steep down there, there can be no easier way to the bottom other than aerial contrivances. It is though you were looking down into a vast bowl, whole round the bottom are various marvellous incrustations among which ants are working with all the usual energy of the ant tribe."

When the early miners struck it rich, they lashed out on lavish spending sprees in Kimberley's dozens of bars and brothels. Raucous laughter echoed through the streets most every evening as instant millionaires lit cigars with bank notes while their ladies of the night literally bathed in champagne.

It was all downhill from there as far as nightlife in Kimberley was concerned. When my family and I came here on holiday one scorching December in the early 80s, rotis-serie chickens passed for live entertainment and things had only picked up marginally since then. Possessing neither the wardrobe nor the inclination to visit the Kimberley Club, which was slipping into decrepitude along with its clients, I headed for the 127-year-old Halfway House bar. It's not the oldest in town – that honour goes to the Star of the West, South Africa's first pub, which was established in 1870 and is said to be haunted by roaming ghosts guarding the fortune in gold coins beneath the floorboards. "The Half" was fairly lively with groups of mildly inebriated men watching a box-ing match on TV as their girlfriends tore apart the fashion sense of everyone else in the room. All I could think was that people in stirrup pants shouldn't throw stones.

I had come to the Half because it had a long-standing rep-utation for excellent service, particularly to one of its early punters who was somewhat vertically challenged. The staff spared Cecil Rhodes the ignominy of mounting and dis-mounting by delivering his tipple to him in the saddle.

Born in England in 1853, Rhodes was sent to work on a cotton farm in South Africa when he was seventeen because of poor health. A year later he skedaddled to Kimberley where he realised that as the diggings were proceeding ever deeper, serious capital was required to overcome the con-comitant challenges of flooding and rock falls. Together with CD Rudd, he bought a number of small claims and formed the original De Beers mining company. Other joint-stock companies followed and Rhodes tapped into his easy access to European capital to bring them into the fold.

Rhodes also formed the Diamond Syndicate, harbinger of today's Central Selling Organisation which oversees almost 80 per cent of current trade and controls the release of stones into the market, thus ensuring it is never flooded and prices remain high.

Another of his company's innovations was the finetuning of a system of wage labour that exploited impoverished Africans. De Beers was instrumental in establishing "locations" that would prevent black workers from pocketing stones and selling them privately. Enclosed by high walls made of corrugated iron, these compounds were in fact prisons where workers on six-month or one-year contracts were strip-searched daily and subjected to summary justice. At any given time, one in fifteen had smallpox or pneumonia, a figure that contrasts sharply with the one in one hundred rate recorded by Kimberley's night-soil removers, who supposedly had the most unhygienic job in town. By the time gold was discovered, Rhodes had created a lucrative model for trimming overheads through cheap labour, minimising stock loss as a result of theft, and regulating supply onto the market so that it retained its value.

His lust for wealth was matched only by his fervour for Empire. At twenty-three he declared, "Why should we not form a secret society with but one object – the bringing of the whole uncivilised world under British Rule – for making the Anglo-Saxon race one empire". Within half a decade Rhodes owned half the De Beers empire, was a member of the Cape Parliament (where he eventually became prime minister) and possessed the kind of wealth that allowed him to import scores of English birds to his garden in Cape Town as he believed their songs would rejuvenate his ailing health. Those which survived the journey didn't so much warble as croak, as did Cecil John shortly thereafter. His legacy is astounding: not only was CJR the first to utter the immortal "Cape to Cairo" vision that caused nocturnal emissions for many an imperialist, he also joined only Simon Bolivar and Amerigo Vespucci in having a nation – Rhodesia – named after him and he established the scholarships to Oxford University that still bear his name.

These days only three mines operate in Kimberley and diamond supply is dwindling. The bustling town where Rhodes reigned has been stripped of the very source of its riches. The plush double-storey clubs adorned with spacious balconies and filigree lacework have long since made way for the concrete headquarters of insurance companies; and where they once occupied block after block, the greatest concentration of bars is now across the windows and doors of homes.

Chapter 16

Where the Street has My Name

Heading north from Kimberley, the town that swelters on a scarred and scrubby plain presented me with an unexpected farewell treat. Marking the boundary between the last fortified cluster of town houses and the bush was a dam teeming with pink flamingos. So thick were they that their massed reflection threw a candy-floss coating over the water through which they waded.

Following the arc of the muddy Vaal River for around 200 kilometres through the towns of Warrenton and Bloemhof, I encountered yet again the most ubiquitous feature of road travel in South Africa: pedestrians.

Even on the most desolate stretches of highway, lone women carrying bundles of wood, washing or shopping on their heads would be ambling along. Often the walkers would appear on the shoulder in groups of two or three: children on their way to school, dawdling teens playing chicken with motorists, immaculately starched congregants en route to church services. Through stinging rain, desert plains, tarmac-melting heat and over muscle-burning hills they plod. As you do when you have only two choices: stay home or not. Often even the modest taxis fees are beyond their means or the region is so remote that there is simply no transport for hire.

Within two hours I arrived at my final destination of the journey. The town of Kroonstad is much like other regional centres that service South African agriculture. Dotted with the churches, parks and sports fields that are the mark of a proud and committed community, it is homely and quietly prosperous. It is also the town in which my father was born and where his family played significant enough a role in early community life to have a street named after them. Said avenue no longer exists but the Smiedt Building on the main street still houses the chemist where generations of towns-folk have turned up with snotty noses, inflamed bunions and all manner of complaints that could be quietly shared with the pharmacist in the privacy of his office out the back.

The dispenser in question is Bram Smiedt, last branch of the family tree in Kroonstad and an engagingly eccentric character. I turned up at the store unannounced and a staff member rang Bram to say someone from Australia was here to see him. As you do in country towns, he had gone home for lunch.

He passed on a message that I should hang around as he would be back shortly. Being something of an ornithologist, Bram had arranged a series of high domed birdcages along the aisles of the pharmacy. These were filled with elec-tric-green lovebirds, sky-blue budgies and parrots that brightened the space with their hues and harmonies.

While I was strolling around, thinking the establishment stemmed from an era when pharmacies served myriad func-tions in a community and slickness was less important than service, Bram returned to tell me he'd figured out who I was. Jovial and engaging company, Bram was patently an esteemed and trusted member of the community he served. He also had a fair streak of the rogue in him and he farewelled a stream of prim and blushing Afrikaner ladies with: "Tell your husband that we now have liquid Viagra in stock so he can pour himself a stiff one".

His way with a one-liner was probably inherited from his father Cyril who ran the pharmacy before him, conducted eye tests on the premises and alerted the community to this service with an enormous billboard reading: "C Smiedt and see better".

Despite my best efforts I could not picture my father as a child on Kroonstad's main street. Aside from mentioning Smiedt Street and his cousin Cyril's sign, he rarely spoke of the place. Nor did he ever take me there. Perhaps he thought there was little to discover here – about himself or much else for that matter. On the first count he was proven correct. But meeting Bram had been worth the detour my father had never taken.

Looking perhaps a little too hard for echoes of hereditary larrikinism, I farewelled Bram and his wife Barbara to set off for Johannesburg, a mere ninety minutes away.

In a little under three months I had travelled over 8000 kilometres, seeing much that I remembered and even more I would never forget. Glimpses of the old South Africa remained, albeit dressed in new criticisms of affirmative action and government corruption. To my own mortification, I also found myself not entirely free of these attitudes. This I discovered in Pretoria when I asked the only white person in a crowded street for directions and he replied, "I don't live here – ask one of these guys".

I had been gladdened by dozens of the new nation's characteristics. My old schools were now multiracial, the national anthem was prized by all South Africans, and the political correctness that characterised the earliest days of majority government had given way to the more grounded reality of getting on with the business of living together. However, the euphoria that had accompanied Nelson Mandela's release had not merely been tempered but rendered brittle by chronic violence, spiralling poverty, the government's indifferent response to the AIDS scourge and an underlying fear that all the mineral resources in the world were not going to stop South Africa's economy going the way of most other African nations.

A decade after the switch to representative government, some black South Africans are undoubtedly better off and can now afford to cower like whites behind electrified security fences patrolled by armed guards. For most, however, life hasn't changed all that much.

Thousands are still fleeing to England, Israel, Canada, America and Australia, just as my father did. That said, I am positive about the future of the land of my birth. Just as it witnessed a bloodless revolution despite all indications to the contrary, I saw enough harmony in my travels to give me hope, albeit tinged with the reality that thousands will not live to see the land South Africa could become. It is a nation of rare resilience, ancient communion with the land and a spirit that blossoms under the harshest of circumstances. As Desmond Tutu noted, "Yes, things could be much better in South Africa – but they could be much worse".

I began my journey in the city where my father died and ended it in the town where he was born. Looking back, perhaps it was naive to think that on some lonely stretch of highway under an African sky I would experience the epiphany of him riding shotgun. Dodging the taxis streaming into

Johannesburg, I had to admit to myself that the presence of the late Sydney Ronald Smiedt was *not* going to materialise. At least not on this trip.

I was, however, certain of two things. The first was that as one of those fathers who viewed travel as an educational experience as opposed to a recreational one, he would have loved this journey. Not least for the fact that I undertook it in his name. More importantly, he was still teaching me the same lesson he had been all along: the more you learn about other people and places, the more you learn about yourself. The second certainty was that although South Africa is no longer home, there's still no place like it.

Epilogue

On Friday 26 July 2003, my brother-in-law Laurence Niselow was at work in his screen-printing business in the Johannesburg suburb of Jeppe. It was lunchtime and staff were coming and going through the security gates. Laurence was probably thinking of the next meal. For devout Jews the Sabbath dinner is a sanctuary from the working week, a time to give thanks for simple gifts like bread on the table and family around it.

Amid the factory chatter, a conversation Laurence was having with an employee was interrupted by two men neither of them recognised. Voices were raised, intervention was attempted, two shots were fired and Laurence was dead before he hit the ground.

I wrote the first words of this book beside him at the dining-room table early one morning: me bleary-eyed and jet-lagged, Laurence on the way to daily prayers at the synagogue.

Second to his devotion to God was that to his country. A champion of affirmative action decades before it was enshrined in law, he championed black empowerment as many other whites whinged that it was impacting upon their livelihood. While he was under no illusions about the problems facing the country he could have left but chose to remain in, Laurence steadfastly believed that these would be overcome. What's more, he would have been disappointed had I let his death overshadow this book being a love letter to South Africa.